A Text Book of Irish Literature

VOL. I.

AMS PRESS
NEW YORK

A Text Book of Irish Literature

Part I.

BY

ELEANOR HULL

Author of " Pagan Ireland," " Early Christian Ireland," etc.

Dublin

M. H. GILL & SON, Ltd.

London

DAVID NUTT.

1906

Library of Congress Cataloging in Publication Data

Hull, Eleanor, 1860-1935.
    A text book of Irish literature.

    Bibliography: p.

    1. Irish literature—History and criticism. I. Title.
PB1306.H75 1974   820'.9   70-153595
ISBN 0-404-09244-6

Reprinted from the edition of 1906-1908, Dublin
First AMS edition published in 1974
Manufactured in the United States of America

International Standard Book Number:
Complete Set: 0-404-09244-6
Volume I: 0-404-09245-4

AMS PRESS INC.
NEW YORK, N.Y. 10003

CONTENTS.

A

PREFACE.

THIS text-book of Irish Literature, which has been prepared at short notice to meet the requirements of the students under the Intermediate Board, takes in, generally, the period up to the early years of the sixteenth century. There are, however, some portions of the Literature which would fall chronologically under that period that it has been found impossible to deal with here. For a great part of the early literature no chronological order can, for the present, at all events, be followed. The earlier existing secular material comes to us for the most part gathered into great vellum compilations made by the assiduity of the scribes of the twelfth and following centuries ; but the contents of these volumes are of various ages ; and the actual date of the composition of any particular piece can only be approximately calculated either by casual allusions contained in it to persons or events whose dates can be verified from other sources, or by the language of the piece itself. Often such calculations can only be fixed within the wide limits of three or more centuries.

It has on this account been thought more satisfactory to group the material under general heads even when this does not indicate the precise chronological order of composition. By this means the student can more readily find any particular piece he may be in search of under its own subject ; and a chronological table has been added to help him as to dates, so far as these are known. The chronology applies chiefly to the poets and poetry and to the religious and historical materials whose dates are to a large extent fixed ; the names and dates of the story-tellers who helped to create and shape the great mass of the romance literature must remain for ever unknown.

The method that has been adopted has necessitated the exclusion from this volume of some material which actually comes to us from before the sixteenth century, and which ought therefore, on chronological grounds, to be found here. The Annals, the Ossianic Literature, and the Classical tales, for example, many of which might appropriately take their place in this volume, have had to be postponed for a second part.

I have thought it inadvisable, in a text-book of small size, to give a large number of footnotes and references ; but I hope to compensate for this by adding a biblio-graphy to the second volume, covering the material dealt with in both Parts, so far as this material has been already published.

I have to thank my friends, Mr. Alfred Nutt for kindly reading through the proofs of the Prose Section, and Dr. Douglas Hyde for looking over the chapters on the Poetry ; also my cousin, Mr. J. D. Hendley, for help in proof-reading.

CHRONOLOGY.

(The dates given are those of the deaths of the poets named.)

GROUP I.—Group of semi-mythical poets connected with the traditions of the Milesian settlers in Ireland. These are AMERGIN GLUNGEL, "White Knee," author of three poems or incantations preserved in the Leabhar Gabhála, or Book of Invasions. He is said to have been son of Golamh or Milesius and brother to the three Milesian princes, Heber, Heremon, and Ir.

LUGAIDH, son of Ith and nephew of Milesius. Lament on the death of his wife.

OLLAMH FODHLA, law-giver and monarch of Ireland, and reputed founder of a College for Law and Poetry.

ROIGNE, or Royne the Poetic. Poem on the partition of Ireland among the sons of Milesius.

GROUP II.—Poets chiefly connected with Ulster during the time of its power in the first century.

ADHNA, chief poet, father of Neidhe.

ATHAIRNE. He belonged to Benn Edair, or Howth, but fled into Ulster when the poets were pro-scribed. Of his cruelty and avarice many stories are told, and his tragic death forms the subject of a separate tale.

FORCHERN. His work is unknown.

FERCEIRTNE. To him are ascribed the composition of the *Uraicept* or primer of the learned, a teaching book for the schools of the poets ; and a poem on Ollamh Fodhla. It was between Ferceirtne and the young poet NEIDHE that the famous contest called the " Dialogue of the Two Sages " took place for the appointment to the office of Chief Poet on the death of Adhna.

MORANN. A law-giver and judge.

GROUP III.—About the year 266 died King Cormac mac Airt of Tara, about the time of whose reign flourished Fionn mac Cumhaill, Oisín, Oscur, Caoilte, and Fergus *finbel,* warriors and poets under whose names a large quantity of prose and verse continued to be composed for several centuries. Fionn was son-in-law to Cormac by his marriage with Grainne ; and Oisín and Fergus *finbel* were sons of Fionn ; Oscur was his grandson.

TORNA, called, like many other poets, by the official title of *Eigeas* or the " Learned," was poet and fosterer to Niall of the Nine Hostages (d. 423). To him are ascribed three poems written to mediate between Niall himself and Corc, Prince of Cashel, in Munster. The ascription is doubtful. These poems are prefixed to those written by the bards of the seventeenth century in the poetic contest known as the " Contention of the Bards."

GROUP IV.—Writers of the Early Christian Period. In the reign of Laeghaire, or Laery (c. 450) three princes, three poets, and three law-givers or Brehons were appointed to revise and compile the Laws of

Ireland. The bishops engaged in the task were St. Patrick, St. Benen, and St. Cairnech; the poets, Dubhtach, Rossa, and Fergus; and the princes, Laery himself, Corc, King of Munster, and Daire, King of Ulster.

d. 461. ST. PATRICK. He wrote the Confession, the Epistle to Coroticus, and the Hymn called the Lorica or Breastplate of St. Patrick.

ST. SECUNDINUS, or Sechnall, nephew to St. Patrick, wrote a Hymn to St. Patrick and (?) a Communion Hymn.

467-8. ST. BENEN, Bishop of Armagh. To him are ascribed parts of the Book of Rights, but the ascription is doubtful.

499. ST. CAILIN, Bishop of Down. A book bearing his name contains prophecies and poems addressed to the heads of several tribes regarding their race and the tributes due to himself from them. Doubtful.

500. ST. FIACC, Bishop of Sletty. Poem on St. Patrick ascribed to him.

525. ST. BRIGIT, Abbess of Kildare. A hymn is ascribed to her.

570. ST. ITA. Poem on the Infant Jesus.

597. ST. COLUMCILLE, Abbot of Hi or Iona. A large number of hymns and poems in Latin and Irish are ascribed to him.

596. DALLAN FORGAILL, or Eochadh Dallan. Wrote the *Amra* in praise of St. Columcille and odes to Aodh mac Duach on his shield and weapons.

b. 543. ST. COLUMBANUS. (Date of death uncertain.) Latin poems on various subjects.

647. SENCHAN TORPEIST of Connaught. Lament over the dead body of Dallan, his predecessor; poem on the battles of Fergus. To him is ascribed the recovery of the tale called the *Táin bó Cuailnge*. Contemporary with Guaire of Connaught and Senchan Torpeist was MARBHAN the poet, half brother of Guaire, a recluse, who wrote a poem in praise of woodland scenery.

656. ST. ULTAN. Irish hymn to St. Brigit attributed to him.

661. ST. CUMMINE *fada*, "the Tall" Bishop of Clonfert. Religious poem.

678. CINNFAELADH the Learned, son of Olioll, or Ailell. Poems on the *Miodhchuarta*, or Banqueting Hall ("mead-hall") of Tara, and on the travels of Milesius. He revised the *Uraicept*, or teaching-book of the Learned.

704. ST. ADAMNAN, Ninth Abbot of Hi or Iona. Works (*a*) Life of Columcille, (*b*) Book of the Holy Places. (*c*) The Vision of Adamnan bears his name, but is probably later.

707. RUMAN MAC COLMAIN, the "Homer and Virgil of Ireland." Song of the Sea.

705. FLANN FIONN, or King Alfrid of Northumbria. Recalled to his Kingdom 685. Poem on the beauty and attractions of Ireland.

746. ST. CUCHUIMNE. Hymn in praise of the Virgin.

800. ST. ANGUS the Culdee "*Céile Dé.*" Compiled a Calendar of Saints, or *Félire*. To him is ascribed also the poem called *Saltair na Rann*, or Psalter of the Verses.

807. The writing of the Book of Armagh was completed in this year by Ferdomnach the Scribe (d. 845).

860. SEDULIUS *Scotus*, or " the Irishman," Abbot of Kildare, 820, Principal of the Royal School of Liége. He wrote Latin poems to the Emperor Lothaire ; also a Dialogue between the roses and lilies, and other occasional poems.

GROUP V.—NORSE PERIOD.

876. FOTHADH " of the Canon " or " Law." Odes to Aedh Finnliath, monarch of Ireland ; he is called " Fothadh of the Law " because he secured the passing of an ecclesiastical canon exempting the clergy from warfare.

884. MAOLMURA OF FATHAN. Historical and genealogical poems on (1) the Origin of the Gael, (2) on the Acts of King Tuathal, or Toole the Legitimate (reigned 130-160), (3) on the Kings of Ireland up to Flann Sionna, his contemporary monarch (reigned 879-914). He is called by the Four Masters " a well-taught, skilful poet and intelligent historian."

908. CORMAC MAC CUILEANAN, King and Abbot of Cashel. He was killed in the battle of Bealach Mughna (Ballymoon, Co. Kildare), fought against Flann Sionna, monarch of Ireland. To him are ascribed (*a*) A Glossary of old and rare words, known as Cormac's Glossary (*Sanas Cormaic*) ; (*b*) The Compilation of the *Saltair Chaisil*, or Psalter of Cashel ; (*c*) Poems. The Annals called *Chronicum Scotorum* describe Cormac as " a most excellent bishop, scribe and anchorite, and the wisest of the Gael."

919. QUEEN GORMFLAITH, or Gormliath, d. of Flann Sionna and wife of Cormac mac Cuileanan.

She was afterwards married to his enemy, King Cearbhal, or Karval, of Leinster, and to Niall Glundubh, who became monarch of Ireland in 914. In her old age she fell from her high estate, and was forced to "beg her bread from door to door." She wrote many "learned and pitiful ditties" on the death of her son, which seem to be lost, but a poem on her second husband, Cearbhal, and a touching appeal after his death to Niall Glendubh, are extant.

918. FLANN MAC LONAIN, poet to the O'Brien family, and predecessor of Mac Liag as chief poet of Munster. He was a native of South Connaught and lived during the lifetime of Lorcan, the grandfather, and Cenneide, or Kennedy, the father of Brian Boru, at their palace of Kincora, near Killaloe, on the Shannon. He is called by the Four Masters the "Virgil of the race of Scotia." He was killed by the Decies of Munster. His death is twice recorded by them under the years 891 and 918. The latter date (or a still later one) is probably correct, as one of his poems is an Elegy on the death of a Prince of Tirconnell who died in 902. He was still living when Mac Liag was poet to the O'Kellys as a young man. Among Mac Lonain's remaining poems are (1) Two in praise of Lorcan, his patron, King of W. Munster; (2) a poem on Kincora (*Ceann-Coradh*, or the "head of the weir"); (3) a poem on the topography of the Clare Hills addressed to Mac Liag. He wrote in a romantic and allegorical style.

946. CORMACAN, or Cormac, son of Maelbrigid, chief
poet to Muirchertach, or Murtough, son of Niall
Glundubh (" Black-knee ") of Ulster. Poem
describing the " Circuit of Ireland " made by
that monarch, from which he gained the title
of " Murtough of the Leather Cloaks."

975. CINAEDH, or KENNETH O'HARTIGAN. (*a*) Topographical poems preserved in the *Dindsenchus*
on " Rath Essa " in Meath ; on " the Hill of
Acaill," or the Hill of Screen in Meath ; on
" Brugh mac-an-Oig " on the Boyne ; on the
" Origin of Tara," on places called after celebrated women, etc. (*b*) Historical poems on
the deaths of Irish kings and warriors ; on
the origin of the stone called the " Pillow of
St. Buite " at Monasterboice in Meath ; on
the death of Niall of the Nine Hostages.

984. EOCHAIDH FLOINN, or O'FLYNN. Chiefly chronological poems on the legendary colonizations
of Ireland, most of them of great length and
tediousness. (1) Poem on the Invasion of
Partholan ; (2) on the coming of Cessair and
Partholan ; (3) on the division of Ireland between the four sons of Partholan ; (4) on
Partholan's druids and artizans ; (5) on the
destruction of Conaing's Tower (Tory Island,
Co. Donegal) ; (6) on the time which elapsed
between the creation of Adam and the coming
of Cessair, Partholan and Nemedh. This
poem has a gloss between the lines. (7) On the
Invasion of the Tuatha Dé Danann ; (8) on
the sons of Milesius ; (9) on the partition of
the Island between the two princes ; (10) on the

Invasion of the Milesians ; (11) on the building of the Palace of Emain Macha ; (12) on the Kings of Ulster ; (13) on Ugaine Mòr, monarch of Ireland ; (14) on the Creation, the Deluge, and the settlement in Egypt of Niul, son of Fenius Farsaidh. Many of Eochaidh's poems are incorporated into the *Leabhar Gabhála*, or " Book of Invasions."

1015. MAC LIAG, Chief Poet and Secretary to Brian Boru. His real name seems to have been Muirchertach, or Murtough mac Chonchertaigh, and he belonged to the Corann country of Mayo and Sligo. He was first attached to the family of the O'Kellys of Hy Maine, on the Shannon, and several of his poems are addressed to them, but he eventually succeeded Flann mac Lonain as poet to the O'Brians at Kincora. Both historical pieces and poems are ascribed to Mac Liag, but several of the ascriptions are doubtful. Of the historical works (*a*) it is likely that a good part of the " Wars of the Gall and Gael," or " Wars of the Foreigners and Irish," may be by his hand. O'Reilly also thinks that he wrote the *Leabhar Oiris*, or Annals of the Wars and Battles of Ireland, but this seems to be rather later. A life of King Brian is said to have been written by him, but if this was the case it is now unknown. Of his poems (*b*) several are extant. (1) On the Sons of Cas, from whom are descended the Dal Cais of Thomond ; (2) on Brian and his brothers, sons of Kennedy ; (3) on the Fall of Brian at Clontarf and the desolation of Kincora,

beginning " O Kincora, where is Brian ? "
(4) poem on the Battle of Clontarf, the account
of which was brought to him by Mac Coise.
It is in the form of a dialogue between the two
poets, beginning " From the East has come the
news of Brian's fall."   (5) Accounts of the
Tributes (*Boromha*) received by Brian at
Kincora and from which he took his title ; (6)
Lament on the fall of Kincora, written from
Innse Gaill Duibh, the Island of the Black
Foreigners, in the Shannon, after his retirement to that place.   Other poems are (7) on
the history of Carn Conaill ; (8) two poems in
praise of Tadhg O'Kelly ; (9) on the death of
Tadhg O'Kelly at Clontarf.   Some of these
poems to the O'Kellys must have been written
in Mac Liag's early days.   They are preserved
in the *Leabhar Ui Maine*, or Book of the
O'Kellys.

1023. URARD, or ERARD MAC COISE, Chief Poet to
Maelseachlann II. (called Malachy II.), the
monarch of Ireland who was deposed by Brian.
He was present among Maelseachlann's hosts
at Clontarf and brought the account of the
battle to Mac Liag at Kincora.   He wrote
several good poems (1) in praise of the monarch
who was his patron and some of his contemporaries ; (2) dialogue with Mac Liag about
Clontarf and the fallen princes ; (3) in praise
of a son of Tadhg of the Tower, King of Connaught ; (4) on the death of Fergal O'Ruaire,
or O'Rorke, who was killed in East Meath in
964 ; a curious prose piece, in which he describes

under the form of an allegory the destruction of his castle at Clartha (Co. Westmeath) by the O'Neills of Ulster, and demands redress. This piece he recited before Donnell O'Neill at Aileach in Donegal and gained his purpose in obtaining restitution for his losses. Mac Coise died at Clonmacnois.

1016. (?) MAC GIOLLA CAOIMH, or Keeffe, a Munster poet who wrote poems in lamentation after the death of Brian and on the deserted condition of the palaces of the South of Ireland. Date of death uncertain.

1024. CUAN O'LOCHAIN, appointed joint Regent of Ireland with Corcran Cleireach, or the "Cleric" of Lismore, after the death of Maelseachlann in 1022. He did not long survive to enjoy this dignity, for he was slain by the men of Teabhtha, or Teffia, two years afterwards (1024), an act which brought that tribe into great disrepute. The interregnum lasted eighteen years after his death, during part of which time Corcran continued to act as Regent.

In the Annals of Clonmacnois Cuan is said to have been a great chronicler, and one to whom, on account of his capabilities, the causes of Ireland were committed to be examined and ordered. The O'Lochains, or O'Lothchains, were a distinguished family of Meath with whom also the O'Garas and O'Haras of Sligo are connected. His extant poems are (1) Poem on Tara in the reign of Cormac mac Airt (d. 266); (2) on the Prerogatives and Prohibitions of the monarchs of Erin; (3) Topographical Poem on the Shannon; (4) on the history of the hill of Druim Criaich (Drumcree, in Co. Westmeath); (5) in praise of Tara under Niall of the Nine Hostages; (6) on the Hill of Taillte (Teltown, in Meath), and the assemblies and sports celebrated there.

1038. MAEL-ISU, grandson of Brolcan of Derry. The real name of the author of the short and sweet religious poems ascribed to "Mael-Isu" is unknown; his adopted name means "Servant of Jesus," or literally, "Tonsured of Jesus."

1056. FLANN MAINISTREACH, or Flann of the Monastery. Fear-léighinn, or Principal of the School of Monasterboice (Mainister-Buite, or Monastery of St. Buite), in Co. Louth. Compiler of synchronisms and historical poems (1) on the burial-places of the Tuatha Dé Danann; (2) on the deaths of the Pagan Kings of Tara; (3) the same, on the Christian Kings; (4) on the names of the persons who composed the "Great Bardic Company" in the seventh century; (5) on the Christian Kings of Munster; (6) on the Kings of Erin descended from Niall of the Nine Hostages; (7) two poems on the origin and history of Aileach, which form part of the *Dindsenchus*; (8) on the household of St. Patrick; (9) an abstract of universal history. These are only some of the compositions of this laborious and voluminous writer.

1072. GIOLLA CAOIMHGHIN (Keevin). His poems are of a similar character to those of Flann Mainistreach and are also of great length.

They deal with the Christian and Pagan Kings of Ireland, whose names are given in chronological order ; the ancestors of the Gaels, etc. These verses are merely aids to memory composed for the use of the schools.

1088. TIGHERNACH, the Annalist, Abbot of Clonmacnois and Roscommon. A learned and widely-read man, as is shown by the numerous and careful citations from foreign authors found in his works. His Annals are the earliest historical compilations that have come down to us in Ireland. They are in mixed Latin and Irish, like many of the compilations and notes of Irish ecclesiastics, and include the period from the earliest times to his own date. They were continued by Augustin M'Grath to the year 1405.

1100. In this year the compilation called the *Leabhar na h-Uidhre*, or Book of the Dun, was completed at Clonmacnois. See Appendix.

1136. TANAIDHE O'MULCONAIRE, or O'Mulconry. Poems on the Firbolg and the Tuatha Dé Danann.

1143. GIOLLA MODHUDA O'CASSIDY, called Dall Clairineach, Abbot of Ardbraccan, in Meath. Poem giving a catalogue of the Christian Kings of Ireland, beginning " Sacred Erin, Isle of Saints," 368 verses ; and two other poems on similar subjects.

1160. GIOLLA-NA-NAOMH O'DUNN, chief bard of Leinster. Poems (1) on the tribes sprung from Milesius, 392 verses ; (2) on the tombs of the Kings of Leinster ; (3) a catalogue of the Kings of Connaught, and other effusions on similar subjects.

1160. In this year the compilation of the Book of
Leinster was completed.   See Appendix.

1100-1200. The Vision of Mac Conglinne, in the form
in which we have it, appears to date from the
twelfth century or earlier.

GROUP VI.—ANGLO-NORMAN PERIOD.   MAURICE
O'REGAN, a native of Leinster, was employed by Dermot
mac Morrough, King of Leinster, as his ambassador to
Strongbow and the Norman nobles of S. Wales to solicit
their aid in the recovery of his kingdom.   O'Regan
wrote in Irish a history of the Anglo-Norman Invasion
as he himself witnessed it, from the year 1168 to the
Siege of Limerick in 1171.

circa 1224. MUIREADACH O'DALY, called Muireadach
Albanach, or " Murray the Scotchman," poet to
Mac William de Bergo of Connaught.   In 1213
he killed O'Donnell's steward and fled to Scotland, where he became chief poet to the Mac
Donalds of Clanranald.   He returned to Ireland
in his old age and died a monk in the Monastery
of Knockmoy.   POEMS: (1) two to Cathal
O'Conor of the Red Hand, Prince of Connaught
(1156-1224), one of them written in the Levant;
(2) poems to Murrough O'Brien and Donough
Cairbreach O'Brien, one of them disclosing his
name and saying that he was just home from
the Mediterranean;   (3) religious poems;   (4)
poetic dialogue with Cathal the Redhanded of
Connaught while they are shaving their heads
before retiring to the Monastery of Cnoc
Muaidhe (" Knockmoy ") built by Cathal. His
original home seems to have been on the shores

B

of Lake Derryvarra, Co. Westmeath, and he calls himself O'Daly of Meath to distinguish himself from O'Daly of Finnyvarra, Co. Clare; but he was living at Lisadill, Co. Sligo, when O'Donnell's steward came to collect his cess or tribute. In his old age he wrote some very tender religious poems, several of which are preserved in the Scottish Book of the Dean of Lismore. He is styled " Chief Poet of Erin and Alba."

1244. DONOGH MÒR O'DALY. The Four Masters speak of this writer as " an expert that in the exercise of the poetic art never has been, nor ever will be, surpassed." He is undoubtedly the greatest member of the ua Dálaigh or O'Daly family, the most important of all the families of hereditary poets in Ireland. He lived at Finnyvarra, in Co. Clare, and from him the O'Dalys of that county are descended. He died at Boyle, Co. Roscommon, and was buried in the Norman Abbey there. From this fact, and also from the devotional character of his extant poems, a tradition grew up that he was Abbot of Boyle, but this does not seem supported by evidence. O'Reilly gives the names of more than thirty extant poems of his containing over 4,200 lines, and there are others in the British Museum not known to him. Many of Donogh's poems are still familiarly repeated in Ireland.

circa 1200-1260. GIOLLA BRIGHDE MAC CONMIDHE, or Gilbride mac Namee, an Ulster poet and retainer of the O'Donnells. O'Curry shows that several poems addressed to the O'Donnells and O'Neills supposed by O'Reilly to be the work of Flann Mainistrech are really written by Mac Namee. (1) Poem on the Battle of Downpatrick, 1260 ; (2) to Hugh O'Conor, of Rathcroghan ; (3) to a helmsman in the Levant ; (4) to Rolfe mac Mahon of Oriel, a vision. Mac Conmidhe is sometimes styled Giolla Brighde Albanach from his frequent visits to Scotland. The date given in O'Reilly (1350) to this poet is erroneous.

1310. TORNA O'MULCONAIRE, or Mulconry. Some of the poems ascribed to Torna Eigeas were possibly written by this poet. There is also a poem extant by him on the inauguration of Felim O'Conor on the hill of Carn Fraoch, in Co. Roscommon.

1315. TADHG MÒR O'HIGGIN. Poem addressed to the young Manus O'Conor of Connaught.

1350. ANGUS ROE O'DALY of Meath. (1) Two poems on the erection of a castle on the hill of Carn Fraoch (1309) are ascribed to him by O'Reilly (" Irish Writers ") ; (2) a spirited address to Hugh mac Owen O'Conor ; (3) address to Art Mòr O'Melaghlin inciting him to drive the English out of Ulster ; (4) poem to Mulloy, whom he had insulted when in a state of intoxication. He beseeches him to forgive him, and instead of revenging himself on his own bard to turn his attention to destroying the English.

1372. JOHN O'DUBHAGAIN, or O'Dugan, Chief Poet of the O'Kellys. Genealogical and Topographical

Poems (1) on the Kings of Leinster ; (2) on the Kings of Erin ; (3) on the battles of Cormac mac Airt, etc. His great topographical poem includes all the septs and families of Meath, Ulster, and Connaught. It was completed for Munster by O'Huidhrin in 1420.

1387. GEOFFREY FIONN O'DALY, a Munster Poet. (*a*) Poem addressed to the Mac Carthys inciting them to vigour, especially against the English ; (*b*) Religious Poems (1) on the limitations of earthly happiness. He contends that to be satisfied with this world is to be like a woman born and bred in a dungeon who has never seen the beauties of the world outside. (2) A poem written after a heavy sickness in gratitude to the Heavenly Physician for recovery.

1390. MAGNUS O'DUIGENAN, one of the great family of scribes of that name. He wrote out a great part of the Book of Ballymote.

1418. GIOLLA ISA MAC FIRBIS, the famous antiquary or scribe of Lecan in Sligo. He arranged and wrote out most, if not all, of the great book of Lecan, and also of the companion compilation known as the Yellow Book of Lecan. A poem on the synchronisms of the Irish Kings with the Roman Emperors is ascribed to him.

1420. GIOLLA-NA-NAOMH O'HUIDHRIN. He completed the topographical poem of John O'Dugan, adding the families belonging to the districts of Munster and Leinster. The poem consists of 780 verses or 3,120 lines, and when joined to O'Dugan's reaches 1,660 verses.

1448. TADHG ÓG O'HIGGIN, Poet of the O'Neills. He
died at Kilconla and was buried in the Monastery of Athlahen, Co. Galway. He wrote (*a*)
poems to the O'Neills and (*b*) devotional poems.
Of the first are (1) on the inauguration of Niall
Oge in 1397; (2) address to the same; (3) on
the death of Teigue mac Cathal O'Conor-Sligo.
This is an affectionate effusion, but does not
forget to mention, by way of business, that the
slain man was accustomed to bestow on him
twenty cows for a composition. (3) On the
death of Teigue O'Kelly, a prince who, according to this poem, had incurred the hatred
of his tribe for the oppressions necessary to
keep up his personal munificence and splendour.
(4) On the death of Ulick mac William-Burke;
(5) on the death of his elder brother and pre-
ceptor, Fergal Rua, full of gratitude and affection for his instructions; begins " To-night the
schools of poetry are dissolved "; (6) on the
struggle of the flesh against the spirit. These
poems are in the British Museum. (See
O'Grady's Catalogue of Irish MSS. at Egerton
III. Arts. 37-43.)

1498. ANNALS OF ULSTER, otherwise called the Sena-
tensian Annals. These important Annals
were compiled from older material by CATHAL
MAC MAGNUS, or Charles Maguire, at Seanaidh
mac Magnus, now Belle Isle, in Lough Erne,
Co. Fermanagh. They begin at the mission
of Palladius and close at the year of the author's
death. Some copies have additions up to the
year 1588.

1459. THE WARS OF TURLOUGH O'BRIEN. This account of the wars against the Anglo-Normans in Munster from 1194-1355 was compiled by JOHN MAC CRAITH, or John Rory Magrath, Chief Historian of the Dalcais of North Munster in this year.

The close of this century and the beginning of the next yield few names of first-rate importance either in poetry or prose, though the family bards continued to produce verse all over the country.

INTRODUCTORY.

THE ancient literature of the Celt leads us into a world of pure romance. To study it, we must be content for a while to loosen our hold upon external fact ; legends of ancient gods, romantic adventures that seem to belong to fairyland, strange over-sea voyages and descents into the mysterious unseen world believed to exist beneath the hills or across the lakes and seas will meet us everywhere. We shall find the tenderest love-tales and songs of love ; we shall find poems on natural scenery, in which there is revealed what Matthew Arnold calls " a magic intimacy with nature " ; we shall hear alike the ring of battle, the bugle-call of the chase, the eulogy of the chieftain, and the passionate lament of the down-trodden and lonely peasant.

In Cuchulain and Conall the Victorious, in Fionn mac Cumhaill and Oisín and Oscar, in King Cormac mac Airt and Niall of the Hostages we shall see set before us the heroic ideals of our forefathers. It is not merely as pretty tales, smoothly or pleasantly told, elopements or fairy tales or descriptions of raids as such, that we prize the old romance as our best heritage from the Gael of an older age ; it is because these stories open up to us not only a picture of his life and social habits, but of his thoughts and ideals, his notions of right and wrong, his conception of chivalry, his dreams of perfection and his pursuit of happiness. They show us what the old Gael was, as no other kind of history can show us, in his home, in his daily life, in his aspirations and the inner dwellings of the soul.

The world conceived of in his literature is far removed
from ordinary life, though it touches it at many points
and throws over it a brilliant fantastic glamour ; it is,
to a large extent, a realm of the imagination, illumined by
the fancies of fairy-land and the traditions derived from
the belief of his forefathers. Everywhere in the literature he has produced we find the same mingling of the
actual and the purely imaginative ; in his serious annals
and historical tracts he surprises us by the perpetual
intrusion of fairy-lore, or by the gravely historic
importance which he attaches to the genealogies and
wars and settlements of the gods ; his legal decisions
and ancient laws have " a thread of poetry " thrown
round them, and his official verse contains the geography,
the genealogies and the historical traditions of Ireland.
One of the difficulties with which the Irish historian
will always have to deal is to discriminate where the
imaginary ends and the actual begins. It, in fact,
ends and begins nowhere ; the two move on through
all the centuries in a friendly union which can only
partially and uncertainly be disentangled. The
accounts of Brian Boru early in the eleventh century
are tinged with fairy-belief just as are the tales of
Conaire Mór at the beginning of the Christian Era ;
nor, when Dr. Geoffrey Keating comes to compile a
connected history of Ireland in the seventeenth century,
does he show much desire to sift the real from the unreal.

But what is undoubtedly a loss to the historian may
be a gain to the lover of literature, and from this point
of view the quite extraordinary proportion of pure
romance coming down from the earliest times to the
present day, as compared with the entire literary output of the country, cannot be regarded as a misfortune.

We are presented with an almost bewildering mass of story and legend and vision and bombastic narrative, which has never entirely ceased to be invented down to close upon our own times ; while if we could reckon up the official poems of the filí, and the more spontaneous productions of the bards and later Jacobite and popular poets, the output of verse would be hardly less surprising.

The untiring and splendid efforts of such scholars as Dr. Kuno Meyer, Dr. Stokes, and Dr. Windisch in the early romance literature, the poetry and the literature of vision ; of Mr. Standish Hayes O'Grady in the historical tales and legends, and the Ossianic and later mediæval literature ; of O'Donovan, Petrie, Todd, O'Curry, and others in the publication of the official and topographical poetry and of works of historical importance, have contributed to open out before us a very considerable portion of the literature in its various aspects. The vast amount of work that has been done is but imperfectly realised by the ordinary student, and much of the lamentation that we hear over the masses of inedited manuscripts might well be spared when we consider that, although there is still material to engage the attention of all the publishing agencies for many years to come, a great part of the remaining manuscripts are duplicates of those already published, and a good number are worthless either from the condition of the manuscripts or from the character of their contents. It is quite as necessary to realise what has been done as to deplore what remains to be done ; and we hope that this little book, which deals chiefly, though not quite exclusively, with material that has, in one form or another, been made accessible to the public, may do something to remove the impression that seems to be abroad that very little has as yet been accomplished. It is a thankless task to underrate the results of those noble and fruitful efforts, which from the time of O'Curry, the Inspirer and Father of a race of laborious sons, until to-day, have done so much to open out before us the literary remains of our ancestors.

Though gaps remain to be filled in every department, we can yet get a fair bird's-eye view of the whole literature in its various aspects.

Old Romance.—A very large body of the Old Romance has been published, and the tales that remain to be edited are many of them duplicates with variations in their details, or short incidents or fragments which would certainly serve to fill up gaps in our knowledge, but which would not greatly extend our grasp of the cycles as a whole. There are still, however, unpublished, several tales belonging to the oldest mythology which would be valuable in extending our very scant knowledge of the oldest folk-lore of Ireland.

Annals.—A most important series of the Annals of Ireland has been issued from time to time under the auspices of the Master of the Rolls, and these are supplemented by the shorter historical tracts brought out among the publications of the Irish Archæological and Celtic Societies, in the *Revue Celtique*, and elsewhere. The general Historical literature is represented by the Annals of Tighernach, of the Four Masters, of Loch Cé, of Ulster, of Clonmacnois, and the Chronicum Scotorum ; the history of special periods by the Wars of the Gael and Gall, the Wars of Callachan of Cashel, and a number of other pieces, usually more or less fragmentary, both in Irish, Latin, and English, which throw light upon contemporary and local events in different periods. The labours of William Hennessy, Drs. John O'Donovan, James Henthorn Todd, Rev. Denis Murphy, Dr. Whitley Stokes, and others, have rendered many of these national annals accessible to the public. Yet several historical tracts and annals of importance still remain to be published. Such are the Annals of Innisfallen, the Annals of Boyle, and of Connaught, and portions of the Munster Annals, which might add considerably to our local provincial information. There also remains to be published the piece known as the " Triumphs of Turlough O'Brien," which gives an interesting account of events in Munster during the Norman period (1194-1355 A.D.*) ; the *Leabhar Gabhála,* or " Book of Invasions " (*a*), and its accompanying piece, the *Reim Rioghraidhe,* or " Succession of Kings " ; Keating's History of Ireland, known as the *Forus Feasa ar Eirinn* (*b*), and some personal and special historical pieces, such as the interesting tract known as the " Flight of the Earls " (*c*), which gives an account of the departure of O'Neill and O'Donnell from Ireland in 1607, and their journey through France and the Low Countries on their way to Rome.†

Several of the more important of these historical tracts are, however, in the hands of Editors, and we may look for considerable additions to the historical

* In course of being edited for the Cambridge University Press by Mr. Standish Hayes O'Grady.

† These tracts are in course of being edited for the Irish Texts Society by Mr. R. A. S. Macalister (*a*) ; Mr. David Comyn (*b*), and Miss Agnes O'Farrelly (*c*). The first portion of Keating's History has already been issued.

Literature during the next few years. Some very important genealogies, such as Mac Firbis' great compilation, are still only accessible in manuscript.

Law Tracts.—Large portions of the ancient Law Tracts of Ireland, commonly called the " Brehon Laws," have been issued by the Commissioners specially appointed for this purpose, and these volumes throw a flood of light upon the early life and institutions of the country.

Ecclesiastical Material.—A great deal of the ecclesiastical material, both in Irish and Latin, including saints' lives and legends, martyrologies and calendars of saints, homilies and passions, sacred poetry, hymns and service books, have been carefully edited for various publications from the time of Colgan to our own day. Among many laborious workers in this field we can only here mention Bishop Reeves, Rev. Dr. MacCarthy, Dr. Whitley Stokes, Rev. Dr. Edmund Hogan, Dr. Robert Atkinson, Rev. Professor Bernard, Rev. F. Warren. Irish and Latin scholars of many different schools of religious thought have nobly united in the effort to lay these documents open to the study and criticism of those interested in Church history.

The Great Collections.—From about the eleventh or early twelfth century, scribes, both secular and ecclesiastical, fearing perhaps the destructive effects of the Norman wars, or actuated by a just pride in the traditions and literary remains of their race, began to collect in large vellum books the old stories, genealogies, historic tales, and poems that had been repeated among the people, and which were probably dying out amid

the inrush of new ideas and customs.   Some of these,
like the Book of Leinster, which was compiled in the
reign and probably for the benefit of Dermot Mac
Morrough, the infamous prince in whose time the
Normans came over to Ireland, are largely concerned
with the traditions and events belonging to their own
province, but all contain a part of the general stock of
the national records and romance, and they preserve
for us these stories and poems in the earliest form in
which they have come down to us.   Among the most
important of these collections are the Book of the Dun
Cow (*Leabhar na h-Uidhre*, *L.U.*) the earliest existing
of these large compilations of material, which was
compiled at the monastery of Clonmacnois about 1100
A.D. ; the Book of Leinster (*Leabhar Laighneach*, *L.L.*),
the Great Book of Lecan (*Leabhar Mòr Lecain*), the
Yellow or Golden Book of Lecan (*Leabhar Buidhe Lecain*,
Y.B.L.), and the Book of Fermoy (*Leabhar Feara-
maighe*), all of which contain for the larger part early
romances, genealogical and annalistic and topographical
tracts and poems, and old historical legends, traditions
and bardic plays.   Besides these we have the Book of
Armagh, the Book of Ballymote (*Leabhar Baile an
Mhota*, *B.B.*), the Speckled Book (*Leabhar Breac*, *L.B.*),
the Book of Lismore, which preserve for the most part
religious and ecclesiastical documents, although they
contain a certain proportion of other matter.   In the
Book of Ballymote, especially, there are several Irish
versions of classical tales, and text books of the instructions given by the poets to their schools of students ; but
on the whole these four volumes may be said to be
chiefly occupied with the lives and legends of the
saints, sermons, passions, and homilies, religious poems,

martyrologies, and the "rules" of various monastic bodies, with much Biblical history. The Book of Armagh contains the earliest and most authentic documents regarding St. Patrick and the tracts believed to have been written by him.*

Scribes.—Though one or two of these collections were written at monasteries or by ecclesiastics, the larger number were the work of successive generations of official scribes who, in different parts of the country, preserved these great vellum manuscript volumes, adding to them from time to time any material which seemed to them of sufficient importance, gathered either from without or contributed by the bards belonging to the different families and septs. The Mac Firbises, the Mac Egans, the O'Duigenans, the O'Mulconroys, the Mac Brodys, and many other noted families of scribes and genealogists have helped to preserve to posterity the traditions of the race. The office of scribe and genealogist was a high one, held in honour in the tribe, and in the ecclesiastical world even bishops were proud to add this title to their names and roll of dignities. Hence the clergy and laity alike contributed to the preservation of the records and to their worthy keeping in large, and, in the case of portions of the Scriptures, often highly ornamented vellum volumes. Some families of chieftains, the O'Donnells, for example, seem to have taken a special pride in the collection and preservation of manuscripts.

Modern Manuscripts.—But besides these well-known books, which bear distinctive names, there are

(* For further details about these books see Appendix).

also a number of hardly less important and lengthy compilations in Trinity College, Dublin, and at the Bodleian Library, Oxford, at Brussels, and elsewhere, formed on the same plan ; and there are, outside of these large vellums, a mass of Irish manuscripts existing on parchment and paper dating chiefly from the seventeenth century and onwards, and becoming very numerous during the eighteenth century, from which time, no doubt, owing to the general loss of the language, the interest in copying and preserving manuscripts gradually dwindled away. The ignorant and wasteful destruction of manuscripts during times quite near our own has perhaps not been equalled in the whole course of Irish history; by persons no longer able to read them they were looked upon as so much waste paper, and ruthlessly flung away. Nevertheless, our readers would probably be surprised at the enormous number of Irish manuscripts still existing, and collected under the hospitable roofs of the Libraries of the Royal Irish Academy, and of Trinity College, Dublin ; of the British Museum, Maynooth, and other home and Continental Libraries. The indices to the manuscript catalogues in the Royal Irish Academy Library alone occupy thirteen large volumes, and these do not contain the more recent additions to the collection. In the British Museum there are one hundred and ninety-eight volumes of Irish manuscripts, each containing a large number of separate pieces. The fact that a copy is comparatively modern in date does not necessarily detract from its value, for the age of the contents of these manuscripts varies greatly, and in some cases a very old story or poem may have survived, as though by the merest chance, in some quite recent manuscript.

There is necessarily a vast amount of repetition, some popular tale or song being contained in as many as twenty or more different manuscripts, but we frequently gain by this means different versions of the same tale, with considerable varieties of style and detail in the method of narration. The different copies, also, frequently help to the elucidation of linguistic difficulties or obscure passages.

A Text Book of Irish Literature

------►◄------

CHAPTER I.

The Early Mythology

So far as the present state of our historical knowledge
enables us to judge, it would seem that two main bodies
of Celts passed over from the Continent and settled in
the British Isles.　The first to come were the Goidels,
or Gaels, the people who now inhabit the Irish-speaking
parts of Ireland, the Highlands and Western parts of
Scotland, and the Isle of Man.　After them came
another branch of the same race, whose language was
akin to, but not the same as, Gaelic, and who called
themselves Brythons, or Britons.　This branch, which
originally spread over the larger part of England, was
eventually driven West by the Saxons, and remained
as a distinct people only in Wales, parts of Devon and
Cornwall, and Brittany, which was colonized by Welsh-
men or Britons, and to which they gave their own name.
Welsh, Cornish, and Breton are allied tongues, as Scotch
and Irish Gaelic and the Manx tongue are allied, and
both branches of the language belong to the same
original stock.　Though the Gaels now inhabit only the
extreme north-western districts of Britain and parts of
Ireland, it is probable that at one time the whole country

was occupied by them, and that they suffered at an earlier stage much the same fate as that which befel the Britons afterwards in being dispossessed and driven West by the second body of invading Celts. The earliest stone inscriptions in Wales and Cornwall are in a tongue that corresponds more closely to the Gaelic than to the Brythonic language, and there are signs in the oldest Welsh literature that Gaelic had originally been understood and used by the people. If this was the case, it will be interesting to ask : "Are there in Wales any remnants of a literature similar in character and ideas to any part of the Gaelic literature of Ireland?" Now, the earliest literature that comes down to us from the past in Ireland is chiefly concerned with three great cycles of romance : that relating to the early prehistoric gods, who are called the Tuatha Dé Danann ; that relating to Cuchulain, who was supposed to have lived in the first century ; and the legends of Fionn and Oisín, heroes who were believed to have existed in the third century of our era. Of the first cycle there are, unfortunately, only a small number of romances left in Ireland, although we know from the frequent allusions to them that there must once have been a great number familiar to the people ; of the second there are over a hundred remaining in Ireland and a few are equally well-known in Scotland ; and of the third cycle there are a multitude of songs and stories common to both Scotland and Ireland, and still told as folk-tales by the Gaelic-speaking people at the present day. The stories of the Tuatha Dé Danann are not known in Scotland.

But when we turn to Wales we find a quite different state of affairs. Cuchulain and Fionn, with all their legends, are quite unknown in Wales : there are only a few casual allusions to them, evidently brought in from outside ; they never played any part in the native legend. But the Tuatha Dé Danann (the Children or Tribe of Danu) are well-known there under the name of " The Children or Tribe of Dôn " ; and in the four tales called " Mabinogion," the oldest tales of Wales, they play the chief part. Several of them bear the same names as the personages in the Irish legends, slightly changed in spelling and pronunciation ; but they are depicted in a different manner and as playing different *rôles*. This interesting coincidence would seem to bear out the testimony of the stone inscriptions in pointing to a period when the inhabitants of Wales and Ireland spoke the same language and had the same traditions ; a period so early that the Cuchulain and Fionn or Ossianic romances had not even been thought of, but when legends of the early gods were familiar on both sides of the Irish Channel. It is of these primeval legends, which possibly hail from a period before the coming of the second Celtic invasion—the Brythonic, or British—to these Islands, that we must first speak. They are the heritage of the undivided Celtic race, and we find both in Gaul and Britain, in Roman times, traces of the worship of some of the gods and goddesses whose memory is preserved in these ancient romances.

Ogma.—Among the Celtic deities known in Classical times was Ogmios or Ogma, patron of Eloquence and Literature, whom Lucian, a second century Greek writer, describes as attired like Heracles, with a lion's skin and club as a proof of his strength. He pictures him as being an old, bald man who drew behind him a willing crowd of people fastened to him by slender golden chains, the ends of which passed through his tongue. Lucian says that a Celt explained this to him as meaning that the race believed that power lay, not in physical strength of body, but in the eloquence and ready wit of the tongue, which drew men gladly after the speaker. The face of Ogmios is towards his captives and he is smiling happily upon them. This Ogmios appears in Irish literature as Ogma, the strong champion of Lugh, in the tale of the " Second Battle of Moytura," in which tale the Tuatha Dé Danann gods are found fighting against the Fomorians. He falls in the battle, but his name survives in the ancient form of writing known as " Ogham," which he is said to have invented. Thus his qualities as a strong man and as one who knew the power of words correspond, as closely as our meagre information will admit, with the Gallic and Greek conception of him.

Brigit.—Several Latin inscriptions in Britain and Gaul mention a goddess called Brigantia, who gave her name to the British tribe of the Brigantes dwelling in the districts of Britain north-east of what is at present known as Wales.

She is a goddess of Wisdom and Knowledge, the presiding genius of arts and industry, and has many of the attributes of Minerva. In Ireland her name is Brigit, and she is a daughter of the Dagda ; in Cormac's Glossary (sec. *Brigit*, p. 23) she is described as " the female sage or mistress of wisdom ; the goddess whom poets adored on account of the greatness of her protecting care, whence she is called the goddess of poets." She is said to have had two sisters also called Brigit, one of whom was a woman-leech or doctor, and the other a mistress of smith-craft or metal-work. This is in accordance with the Irish custom of breaking up single personalities into triads, and signifies that Brigit, in her capacity as goddess of wisdom, presided over the three great departments of ancient knowledge—philosophy or poetry, medicine, and metal-work. Brigit, the Saint and Abbess of Kildare, was doubtless named from her.

War Goddesses.—So also Nemetona or Nemon, whose name is found on a monument at Bath, seems identical with the fierce wife of Neit or Nét, the god of battles of the ancient Irish. In Cormac's Glossary (sec. *Be-nét*, p. 25) Nét, and Nemon his wife, are called a "pestilent or venomous pair," wars, rapine and blood-shed being caused by them. Nemon, who is also known as Badb, is one of a triad of war-goddesses whose only distinction is in the difference of name, Badb, Macha, and Morrigan, and she is constantly called the Badb-Catha or Badb of Battles, *i.e.*, a war-fury. A battle-field is called "the fold of Badb," and the slain are her "circle;" after a bloody fight her hunger is said to be "sated;" when a hero is overthrown, she "shrieks from the corpses," and before the destruction of a building it is said, that "the Red-mouthed Badb will cry around the house; for bodies she will be hungering." This terrible triad of goddesses are usually present before or during any battle where there will be destruction of life; they have the power of changing themselves into ravens or royston crows, and flutter screaming over the heads of the warriors or the points of their spears, driving them mad with terror. It is possible that

the awe-inspiring personage known as " the Washer of
the Ford," who appears in many of the tales to warriors
and hosts going out to battle, washing and wringing
at a stream the bloody garments of those who will
be slain in the fight, is another aspect of the Badb.
Some years ago a small pillar-stone, about thirty inches
high, bearing an inscription to this goddess under the
name of Cathubodvae (the Irish Badb-Catha), was found
in Haute-Savoie in France, proving that she was known
also in Gaul, and possibly worshipped there.

But it is remarkable that these gods, so well known
to the Romans, and whose cult was spread over Britain
and Gaul, are by no means the members of the Tribe
of Danu best known to us in the romances. We
possess no long tales of Nemon and Ogma and Brigit,
or of many of the other gods whose worship is recorded on
Gaulish and British inscriptions. We should indeed hardly
be aware that such great personages had ever existed
but for casual allusions such as those in the topographical poems or in Cormac's Glossary and the *Cóir
Anmann*, the " Explanation of Names," in which their
titles and attributes are interpreted to a people already,
in the ninth or tenth century, half-forgetful of their
existence. These hoary gods of the primeval time
made way for the youthful Angus, Manannán and Lugh,
a younger and more attractive race of deities. Yet
that they once occupied a large place in the conception
of the people is shown by the multitude of place-names
which in early times were derived from their traditions
and connected with their names, and by the frequent
casual allusions to them in the romances, allusions
evidently well understood in the day in which these
tales were recited and written down, but to the meaning

of which we have now no clue. When Emer and Cuchulain converse about the route he has taken from Emain Macha to Lusk, a route every name of which enshrines some old tradition of ancient gods evidently familiar to both ; or when the two Sages utter their mystic poet's dialogue, we are in a world of legend of which we know hardly the barest outline. If ever the traditions of these ancient deities were enshrined in writing at all, and it is unlikely that they were, they have been almost entirely lost to us. Even the romances connected with the younger gods are rare ; those of the most remote age hardly exist at all To us, Eochaid Oll-athair, " a great father to the Tuatha Dé Danann ; " Adammair Flidaise, " Queen of the Tuatha ; " the three Brigits ; Delbaeth, or " the Shape of Fire ; " Bil or Bial, who is supposed to have given his name to the " beltine " or fires of Bel ; Midach, a Dé Danann physician, son of Diancecht, or Etan, the poetess, his daughter, are mere names. Even of such great personages as Lir or Llyr, god of the ocean, who is better known in Welsh mythology, but who has in both abdicated his supreme position in favour of his son, Manannán mac Lir (Manawyddan mac Llyr), we know little beyond the modernised story of the " Fate of the Children of Lir," in which his connection with the ocean seems forgotten ; but even in late Irish poetry the billows were known as " Lir's Plain," while the hoary ancient god plays his tempestuous and storm-tossed part in tragedy, as the original of Geoffrey of Monmouth's and Shakespeare's " King Lear."

I am inclined to think that there must have been some intentional omission of romances or destruction of manuscripts relating to the Tuatha Dé Danann, otherwise it is difficult to account for so complete a disappearance of what must once have been a large cycle of tradition. To the populace of later times the gods became fairies or *sidh* (shee) folk, harmless, beautiful and dignified troops of beings who inhabited the hills and fairy-mounds ; but the scribes and Christian teachers regarded them as evil spirits and spoke of them as demons. It is more than possible that these stories were discouraged, just as the old pagan incantations and sooth-saying were rigorously put down. From whatever cause, we have only casual allusions and stories remaining of a great cycle of old romance.

Nuada.—Another personage who was apparently known to the Romans as a god is Nuada of the Silver Hand. In an inscription in Gloucestershire, found in what is believed to be a Roman temple dedicated to this god, the words D. M. Nodonti are inscribed, while in a mosaic pavement on the ground occur the same letters D. M. N. They are surrounded by a border representing two water-monsters with intertwined necks and salmon playing about. In another spot is to be seen a fisherman hooking a magnificent salmon. These emblems point to the probability that the god here worshipped was a water deity. This god, called Nodens by the Romans, is thought to be the same personage who in Ireland is called Nuada and who was wedded to Boand, the goddess who gave her name to the river Boyne, which is said to have risen out of a secret magic well that no one was permitted to look into. In her pride of heart, Boand looked into the well, saying that it could not harm her, but the water rose and over-flowed, following her as she fled to the sea, where she was drowned. Of Nuada we know little, save that he appears as King of the Tuatha Dé Danann in the late tale of the First Battle of Moytura, fought, it is said, at Cong on the east of Loch Corrib, in Co. Mayo, between the Dé Danann and Firbolg races. In this battle he is said to have lost an arm which was replaced by Diancecht, the physician, with a movable arm of silver, whence his name Nuada *Airgetlám*, or Silver Hand. This, however, is not an ancient story but belongs to the later attempt to explain the old traditions of the gods by a succession of invasions of Ireland. There is only one battle of Moytura in the primitive belief, and in this battle Nuada is said to have been killed by Balor of the Hard Blows and Evil Eye. Professor Rhys thinks that Nuada is the same personage as Nudd or Lludd, a god over whose early temple the Cathedral of St. Paul's was afterwards built and who gave his name to Ludgate Hill.*

In later centuries, when the belief in pagan gods was beginning to fade away, it is probable that there were added to the family of the Tuatha Dé Danann the names and traditions of many local and tribal deities, who had been worshipped for centuries, but who had no real place in the cycle. The official collector and recorder of traditions knew that different places were centres of special cults, and he threw the names of these various local gods into the one great family called Dé Danann, which had come to include for him the whole primitive pagan hierarchy. These local native cults were perhaps

* Personally, I feel doubtful about the identification of Nuada either with the Roman deity or with Nudd. The attributes do not agree, and Nuada appears to belong to a later or different order of ideas.

the most ancient of any that we know ; earlier, it may be, even than the coming of the Gael or Briton to the land.

The head of this primeval family of the gods was called Ana or Anu, goddess of Wealth and Prosperity, the " mater deorum hibernensium " from whom the Tuatha Dé Danann, that is, the " Children " or " Tribe of Danu " or " Anu " are sprung.   Two hills called " The Paps of Ana," near Killarney, are named from her, symbols of productiveness and life-giving ; and, according to an ancient though doubtful derivation, the name of Munster is taken from *mó* " greater " and *Ana* " wealth " or " prosperity," because of the great fertility contributed by her to the province.

Dagda Mór.—Among the ancient gods an important place is assigned to the Dagda mór, who in one place is said to have been worshipped by the Tuatha Dé Danann themselves on account of the vastness of his powers. His name seems to mean the " Good God," and he is elsewhere spoken of as " Cera," which Dr. Stokes takes to mean " Creator."   He is called also " Ruad-Rofhessa," the " Lord of great knowledge," or the " All-knowing One," because he knew perfectly all pagan wisdom.   He is represented in the piece called " The Second Battle of Moytura " as a grotesque and cumbersome old man, so fat and unwieldly that men laughed when he attempted to move about.   From the hugeness of his body he could hardly walk, and his club was so massive that it took eight men to draw it on a wheeled car behind him.   As it rolled along it left tracks as broad and deep as the boundary-dyke between two provinces.   He had a cauldron which held fourscore gallons of new milk and a similar measure of meat and fat. Whole goats and sheep and swine were put into it, and of this the porridge of the Dagda was made. Before the " Second Battle of Moytura " the Fomorians filled his cauldron with porridge and bade him eat the whole of it on pain of death. Each bit as he brought it up was a half of a salted pig or a quarter of beef, and he ate it with a ladle big enough to hold a man and woman lying in the hollow trough of the spoon. He possessed, too, a magic harp into which he had so bound the melodies that they sounded forth only when summoned by his call, and the harp would move of its own power from the wall to his hand when he summoned it, overthrowing all that stood in its way. He played on it the three strains known to the perfect musician ; the sleep-strain, which brought slumber on the hosts and on invalids in pain or trouble ; the wail-strain, which made men and women weep ; and the laughing-strain, on hearing which all who listened to it laughed aloud. This monstrous and grotesque figure of the Dagda, who reminds us in many respects of the Greek Cronus, is only one of a large group of the ancient deities who are possessed of prodigious powers. Each represents some quality ; as the Dagda is Lord of all Science, and Brigit of Philosophy and Poetry, so Diancecht is master of Leech-craft or Medical Arts, Ogma of the force of Eloquence, Credne and Goibniu of the arts of Smithery. In the Second Battle of Moytura, in which they all engage, their various powers are put to the test. The club of the Dagda, like the thunderbolt of Jove, rattles down upon the enemy, crushing their bodies as " the hailstones are crushed beneath the feet of a herd of horses."

The smith, Goibniu, forges spears that never make a
missing cast, and no skin was ever pierced by them
without the death of its owner following.   When the
spears were broken in conflict they were renewed again
by three casts of the spear-heads the shafts and the
rivets made successively by Goibniu and Credne, the
smiths, and Luchtine, the carpenter.   This Goibniu
became known in later times as the mysterious wandering
architect called the Gobhan Saer, to whom a popular
tradition ascribes the invention and construction of the
first of the Round Towers.   He belongs, however, to a
far earlier stage of tradition.   The powers of Diancecht
in battle were no less valuable to his friends, for he
prepared a well with magic herbs, and every wounded
warrior who was put into its water overnight was fit
for conflict again on the morrow ; while Bé-chulle and
Dianann, the two witch-folk, brought up hosts and
battalions of armed men formed out of the trees, and
stones, and sods of the earth.

The Second Battle of Moytura.—This battle, the
account of which is one of the few long romances which
give us details of the personages in this ancient
Pantheon, was a terrific conflict between the Tuatha Dé
Danann and the Fomorians, fought on the coast of
Ballysodare, in Co. Sligo.   The Fomorians were sea-
giants, descending upon and depredating the North
of Ireland.   These terrific beings, who ultimately
merge into the Lochlannachs or Norsemen, were,
according to some accounts, monsters with one hand
or one foot, or with the heads of horses and goats.
They demanded the offering of healthy human children,
and of two-thirds of the corn and wine of Ireland

as a tribute.   According to the old legends, these
fierce pirates of vast stature and terrifying appearance
infested the northern coasts of Ireland for over two
hundred years.   At the time we first hear of them
they are led by Ciocal *cen chos*, or Ciocal the " Footless,"
son cf Garbh the " Rough," son of Ughmor, or " Great
Woe."   In the Battle of Moytura their leaders are
Breas, who is half a Fomorian and half a Dé Danann,
and had been Regent of Ireland, but whose cruelty
and parsimony were such that he was driven out of the
kingdom ; and Balor, a terrible monster with a single
eye in the middle of his forehead, who was known as
" Balor of the Evil Eye."   Save on a battle-field
that eye was never opened, and it needed four men to
lift the lid with a polished rod that passed through it.
Before its poisonous glance a host of men would fall.

Opposed to the Fomorians are the Tuatha Dé Danann,
the children of light and knowledge, whose coming to
Ireland had been in a magic mist, so that men knew
not whether it was from the heavens or from the earth
they came, or whether they were phantoms or men.*
They were possessed of the knowledge of arts and
sciences, so that men regarded them as magicians and
wizards, to whose powers all things were possible.

Lugh.—They are led in the Battle of Moytura by
Lugh, son of Cian, the brilliant youthful god whose

---

* The later annalists, who looked upon these old gods of their
nation merely as so many different races of men who settled at
different times in Ireland, are quite clear as to who each was
descended from and whence each came.   We have nothing
to do in this chapter with this later rationalized account.   Here
we are regarding them entirely in their original light as parts
of an ancient mythology.

widespread cult has left his name in the towns of
Laon, Leyden and Lyons (*i.e.*, *Lugu-dunum*, the dún
or town of Lugh), and whose sports and festival on
August 1st, called in Ireland Lúghnasadh, the Feast
of Lugh, were by no means confined for their celebration
to the Irish Gael. Lugh *Lámh-fhada* " of the long arms "
was the god of light and knowledge among the ancient
Irish ; he is often called *Ioldánach* or *Samildánach*,
as being possessed of many arts, and when he presents
himself at the door of Tara and is challenged as to
his powers, he proves that he is the superior of each
expert in his own special branch of knowledge.   The
brilliance of his form and countenance betokened the
splendour of his mental qualities.   In the " Fate of
the Children of Tuireann," he is described as " a young
man high in authority over all ; like to the setting
sun was the radiance of his face and brow, and they
were unable to gaze upon his countenance for the
greatness of its splendour."   Later in the same tale
we read that as he was approaching Breas, son of Balor,
from the west, the Fomorian king mistook him for
the rising sun.   " It is strange," he said, " that the
sun should rise in the west to-day and in the east every
other day."   " It had been well for us if it were the
sun," say the Druids.   " Why, then, what else can
it be ? " said he.   " It is the radiance of the face of
Lugh *lámh-fhada*," they reply.   His long arms may
represent the outstretched rays of the rising and the
setting sun.   He is " the gifted child " who both
in Welsh and Irish story reached full growth and
development when he was yet but a babe.   His magic
spear flashed fire and thirsted for blood ; in battle it
roared and struggled to get free, for it had life within

itself.   In Welsh literature he is known as Llew, the
god of light ; he marries a maiden formed of flowers,
and he rises up towards heaven as an eagle.   All his
race were gifted, but none so excelled as he.   When
he encounters Balor of the Evil Eye on the battle-field,
the One-eyed said to his servant, " Lift up mine eye-lid,
lad, that I may see this babbler who is talking to me."
The lid was raised from Balor's eye, and Lugh cast at
him a sling-stone which carried the eye right through
his head behind, so that its poisoned glance fell on his
own host and they fell dead before its venom.

It seems clear that the great mythological warfare
between the Fomorians and the Tuatha Dé Danann,
which culminated in the second battle of Moytura,
represents the contest between the forces of light and
knowledge on the one side and the powers of darkness
and ignorance on the other.   It describes, under the
form of a myth, the struggle which the advancing
intelligence and skill of man wages against the brute
forces of nature, subduing them to his will.   With arts
that appeared to their ignorant predecessors magical and
superhuman, the people of knowledge drove out before
them the days of barbarism, when nature presented
itself to man merely as a cruel and devouring foe, taking
from human beings all that their industry had gathered
of corn and produce, and demanding even their offspring
in toll.   But brute force had eventually to give way
before the light but efficient weapons of civilization
and progress in knowledge.*

Lugh belongs to the younger race of the gods, but

* Later legend added another Battle of Moytura Cong, in
Galway ; but it has no place in the original mythological conception.   It belongs to the annalistic account of the Settlements.

there are one or two of the older race of whom some traditions and stories are left, which must be mentioned before we pass on.

Midir.—Midir, the "Very Proud One," who dwelt at the *sidh* or shee-mound of Bri-Leith, is chiefly known as the husband of Etain, the goddess, who became a mortal and was wedded to Eochaid, King of Ireland (Wooing of Etain, p. 83). Even in her human state Midir still loves Etain and watches over her, and from time to time he appears to her and prays her to return with him, but she will not part from Eochaid. Finally, in a beautiful and dramatic tale, it is told how Midir wins back his wife as the stake in a game of chess played with Eochaid and bears her off through the air to the fairy-mound. He is said to have possessed " three cranes of inhospitality and churlishness," but this does not seem to accord with his character.

Cian.—The father of Lugh, and son of Diancecht. It is he who was cruelly murdered by the three sons of Tuireann when to escape them he had changed himself into one of a herd of swine. One of the three, suspecting this, changed his two brothers into hounds, who pursued the boar, and one of them ultimately killed Cian by stoning him. The earth refused to retain his body, so horrified was it by the savage deed, and Lugh, on discovering the death of his father, demanded of them a heavy fine or eric, which brought them all to a miserable end. There are ugly and curious stories told of Cian in the tale of " The Pursuit of Diarmuid and Grainne " ; he would appear to have been regarded as an unquiet and gruesome being.

Lugh is also called, according to other accounts,

Lugh mac Ethlenn, from the name of his mother, who seems to have been daughter of Balor and Cian's wife. A folk tale in Donegal calls Lugh's father and mother MacKineely and Ethnea, evidently forms of Cian and Ethlenn; in this story MacKineely is killed by Balor, his father-in-law, and it is on this account that Lugh revenges himself on the one-eyed Fomorian tyrant. Lugh himself was father of Cuchulain, in whom were reproduced many of the qualities of the brilliant Irish sun-god.

The three sons of Tuireann who killed Cian were named Brian, Iuchar and Iucharba.   In the annalistic accounts they are known as Mac Cuill, Mac Cecht, and Mac Greine, who were wedded to Banba, Fodla, and Eriu, the three princesses who gave their poetic names to Ireland.   Here we see the Irish passion for triads in full force, for these are all evidently forms of single personages, having three names of similar meaning to designate them.   The Dagda himself is called also Cera, and Ruad-rofhessa, to express his different qualities as Creator and All-knowing One, as well as that of the Good God; and his wives bear three melancholy names denoting Lying, Deceit, and Shame, pointing to an early conception of the union of good and evil forces.   These three princes, Mac Cuill, Mac Cecht, and Mac Greine were the three Tuatha gods, the Dé Danann, *par excellence*, according to the annalistic accounts, and it was they who led the settlement to Ireland and reigned there together; their mother was Danu or Anu, the mother of the gods, of whom we have already spoken. The account of their miserable end in the story of the Children of Tuireann does not agree with their province as gods of literary and artistic inspiration, and seems to

D

belong to a different order of ideas about them. They are elsewhere called sons of Brigit, in her capacity of goddess of poetry and philosophy, and grandsons of the Dagda. The attempt to make them into historical princes of human origin has confused the interesting symbolism of the mythological accounts.

Angus.—A legend of Angus, one of the younger gods, whose attributes of beauty, youthfulness and love make him the Adonis of the Irish Pantheon, seems to describe symbolically the transference of authority from the elder to the second race of deities. The great range of tumuli which lie along the north bank of the sacred river Boyne, near Drogheda, known as New Grange, Dowth and Knowth, with a number of lesser mounds in the vicinity, became associated in the minds of the people with the Tuatha Dé Danann. They are evidently very ancient royal tombs, for skeletons have been found in their domed chambers, but to the early Irish they represented the dwellings of the gods. Angus, especially, was always called Angus na Brugh, because he was conceived of as inhabiting the mansion or Brugh on the Boyne, which was supposed to be always adorned with flowers and decorated with the greatest splendour. Brugh na Boinne originally belonged to Elcmar, the foster-father of Angus, whose real father was the Dagda mór, to whom he was the youngest son. Manannán Mac Lir suggested to Angus to ask Elcmar to allow him the possession of the Brugh for a night and a day ; but when this was granted he refused to give it up again, averring that all time was made up but of nights and days. Then he surrounded himself with an invisible wall which none might pass, and he lived henceforth in splendour, drinking the ale of immortality and eating of the pigs that never failed.*

Of Angus, the youthful God of Love, many love adventures are told.   It is said that the four kisses of Angus were changed into birds " who haunted the young men of Erin."   When Etain, wife of Midir, was separated from her husband by the evil wiles of Fuamnech, her rival, Angus placed her in a *grianán* or sunny chamber of crystal which he always carried about with him.

As Lugh was re-born in Cuchulain, so Diarmuid, in Ossianic legend, was looked upon as a second and more human Angus, whose " love-spot," that is, his beauty, caused every woman who saw him to fall in love with him.   Angus guards and watches over Diarmuid and Grainne, and when they are in danger carries Grainne off with him to Brugh na Boinne.   All the stories of Angus that have come to us represent him in the same aspect.

Manannán Mac Lir and Bran.—We learn more of the family of Lir in Welsh story than we do in Irish legend, for except from the single modernized tale of the " Fate of the Children of Lir," which in no way represents the old beliefs regarding him, we have few references to this ancient Ocean-god.   In Ireland his characteristics were carried on in Manannán, his restless, wandering, shape-shifting son, whose changing moods and dwelling-places well represent the moving, unstable ocean.   Llyr, in Welsh story, was the father of several children, the most important of whom were Bran or Bendigeid Vran, Manannán (called in Wales Manawyddan), and

---

* Another account says he got the Brugh directly from the Dagda, who had forgotten to provide a home for Angus.

Branwen, a daughter, who wedded an Irish king. Bran and Manannán are both known in Ireland, but their relationship is not so well defined. They have many characteristics in common, and in Irish legend Manannán seems to have taken the place of Bran in the imagination of the people as he did that of his father Lir. He is a great favourite with the Irish race, who have always loved this wandering tricksty god, whom they thought of later as " a celebrated merchant in the Isle of Man," and " the best pilot of the West of Europe, who could tell the periods of fine and wet weather by studying the sky." He is usually connected in Irish legend with the Isle of Man, which an old Irish Glossary tells us was named after him ; while Loch Oirbsen, the more ancient name for L. Corrib in Galway, recalls another name of this god. In the Isle of Man, where also there is a tradition that he was their first ruler, his grave, thirty feet long, is shown outside Peel Castle. He kept the island always under magic mists raised by his wizard arts, and it is said that the curious sign of the Island, three legs joined like a wheel, are the legs of the ocean-god rolling through the mists. Possibly they represent the rise, full meridian and setting of the sun. This god was possessed of two magic cows brought by him from India which supplied an inexhaustible flow of milk, and at his banquet, the " Feast of Age," every comer was satisfied, for, like the Dagda, he possessed the " Undry cauldron," or " Cauldron of Restitution," so called because it never failed until each had had his fill. There was neither more nor less than was needed for every guest. The cauldron was called also the Cauldron of Truth, because if anyone present spoke falsehood, the pig that was in it could not be cooked, and each must tell a true story before the cooking was finished. Manannán possessed also the Helmet of Invisibility, in which he could not be seen ; and he travelled in a magic copper boat, the " Wave-Sweeper," which needed no oar or rudder, but went directly to whatever place its master desired. His spears were " Yellow Shaft " and " Red Javelin," and his swords were " Great Fury " and " Little Fury." His shield, which in after days became the Shield of Fionn mac Cumhaill, was made from the wood of the Dripping Ancient Hazel, the withered leafless tree which bore the head of Balor of the Evil Eye, after Lugh cut it off at the Battle of Moytura, and from which a baneful venom dripped.*

The legends of this restless deity are in Ireland not always to his credit, but the most important *rôle* he fills is that of King of the Land of Promise (Tir Tairngiri), or, as it is sometimes called, the Land of Sorcha or " Clearness," or Magh Mell, the " Honey Plain."

The idea that this land of everlasting youth and beauty lay under or beyond the water of lakes or of the ocean coincides with Manannán's connection with islands and distant places in the sea. It is always reached by a boat or coracle, and is invisible to ordinary mortals. Sometimes it is called " Emain of the Apples," a name applied to the Islands of Mull or Arran in Scotland. Both Bran and Manannán are connected in the Over-sea Voyage tales with this blissful elysium, of which we have to speak later. Bran makes a voyage thither, its beauty being described to him in exquisite verses sung by the princess who entices him away. Manannán is found reigning there by Cormac when he

* Poem on the " Shield of Fionn," in the collection of Ossianic poems called *Duanaire Fhinn.*

goes away into the invisible land ; and in the story of Cuchulain's Wasting-away or Sickbed he is the husband of Fand, the Queen of the fairy-world.   It was because he had forsaken her for a time that she appealed to Cuchulain to come to her.   He, however, claims her again and takes her back to his invisible realm.   The name Fand is said in the old story to mean a " tear," " the moisture or water of the eye ; " it seems to mean simply water, and is an appropriate designation for the wife of the Ocean-god.

In Welsh legend he is not connected with the ocean ; he is rather an agriculturist and an expert shoemaker ; a gentle and kindly character who was robbed of his throne by an intruder.   He is not so important as Bran, his brother, who is " King of the Island of the Mighty," or Britain ; and whose head, buried on the White Mount in London, with the face turned towards France, pre-vented any invasion coming across the sea so long as it lay in concealment.   No house that ever was made could contain Bran, and to him belonged a Cauldron of Renovation.   It was brought to him from Ireland, and revived dead men who were cast into it in time of battle, so that " save that they had not the power of speech, they were as good fighting-men as before." For over fourscore years after he was dead, Manawyddan and Pryderi and Taliesin, and four other nobles carried the head of Bran with them from place to place, till they came in joy and peace to the shut door that looked towards Cornwall.   In Harlech they feasted seven years, the birds of Rhiannon singing unto them the while ; and for fourscore years at Gwales in Penvro, in a fair regal spot overlooking the ocean, and they were unconscious of ever having spent a time more joyous and mirthful ; and the head with them all the time, as pleasant company as ever it had been in life. This sojourning of theirs is spoken of in a tale called "The Entertaining of the Noble Head." And until they opened the door that was shut they knew no sorrow, but when they looked through it all the evils that they had ever sustained came back upon them again, and they hastened to bury the head, as Bran had commanded them. This Welsh version of a sojourn in an earthly Magh Mell is interesting as being connected, like the Irish visions, with Manannán and Bran.

In later days Bran is introduced into authentic history as Bran the Blessed, the Father of Caratacus, the British chief who made his noble protest in chains before the Emperor Claudian at Rome.

The Retirement of the Gods.—In later times, when the pagan gods no longer held their old place in the thought of the people, the annalists and poets told how, after the battle of Taillte (Teltown, in Co. Meath), in which the Milesians defeated the Tuatha Dé Danann hosts, they retired into the green valleys and hills of Erin and set up new kingdoms underground. They gave the Sovereignty to Bodb Derg, son of the Dagda, and they settled down, each with their own chiefs and hosts, in different parts of the provinces of Ireland. The *sidh* or fairy-dwellings of these invisible chiefs were as well-known as the palaces of the princes who reigned above ; and the hosts appear as fairy cavalcades of noble and beautiful beings who mix from time to time with men and women, and even intermarry with them ; but who retain always some special dignity of form and expertness in magical arts which mark them out as being above and independent of the limitations of mortal life.

CHAPTER II.
The Red Branch Tales

This great group of tales, comprising some of the finest literature that Ireland has produced, seems to have arisen in and to have been confined to Ireland. Except for two or three Welsh songs, connected principally with Curói mac Daire, and for a few incidents, such as the tale of the Sons of Usnech and the Death of Conlaech, which are found in their late mediæval forms in Scotland, the Cuchulain stories are unknown outside Ireland. In the Highlands and Western Isles these stories have become so mixed with the tales of Fionn and his compeers that MacPherson, when he came to re-cast the legends, believed that they formed part of the Saga of the Fianna.

At the present day they are even little remembered in Ireland itself. But at the time when the Book of the Dun (*Leabhar na h-Uidhre*), the Book of Leinster, and the Yellow Book of Lecan were compiled, that is, from the beginning of the twelfth to the close of the fourteenth century, these tales formed the bulk of the romance of the people, or, at all events, of the nobles and chiefs. They fill a great portion of the pages of these volumes and they held a large place among the " Chief " and " Secondary " stories which it was the duty of the *seanchaidhe* or Story-teller to relate at feasts and entertainments, as is shown by the lists that still remain of the titles of these stories in the Preface to the Ancient Laws of Ireland, in the Book of Leinster, and elsewhere.

The Ulster Cycle.—These tales hail from and deal with Ulster : not with the whole of Ulster, but exclusively with that eastern portion of the province known in ancient times as Uladh, lying east of Lough Neagh and the River Bann.   It is curious to us, to whom this particular district, the neighbourhood of Belfast, Lurgan and Newry, with their surrounding manu-facturing towns, represents the most commercial and industrial, perhaps, we may even say, the most prosaic centre of Ireland, to reflect that it was from this very area that the finest of our old romances and the most splendid Gaelic conceptions of chivalry, valour and honour emerged and took shape.   This district, which was, in the time of which we speak, politically distinct from the rest of the province, had for its capital Emain Macha ; the outlines and raths of this ancient palace of its kings still remain and are known by the name of Navan Fort, a few miles south-west of Armagh.   The whole action of the stories is, so far as they deal with Ulster, confined to this narrow strip of country and the district immediately south-east of it.   Here the various chiefs and heroes who play their part in the stories had their dúns or forts ; here, along the southern skirts of the province, took place the entire raid known by the name of the *Táin bó Cuailnge*, which forms the central pivot of the entire series of Ulster tales.

Historically, the palace of Emain Macha was destroyed in 332 A.D., and later we find the balance of power shifted to the opposite end of the province. The O'Neills of the Norse period are found holding their court and exercising a powerful sway from their solid and still very remarkable fortress of Aileach, six

miles S.W. of Londonderry in the present County of
Donegal, and thenceforward, up to the dispersion of
the clans, the O'Donnells and O'Neills of Western and
South-Western Ulster brought their tribal districts
into a position of influence which made this the most
stirring portion of the whole country; princedoms the
sturdiness of whose independence centuries of effort on
the part of England failed to subdue.

Ancient Boundaries of Ulster.— In the first
century, when the deeds of the Ulster champions
are supposed to take place, the province of Ulster
extended much farther in a southward direction
than it did after the formation of the kingly province
of Meath, about the middle of the second century,
and it is a mark of the great antiquity of the tales
that they show no knowledge of Meath as a separate
province. According to tradition, the centre of Ireland
was erected into a distinct province by a king called
Toole (Tuathal) the Legitimate, about 130 A.D., a
portion being taken off each of the existing provinces
for this purpose round a great stone on the Hill of Usnech,
in Westmeath, still called the "Stone of Divisions."
But at the time in which these stories arose Ulster
stretched southward to the borders of Munster and
Leinster, and included the district of the Eastern
sea-border (the present counties of Louth and Down)
which formed the tribe-lands of Cuchulain, the chief
hero of the tales. His fort or dún was at Dún Dalgan
(now Dundalk) and his district was called Cuailnge
and Magh Muirthemne. It was on Cuchulain's own
ground that the chief incidents of the Táin took place.

The five provinces spoken of in the Táin do not,

therefore, include Meath, which had not then come into existence. They are Ulster in the North, and Leinster, Connaught, and East and West Munster in the South. Munster was, throughout the whole course of mediæval history, and into comparatively modern times, divided into two practically independent portions ; in the earliest stage and during the Norse period we find the division existing between the East and West, with Cashel as the capital of the Eastern, and Kincora, at least in the time of Brian, of the Western portion ; but later the balance of power lay between the Northern and Southern Kingdoms, known as Thomond and Desmond.

We have, then, reason for believing that the principal tales of this cycle arose at a period (1) when the Province of Meath was unknown ; (2) when the centre of power in Ulster lay in the eastern district of the province, and the traditions of Emain Macha as its capital were alive among the people.

The second point leads us somewhere back before the end of the fourth century, the first before the middle of the second century. The purely pagan character and flavour of the tales themselves and the archaic stage of civilization they reveal, tends to confirm the traditions of their early origin. They present us with a picture of life drawn from a stratum of society coeval with that of the Homeric age in Greece. The chariot-driving instead of riding, the methods of warfare, the series of single hand-to-hand combats of which every battle was composed, the open-air roving life made up of raids and cattle-driving, the quickly-aroused passions and swift retaliation, all these and many other points make up a picture of a society in a primitive stage of development. This fact would give to the early romance of Ireland a position of unique importance, even if it had no special beauties and excellences of its own to recommend it, such as it undoubtedly possesses.

Moreover, in many details, such as the use of armoured war-chariots in battle, the warriors fighting naked in the heat of conflict, the use of hounds as well as horses in warfare, the preservation of the skulls of slain enemies as trophies, the part taken by women in warfare, besides numerous details of personal appearance and habits, the Irish accounts correspond in a marked way with the observations made by classical writers of the first century or thereabouts regarding the Celtic peoples with whom they came in contact. Cæsar, Livy, Poseidonius, Strabo, Diodorus the Sicilian, and Tacitus, give detailed reports of the Britons and Gauls with whom the Roman armies were so often at warfare and many of whom they absorbed among their fighting legions; and these descriptions tally closely with what we know from these native stories about the conditions of life among the ancient Irish. This tends to confirm the supposition that the traditional date of the origin of the tales, that is to say, about the beginning of the Christian era, cannot be very far astray.

The Red Branch.—The stories relating to Cuchulain and his champions, like those of Arthur and his knights, form an entire cycle; but they hail to us from an earlier age, and represent a more archaic system of life and thought. Some of them, like the Arthurian tales, have gone through successive changes and developments in the course of centuries of repetition; but the larger number bear the impress of a very early stage of society and primitive thought. It would seem that these stories, which relate the deeds and achievements of the champions of Ulster, or the Northern half of Ireland, fell gradually out of popular favour, and that the tales of Fionn and Oisín (Ossian) to a large extent replaced them. Few, if any, new stories were added to this cycle later than the twelfth century; whereas Ossianic stories and poems continued to be produced and invented up to recent times, and the recollection of the older Ossianic tales is still fresh in the minds of the peasants of Ireland and Western Scotland wherever Gaelic, either Scotch or Irish, is spoken to-day. Up to the time of king Brian Boromhe (Boru), who was killed at the Battle of Clontarf in 1014, the Overkings of Ireland were, with two insignificant exceptions, always chosen from the Northern race, and, naturally, the heroic deeds of the North were those recited in the palaces and houses of the chiefs belonging to the dominant party.

The Cuchulain cycle of tales relates the deeds and adventures of a group of heroes called "The Champions of the Red Branch," so named from one of their three halls of assembly. Chief among these heroes was Cuchulain, whose prowess began to show itself in his earliest youth, and whose courage and powers were so extraordinary that in the long and archaic tale which forms the pivot and centre of the series, called the *Táin bó Cuailnge* or "Cattle-raid of Cooley" (in Co. Down), he is represented as holding at bay single-handed the allied forces of Ireland through a long series of single combats which occupied a whole winter; and this at a time when he was but a youth and beardless.

Next to him in the order of their achievements came Conall *cernach*, or Conall " the Victorious," and Laeghaire *buadach*, or Leary " the Triumphant," two chieftains of almost equal valour. The contests of strength between these three famous champions form the theme of many of the tales. The heroes were supposed to have lived during the reign of a king called Conor or Conchobhar mac Nessa, who is said to have died of grief and fury at the news that Christ had been crucified in Judea—therefore about 30 A.D.

Historical Foundation of the Tales.—It is diffi- cult to decide how far the exploits and adventures of the Champions of the Red Branch cycle had an actual foundation in historic fact.

These chiefs and champions are, as we said, almost entirely unknown outside Ireland, and they are also but loosely connected with the history of Ireland in the Irish historic records. The casual mention of such personages as Fachtna *fathach*, who in some tales is spoken of as father of King Conor or Conchobhar (though he is said in the older versions of the tale to be son of the Druid Cathbadh), or of Cairbre *niafer* or Lewy of the Red Stripes (*Lughaidh Sriabh n-Dearg*) or of Congal *claringnech*, Conor's son, who are all mentioned in the Annals or Lists of royal personages, does not warrant us in concluding the whole series of characters and adventures to be based upon fact.

In the Nibelungenlied or the Dietrich Saga, it has pleased the later historians to give an appearance of historical consistency to the old mythology by trying to fit it into an actual place in their country's development; and so also in Ireland the personages of the Cuchulain

cycle are loosely connected with the history of the race,
but no system of interpretation will really make them
synchronise.   Indeed, the careers even of these semi-
historic personages are so mixed with fable that it is difficult to tell how much of their history may be believed.
Clearly the larger part of it is mythical.   Still we incline to
think that the general framework of the story may have
arisen out of actual circumstances, enlarged and
fashioned by centuries of re-telling, although reliable
history does not go back far enough to tell us what
these circumstances were.   Probably, also, some of
the characters, such as the warrior-queen Meave
(Medb), the Irish counterpart of Boadicea, and
those of King Conor or the chief heroes, owe their
conception to the traditions of actual personages
whose exploits had impressed themselves upon the
imagination of the race.   It is quite evident that such
ancient regal dwelling-places as Emain Macha and
Rath Cruachan of Connaught have been at one time,
far back in the dim memories of the past, places of
importance and centres of brave deeds, and that these
traditions should have lingered on and taken an imaginative form is only what we might expect.   Whether
this is so or not, these heroes have left their traces upon
the literature of their native soil in a far more marked
manner than many more recent and authentic chieftains
who have played their part in the history of their country.
The deeds of the O'Byrnes and O'Mores, the feats of
O'Sullivan Beare, nay, even the heroism of the O'Donnells and O'Neills may be forgotten by the Irish race
at large and but faintly treasured even locally about
their own country-side, but the legendary combats of
Cuchulain and Conall the Victorious, the pride of Meave

and the evil tongue of Bricriu remain still, like the wiles of Manannán or the loves of Angus, as a national heritage from the most distant past.

Mythology.—The Red Branch tales bear a close relationship to the earlier legends of the Tuatha Dé Danann ; indeed, a few of them, both in style and subject, such as the " Wooing of Etain " or the " Dispute of the Swineherds," belong equally to both cycles. The second series of legends was looked upon as the natural outcome of the first, and is dependent upon it for its significance and meaning. All the chief heroes of the Cuchulain cycle traced their origin and owed their birth to the earlier gods ; Cuchulain himself was, on one side, the son of Lugh *lámh-fhada*, and was possessed of many of his supernatural powers, although he had also on the earthly side a mortal father, named Sualtam or Sualtach, who is said not to have been of the race of Ulster.   Why Cuchulain, the chief champion of Ulster, is represented as being of another race, is obscure, but he is occasionally spoken of in the tales as being, unlike the majority of the heroes, who were fair or ruddy, " a little dark man," which emphasizes this distinction.   Elsewhere, however, he is described as fair, and possessed of hair of three different hues, golden at the tips and darker beneath.

It was supposed that all the Red Branch heroes were descended from the Tuatha Dé Danann gods, and their extraordinary feats and prowess are supposed to be accounted for by their divine origin.   The descent of the chief heroes, Fergus, Conall the Victorious, the Sons of Usnech, Conor and Cuchulain is traced from

Rury (Rudhraigh) the head of the family in the male line, and in the female line from Maga, a daughter of Angus na Brugh. Some of the personages, such as King Conor and Dechtire, his sister, are spoken of as gods and goddesses themselves, though this is qualified by the statement that they were " gods of the earth," which seems to imply that they occupied a different position to the earlier gods and were looked upon as intermediate between the old gods and ordinary men. It is not to be supposed that they either were worshipped themselves or worshipped the Tuatha Dé Danann. There is no sign whatever of such worship ; they were on a footing of intimacy with the gods far removed from the awe which shows itself in worship or from the terror which leads to sacrifice and propitiation. The early gods play a conspicuous part in the Cuchulain tales, but it is a part very similar to that taken by the Greek gods in the Trojan war. They take sides for or against Cuchulain, who is specially guarded and watched over by Lugh, his supernatural father, but attacked and harrassed by the Morrigan, or Goddess of War, who takes advantage of his moments of weakness to endeavour to destroy him. The champions address and challenge the gods on almost equal terms ; they regard them as more powerful than themselves, but otherwise as being simply their friends or foes ; indeed at times, as in the piece called the " Wasting away of Cuchulain," we find the gods appealing for help as well as for affection from the race of god-like heroes.

Each tribe seems to have had its own local deities, for the common form of asseveration is " I swear by the gods of my people " or " of my tribe ; " and it is probable that these tribal gods were worshipped. Certain folk-

E

customs retained to this day locally among the peasantry seem to carry down to us the memory of ancient rites. Such are the annual St. John's Eve festivities in the neighbourhood of Cnoc Ainé in Munster.   Ainé is Queen of the Munster fairies, and at midsummer the villagers carry burning bunches of hay and straw on poles to the tops of the hills, and scatter them over the land, hoping thereby to secure fertility.   The occasional mention in the old romances of " the gods to whom I pray " probably has reference to these family or tribal gods, while the Tuatha Dé Danann were looked upon rather as the presiding geniuses of war, arts and agriculture.   There was also in Ireland in very early times an appeal to and worship of the Elements, the Air, Fire, and Water, and the people are said to have " carved on their idol-altars the forms of the elements they adored, especially of the sun." (Cormac's Glossary, Ed. Stokes, p. 94.)

There are over a hundred tales belonging to the Red Branch cycle, and from these tales, which dovetail into each other with great exactness, we get a complete history from birth to death of each of the principal actors in the series.   It was the pleasure of the story-tellers to invent and follow up, bit by bit, an appropriate life-history for each of the characters in which they were interested.

The series centres in the great epic of the *Táin bó Cuailnge*, which in regard to the ancient literature of Ireland holds a place similar in importance to that occupied by the Iliad in the literature of Greece.   It is the pivot round which the whole cycle moves, and in it Cuchulain is the central figure and chief hero.   It will, therefore, be well to study it first of all.

CHAPTER III.

The Táin bó Cuailnge : its Mythology

Táins or Cattle-Drives.—It is very characteristic of the conditions of life in early Ireland that the most important of its romances should arise out of a Táin or Cattle-driving between the South and Ulster. These "táins" or "creaghs" were, as our annals show, of the most frequent occurrence between the clans. Every great war was preceded by a series of cattle-raids, which were designed to collect kine and other live-stock to serve as provisions for the army, and many lengthy campaigns consisted either entirely or for the main part not of a series of battles, but of a series of excursions into the enemy's country, accompanied by the burning and depredation of villages, and the carrying off of heads of cattle. To harry for "wives and kine" was part of the employment of a gentleman, and was considered as a natural and inevitable part of life, exciting neither anger nor surprise, but liable to be followed by reprisals on the part of the defrauded family or clan. In early Ireland the main part of the property and wealth of either a private person or of a sept consisted in the possession of horses and of herds of sheep, cattle, and swine. There was no money, and land was plentiful and of little account. There seems to have been little desire to add fresh extensions of territory to the tribal lands ; each chief was, as a rule, contented within his own limits, and even when a whole sept migrated, as in the case of the Deisi of Meath, there was no lack of space for them to settle

down elsewhere.   In proportion to the population,
land was plentiful ; the difficulty was to get sufficient
live-stock to place upon it.   It is to be remembered,
too, that private property did not in ancient times
consist in the possession of land ; except the actual
space around the fort or farm-house, land was not
separately owned, it belonged to the entire tribe and
was loaned out for cultivation to the heads of families.
No one might sell or alienate his piece of land ; it
still remained in the possession of the chief and could
be reclaimed by the tribe.   Any man could have " a
piece of bog, a piece of arable land, and a piece of
wood " for the asking, and on it he reared his family,
paying for it by tribute or by body-service to the chief.
But for chief and farmer alike the attainment of cattle
was a necessity, and the most powerful chief was he
who was possessed of the largest herds and flocks.
There is even an instance of a private farmer rising to
be monarch of Ireland merely through the accumulation
of great personal possessions.   These consisted in live-
stock, household utensils, ornaments and female slaves,
to which a chief would add as a title to consideration
the number of his fighting-men.   In these, and not in
land or money, wealth consisted, and a purchase
was effected by parting with these commodities in
exchange for other goods.   All this comes out with
great clearness in the Prologue to the *Táin bó Cuailnge*,
where Queen Meave, in calculating her possessions,
counts over the number of her flocks and herds, her
utensils, ornaments, and garments, but neither makes
protest as to the increase of her territories nor of the
number of the inhabitants under her sway.

Thus, by fair means or foul, a tribe or chief or farmer

must acquire cattle, and out of this necessity arose those raids into neighbouring territories, which were through centuries a normal part of the system of things. The Annals sometimes mention as many as four, six, or even eight plundering expeditions in different parts of the country in one year; and as we may conclude that only the larger provincial or tribal " cattle-liftings " and " hostings " were considered of sufficient importance to be included in the general Annals of Ireland, we must picture to ourselves a very restless and unsettled condition as prevailing throughout the country. The hand of every chief and lord was perpetually against his neighbour.

A great number of romances have as their subjects these " táins " or " creaghs; " the great romance of the *Táin bó Cuailnge* being preceded by a series of lesser Táins, relating, sometimes with much humour and gaiety, the series of lesser expeditions undertaken by Queen Meave to collect provisions for her host.

The Táin bó Cuailnge.—But in the Epic of Ireland the common topic of a cattle-drive is lifted far above the level of a tribal or local episode; it takes the form of a mythological warfare in which gods and god-like heroes alike struggle for mastery. Although it cannot be understood at all without an accurate conception of the simple pastoral conditions out of which it grew, and of the primitive state of the people to whom the tale of a cattle-lifting could assume an importance so vast and all-absorbing as to become the national epic, yet we feel, as we read it, that we are in the presence of ideas that have for the creators of the story a meaning and signi-

ficance far beyond the actual events recorded. Though
it has its origin in conditions of life familiar to the
nation it is not as a cattle-raid, pure and simple, that
we are expected to regard it.   There is an effort shown
throughout the story to make us conscious of the
presence of the supernatural, the vast, the abnormal.
The two Bulls, about whom the war is undertaken, are
of superhuman birth ; they have existed under many
different forms before they are re-born as bulls ; first
as swine-herds of the gods of the under-world, then as
ravens, as warriors, as sea-monsters, as insects.   Under
each of these forms they have lived through vast spaces
of time ; out of them they have come, always after a
terrific struggle which shook the borders of Ireland,
only to pass again into some new transformation.   Their
contests under these various aspects prove to be but a
prelude to the final war of the *Táin bó Cuailnge*, in
which all Ireland is destined to be engaged, and to the
gigantic struggle at its close between the two Bulls
themselves, wherein both of them are torn to pieces.

These Bulls are called the " Dond " or Brown One
of Cuailnge, Cuchulain's country (in the present Co.
Louth), and the " Findbennach " or White-horned, who
belonged to Meave (Medb) of Connaught.   It was her
ambition to become possessed of the second Bull, and
for this purpose she collected the united hosts of Ireland
to raid the province of Ulster and carry it off.

Both of these mysterious kine were of immense size
and possessed of prodigious ·powers.   In the final
passage of the piece which relates the birth and transformations of the Bulls, the Dond is thus described :—

> " With bull-like front,
> With the pace of a billow,

> With the pride of kings,
> With the loose plunging of bears,
> With the fury of dragons,
> With the impetus of robbers,
> With the savagery of lions, etc."

On his back or between his horns fifty little boys might every evening play their games. His bellowings strike terror into all who hear them, and after his final battle with the Findbennach, in which he gores and tramples his adversary to death, scattering its parts over the four provinces of Ireland, he returns, head erect, into Ulster, destroying all who come in his way; and finally, placing his back to a hillock and " vomiting his heart up through his mouth, with black mountains of dark-red gore," he so expires.*

Cuchulain.—The hero, Cuchulain, who has to defend alone and unaided the province of Ulster against the united hosts of Ireland, is also possessed of superhuman powers. He is the offspring of Lugh, the Irish sun-god, and he inherits the capacities belonging to his divine origin. From his birth he is of abnormal development. As a child of five he puts to shame all the boys of Ulster in their various sports; at six years he slays the terrible watch-dog of Culann the smith, from which feat he gained his name Cú-Chulainn, or "The Hound of Culann;" † at seven years he has already taken arms and slain prime warriors in single combat; and he is still a beardless boy of seventeen during the long winter throughout the whole of which he holds the hosts of

---

* Comp. in Vedic Mythology the deeds ascribed to Indra or the Sun. Rig-Veda i. 54, 4; *ibid* iii. 31, 6; *ibid* x. 75, 3, 4.

† See the section of the *Táin bó Cuailnge* entitled " The Boy-deeds of Cú."

Ireland in check, nightly and daily slaying and destroying great numbers of them.

When he puts forth his strength, his appearance is so terrific that no one can stand before him ; his very look destroys his foes, not by ones or twos, but by hundreds ; his whole person undergoes an extraordinary distention and change so that his very friends cannot recognise him ; his body gives off a terrific heat. Throughout his whole career, which ends at the early age of twenty-seven, his acts perpetually remind us that we are in the presence of a being more than mortal.

Debility of the Ultonians.—The cause of Cuchulain's single-handed fight is explained in one of the ten (or twelve) *remscéla* or introductory tales to the *Táin bó Cuailnge*. The legend is that a curse had been pronounced upon the king and warriors of Ulster by Macha, one of the three war-goddesses, on account of an act of cruelty practised upon her by King Conor. The curse she laid upon Ulster was that at the time of its direst need and danger the king and all his hosts should be prostrated by weakness and be unable to take part in defending the Province ; thus, during the whole course of the war, which occupied an entire winter, from Samhain or November, the beginning of the winter months, to Imbolc (2nd February), which in the ancient Irish calendar was the opening of the spring season, the whole of the men of Ulster, except Cuchulain, were lying prostrate in their houses and unable to go forth to fight. Hence, alone and single-handed, the youthful figure of Cuchulain is found holding back the hosts of the four provinces, guarding the frontiers of the Northern Province and dealing destruction among the enemy. The exemption from the curse made in the case of Cuchulain is said to have been " because he was not of Ulster," but it is not explained whence he came, or why, not being of Ulster, he on all occasions represents the Northern Province. Possibly this is only a late attempt to explain a phenomenon which the scribe himself could not understand ; or it may be intended indirectly to emphasize Cuchulain's supernatural origin.

Isolation of Ulster.—The *Táin bó Cuailnge* is, then, the history of a raid made by Queen Meave (Medb) of Connaught with the united hosts of Ireland into Uladh or Eastern Ulster to attempt to acquire possession of the Brown Bull or Dond of Cuailnge. Even at this early period we find Ulster standing alone, the foe and haughty antagonist of the rest of Ireland. This isolation and proud independence of the Northern Province is one of the most curious and persistent facts in Irish history ; it can be traced step by step backwards from the present day through the historical period and through the semi-historic stories of the kings, to the still more remote epoch of which these romances form a sort of pictorial record. This independent and haughty spirit goes back far beyond any differences of race, politics or religion, of which we have any historical knowledge ; it may perhaps arise from some very ancient difference of nationality whose beginnings have long since faded out of the memory of the race.

The hosts of Meave are led by the Queen herself under the direction of Fergus mac Roich, himself head of the Red Branch House of Ulster, and once king of the Province. When dispossessed of his Princedom by the wiles of King Conor he took refuge with Meave

and her consort, Ailell, and was induced by them to
take the conduct of her hosts against his own people.
The unwillingness of Fergus to aid the enemies of his
country, his affection for his foster-son Cuchulain,
and his efforts to spare and aid him, form one cf the
important side-issues of the tragedy.

Course of the Troops.—The course of the troops
is from Rath Cruachan (now Rath Croghan), Meave's
palace, in Connaught, by a fairly straight easterly route
towards Cuchulain's country, then called Cuailnge and
Magh Muirthemne, whence they strike up northward,
passing through the whole of Uladh or Ulidia in a direct
course to the extreme northerly coast at Dun Sobhairce
(now Dunseverick) in Co. Antrim ; returning by a line of
march keeping rather south of their former course, and
so back across the Shannon at Athluain (Athlone).

CHAPTER IV.

The Tain bo Cuailnge : its Literary Form

Two Main Recensions.—The *Táin bó Cuailnge* comes down to us in two main recensions,* which differ from each other not only in style and aim but in the arrangement of the incidents, and the matter which they include and exclude.   This long and popular story has not only gathered round it the group of shorter explanatory tales which are called the *remscéla*, or " foretales," but it has gathered into the body of the story itself fresh episodes as time went on, and has by the moulding and poetic additions of successive generations of story-tellers partly also changed its character and scope.   The old legend which traces the recovery of the original story to Senchan Torpeist, towards the end of the seventh century, has the support of linguistic evidence.   By the test of language the earliest version that we know would also be placed about this period. This earliest version is preserved in two vellum books known as the *Leabhar na h-Uidhre* (L.U.) or " Book of the Dun," written at Clonmacnois about 1100 A.D., and the " Yellow " or " Golden Book of Lecan " (Y.B.L.) written late in the fourteenth century.   Though neither of these copies is complete, they follow the same general outline, the copy preserved in the Yellow Book of Lecan being, although the manuscript is later, rather the older of the two.

---

* Some critics would add a third recension represented by some less-known manuscripts, but the above will be sufficient for the general student.

But a good deal of change, even in early times, went on in parts of the story in the course of repetition, some episodes being enlarged and adorned with fuller descriptions, poems being added, and the general arrangement being altered into a more homogeneous form. Some passages, such as the combat of Cuchulain with Ferdia became immensely extended and formed almost a separate story, filled with beautiful poems. About the eleventh century a new arrangement or " redaction " of the story was made, and the oldest version that we have of this secondary form is that found in the Book of Leinster (L.L.) written down before 1160. This is much more extended, complete and picturesque than the version in L.U. ; the author seems to have aimed at producing a literary version, and instead of the abrupt, condensed passages and archaic form of the Book of the Dun recension we have a finely artistic rendering of the whole story. From the copious materials before him the writer selected and arranged his material, giving full play to his artistic faculty and including all the poems and descriptive passages that seemed to him to heighten the interest or the pathos of the story. Though the language of this version, as we have it in the Book of Leinster, is not so old as the others of which we have spoken, the form of the story need not necessarily be later ; it may represent the manner of its recitation in Leinster while the other form may represent the manner in which it was usually recited in Connaught. From the solemnity with which the writer concludes his copy we should infer that the arrangement was not his own invention but was the one which, after due thought, be believed to be the most accurate which he could find. In a note

at the end, he adds, " a blessing on all such as con-
scientiously shall recite the Táin as it stands here,
and shall not give it any other form." It is evident
that he hoped by his version to restrain the tendency
to corruption which was going on.

Construction of the Story.—The *Táin bó Cuailnge*
divides itself into several sections, each of which has a
definite place in the building up of its composition.
Though its great length prevents us from easily analysing
its structure, to the old story-teller it had a very clear
construction, moving on from the light and playful
episodes of the opening passages through the deepening
seriousness of the single combats (which culminate in the
fight of Cuchulain and Ferdia), to the awakening of the
Ulster hosts and their general gathering on the Hill of
Slane. Following on this comes the final battle of the
Táin, in which the whole of the hosts of Ireland were
engaged in terrific conflict, and the ultimate dispersion
of Meave's forces, as they returned broken and flying
in rout across the Shannon at Athlone. Thus ends
the human portion of the conflict, which is appropriately
followed by the onset of the two Bulls against each
other, and their final destruction.

Exaggerated and tedious as parts of the story are,
the general outline and purpose of the theme is clear,
and the construction is carried out on a literary plan,
which remains distinct and well-defined in spite of
minor changes in the arrangement of the parts in the
different versions.

The outline is as follows :—(1) The Prologue, relating
in the form of a night dialogue between King Ailell
of Connaught and his wife, the causes which brought

about the raid, and Meave's consultation with a sooth-sayer as to its chances of success ; (2) the collecting of Meave's hosts and the preliminary movements of the army, during which period she first becomes aware of the presence and powers of Cuchulain.   Her enquiry of Fergus as to who this formidable foe, Cuchulain, is, leads to a long section called (3) Cuchulain's Boy-deeds, in which Fergus relates the remarkable prodigies of Cuchulain's youth, and warns Meave that though the hero is but a beardless youth of seventeen, he will be more than a match for all her forces.   Then come (4) the long series of single combats of which the first part of the tale is made up ; they are at first gay and bombastic in their character, but become more grave as they proceed, and culminate in the combat of Cuchulain with his old companion, Ferdia.   This section contains the account of Cuchulain's " Distortion " (*Riastradh*) which always occurred before any great output of the hero's energy, and of the rout of the hosts of Meave which followed it, called the *Brislech Mór* or " Great Rout " of Magh Murthemne.   After this come (5) the general awakening of the warriors of Ulster from their lethargy, and their gathering by septs upon the Hill of Slane, clan by clan being described as it comes up in order ; and (6) the final Battle of Gairech and Ilgairech, followed (7) by the rout of Meave's army and (8) the tragic death of the Bulls.

Thus, the story develops along natural lines of evolution, and we can study the parts in detail without losing sight of the continuous progress of the whole. This is much more marked in the Book of Leinster version than in that of the Book of the Dun, which exhibits rather the aspect of a series of disconnected episodes than that of a literary whole grasped by the mind of the writer as such. Of the one we may say that the composition is of the nature of a musical suite ; of the other that it corresponds to a musical symphony. Yet in the episodes in the older version, disjointed as they are, there are signs that the writers were aware of the more literary arrangement and have incorporated some parts of it into their text.

We can now study this story, the Iliad of Ireland, in some detail, giving a few examples of the manner and contents of the different episodes in their natural order.

The Prologue.—The Prologue opens with a curious and amusing " Bolster Conversation," or as we might term it, a "Curtain Lecture," of a sufficiently acrimonious sort between Queen Meave of Connacht and her spouse. The point in dispute is whether Meave, whose pride and arrogance are a marked feature in all the stories, has improved her position by marriage with Ailell, or the contrary. In an assertive manner she assures her husband that she might have wedded many men of higher position than himself, and that she had preferred him chiefly because she believed that he would let her have her own way and not interfere in any course of action that she might choose to pursue. The conversation, which is carried on at some length and with great spirit, ends in Meave sending out through the whole district to gather in her flocks and herds, her horses and pigs, and spreading out her household utensils and other goods to be reckoned over against those of Ailell that it might be seen which of them had the greater number of possessions. These proved to be in every way equal in amount and value, save that one Bull had of his own free will, and because, as the story quaintly puts it, " he deemed it unbecoming for a bull to be under the management of a woman," gone over to the cattle of Ailell. When this was made known to the Queen, she was so seriously annoyed at being found to be in any way poorer than her husband " that she deemed that she owned no pennyworth of stock." It was on account of this deficiency that she made up her mind to send to Cuailnge and try to gain possession of the most famous bull in Ireland, the Dond, and she instantly laid her plans for obtaining her purpose either by fair means or by foul. Thus the Epic of Ireland arose out of the pride and jealousy of a woman, as the Epic of Greece had its origin in a woman's beauty and frailty.

Humour of the Táin.—The Prologue gives the key-note to the whole of the earlier sections of the Táin, the characteristic feature of which is their buoyant, careless humour, a humour which everywhere breaks the monotony of Irish literature by the lightness of its touch. Later on in the story, when the central interest deepens, we lose these gay episodes, and the stress of the situation increases up to the end of the tale.

Take the account of the meeting of Cuchulain with the charioteer of Orlam, one of Meave's sons, just after the episode of the " Boy exploits " related by Fergus. The charioteer has been sent by his master to cut down a holly tree to make fresh chariot-poles for one of Meave's chariots, ruthlessly broken up in the rapidity of the pursuit entailed by Cú's sudden movements. While he is busy in the wood, Cuchulain comes up to

him and asks him what he does there ? The lad
innocently replies, " I am cutting chariot-poles to
repair our chariots, because that in chasing that famous
wild deer, Cuchulain, we have damaged them sorely ;
therefore, O Youth, lend me a hand, for I am each
moment in dread lest this same noble Cuchulain pounce
down upon me here." " Take thy choice, lad," says
Cuchulain, " shall I cut down the holly-poles or shall
I trim them for thee ? " " To trim them would
help me most," replies the boy. With all his wonted
energy, Cuchulain sets to work to smooth and trim
the holly-poles that are to be used against himself,
and so skilfully and rapidly does he turn them out,
that the charioteer, watching him closely, says at last,
" I incline to think that thou art accustomed to some
higher trade than cutting chariot-poles ; who art thou
then at all ? " " I am that notable Cuchulain of whom
just now you were speaking," says the hero. Terrified
out of his wits, the driver exclaims that he is but a
dead man ; but Cú comforts him with the assurance
that he hurts not charioteers, nor unweaponed men,
and sends him off with a message to his master Orlam
to tell him that he had better not come that way, as
he would certainly not return alive. The quaint
incident concludes by recounting how Cuchulain,
passing the messenger as he is going with the message,
arrives first and strikes off Orlam's head, and holding
it aloft, he shows it to, and shakes it before the faces
of the men of Erin. We are perpetually confronted
by this curious mixture of savage action and chivalrous
consideration.

Again, shortly afterwards, before the valour of the
Ulster hero has been proved to the Connaughtmen,

F

a certain massive, strong fighting-man, named Nachrantal, goes out to fight with Cuchulain, whom he despises
as a mere boy, with no arms but a sheaf of holly-spits,
prepared with fine points, hardened in the fire.
Cuchulain meets him at the ford, but when he sees the
weapons of his adversary, he takes no trouble to fight.
Nachrantal flings the wooden spits one after another,
and Cuchulain lightly catches them in his hand, or
leaps over them as they come against him.   In the
middle of this performance, a flight of wild-fowl swoop
down upon the plain.   Cuchulain, mindful of the
necessities of the evening's meal, for he was dependent
on his own exertions to sustain himself, and lived on
fish, birds and wild things caught by himself and his
charioteer through the entire winter, flies off and begins
to hunt the birds, quite forgetting Nachrantal, who
is left standing in the water.   Making the best of a
bad business, the warrior returns to Meave and boasts
that as soon as he saw him, Cuchulain ran away. " This
renowned Cuchulain, as he is called," he brags, " has
this morning behaved like any runaway or coward."
" We were quite sure," replies Meave exultingly, " that
as soon as a capable warrior and good battle-soldier
attacked him, this beardless young fury would make
no stand against him ; and now the first time a good
man of war has gone against him, he has straightway
run away ! "   Fergus heard this, and he was ashamed
that the young hero should give way before a single
warrior, however strong.   He sent a private message
to Cuchulain, to upbraid him. The message is delivered,
and Cuchulain is surprised.   " What do you mean ?
Who has been prating in this fashion ? " he asks.   When
told that it is Nachrantal, he exclaims : " Surely

Fergus and the nobles of Ulster know by this time that I fight never with charioteers or with men unarmed. I could not kill Nachrantal, because he had no weapons of defence; he brought with him but a few spits of holly. But tell him to return to-morrow morning, fully equipped, and we will have it out." Next morning the warrior goes forth, fully armed; but so changed is the aspect of Cuchulain (for his battle-fury had come upon him) that the man fails to recognise him. Needless to add, Nachrantal did not a second time return alive.

Central Episodes.—The central section of the Táin opens with the driving away of the Brown Bull northward from Cuchulain's country into the district northeast of Lough Neagh, and its refuging itself in Meave's camp, " the greatest insult that in the whole course of the raid was put upon Cuchulain." This ominous event gives the keynote to the whole of this section, which is one of stress and exhaustion to the hero, who, as we shall see, is, through the fatigue of the lengthened conflict sustained by him single-handed all through the winter, almost obliged to retire from the struggle. At this point also the Morrigan, or Goddess of War appears, and reiterates a former threat that she will take part against him in the moment of his greatest need; a threat which is afterwards fulfilled in her efforts to overwhelm him during his conflict with Loch Mór. The two severest combats sustained by Cuchulain in the course of the raid are this combat with Loch Mór and that with Ferdia. The accounts show several features in common; both men are first-rate warriors; both had learned the art of war from the Amazon Scathach in Alba (Scotland), and

in both episodes recur those touches of chivalrous consideration of the combatants for one another which gives
a tenderness to even the roughest and most barbarous
passages of this story.   There is a sort of lovable, boyish
swagger in the insistance of these heroes on carrying
out their absurdly exaggerated code of chivalry;
Cuchulain goes out of his way to send greetings by his
charioteer to his foster-brothers and comrades among
the hosts of Meave, who are now fighting against him;
most reluctantly, and only when forced to it, does he
allow himself to be drawn into combat with any one of
them, and on every occasion he gives them an opportunity to escape unharmed.   When Loch Mór, as a
dying request, prays him to permit him to rise, so that
he may fall on his face, and not backwards towards
the men of Erin, lest hereafter it should be said that he
fell in flight: " That will I surely," said Cuchulain,
" for a warrior's boon is that thou cravest; " and he steps
back to allow the wounded man to reverse his position
in the ford.   Yet it was in this combat that Cuchulain
was himself most nearly overcome, for the Morrigan,
appearing as a black eel, twined herself round the hero's
legs, so that he could not keep his feet; as a heifer,
followed by a herd of young cattle, she rushed through
the ford, upsetting him, while Loch Mór inflicted on
him wound after wound; as a rough grey she-wolf she
attacked him, and while he was dispatching her, again
the warrior wounded him.

It is this constant note of native chivalry which
differentiates Irish romance literature from the literature
of Greece, or even from the Arthurian cycle.   There we
get occasional examples of it, but here it stands out as
a prime consideration on every page.   These barbarians

are barbarians with the instincts and feelings of gentlemen.   In the combat with Ferdia, Cuchulain's former
friend and fellow-pupil, this chivalry finds its culmination.
The courtesy which day by day leads each to defer to
the other as to the choice of weapons, which night by
night makes them put up their horses in the same
paddock, while their charioteers lie beside the same
fire ; which, when Ferdia is wounded, makes Cuchulain
send to him healing balms and medicine men, and
when Cuchulain lacks food, makes Ferdia send provisions and pleasant drinks over the ford to him, cannot,
we should imagine, be surpassed in any literature.
It is as unlike as is possible to the treatment by the
Grecian warriors of their foes in the Wars of Troy.   It is
a sign that the conflict is nearly ended and has assumed
a deadly intensity when these kindly courtesies are,
on the last day of the fight, no longer resorted to.
In the fine though, as usual, exaggerated language of
the tale, " so close was the fight they made, that it seemed
(to the onlooker) that their heads met above, and their
feet below, and their arms in the midst over the rims
and bosses of their shields.   So close was the fight
they made, that they cleft and loosened their shields
from their rims to their centres.   So close was the fight
they made, that they turned and bent and shivered their
spears from their points to their handles.   Such was the
closeness of the fight that the phantoms and spectres
of the glens, and demons of the air, screamed from
the rims of their shields, and from the hilts of their
swords, and from the shafts of their spears.   Such
was the closeness of the fight that they cast the river
out of its bed, and out of its course, so that it might
have been a reclining and reposing couch for a king and

queen in the middle of the ford, for there was not a
drop of water in it, unless it dropped into it by the
trampling and hewing made by the two champions
in the middle of the ford.   Such was the intensity of
the fight they made that the steeds of the Gaels darted
away in fright and shyness, with fury and madness
breaking their chains and their yokes, their ropes and
their traces ; and the women and youths and little
people and camp followers and non-combatants of the
men of Erin fled out of the camp south-westwards."

The sustaining of the lengthened combat through the
whole course of the winter at length begins to tell upon
the hero.   He is exhausted and overcome both by the
actual conflicts in which he has engaged day by day,
and by the aerial warfare kept up by those mythological
beings who bear their share in the struggle.   But at
the moment of his greatest distress, his supernatural
father, Lugh, comes to his help.

' Laegh, Cuchulain's charioteer, being in his place,
descried a lone man that out of the north-eastern
quarter came obliquely through the camp of the four
great provinces directing his course in a straight line
towards him.   "A man comes to us, little Cú ! " he cries.
" What manner of man is he ? " Cuchulain asked.   " A tall
and comely and impetuous man, wearing a green mantle
fastened at his breast with a silver brooch.   Next to his
skin, and reaching to his knees, is a shirt of regal silk
embroidered with red gold.   He carries a black shield
with hard rim of white bronze.   In his hand is a five-
barbed spear ; beside him a pronged javelin. Wonderful,
indeed, is the manner of his progress, the mode and
semblance of his action.   Him no man notices, and no
man, too, he heeds, even as though in that great camp

none saw him." "True it is, my servitor," said
Cuchulain, "'tis some one of my fairy kin that comes
to succour and to solace me, for well they know the
tribulation in which upon this raid for the kine of
Cuailnge, I, warring alone against the four great
provinces of Ireland, am involved.'"

' Cuchulain was quite right ; the approaching warrior
when he was come up to him spoke to him, and for the
greatness of his toil and the length of time for which
he had lacked sleep, condoled with him, saying : " Sleep,
then, Cuchulain, and by the grave in the Lerga slumber
deeply, until three days with their three nights be
ended. During which space, upon yonder host I
myself will exercise my skill in arms." By the grave
that is in the Lerga for three days accordingly Cuchulain
slept a torpid sleep. Nor are the duration and pro-
foundness of his stupor things at which to marvel,
considering how great his weariness necessarily must
have been.

' For from the Monday immediately before *Samhain*
to the Wednesday next after the Feast of Bridget—
during all that time, I say—saving only a brief snatch
at midday, he never slept ; and even that was taken
as he leaned on his spear, his head resting on his fist,
and his fist closed around the spear-shaft, this last also
resting on his knee. Rather did he employ that
interval in hewing and in felling, in slaughter and in
ruin of the four great provinces. Cuchulain thus being
lulled to rest, to his wounds and hurts that warrior
laid balsams and healing herbs of fairy potency, so
that while he slept, not knowing that which was wrought
in him, the hero made a good recovery.'

Cuchulain's " Riastradh."—The repose of the hero is followed by an abnormal display of renewed energy. Hardly has he awakened from his trance than he calls upon Laegh to bring him his " scythed chariot," a vehicle which appears only to have been used on occasions of special urgency, and in it he delivers a terrific charge which works havoc in the ranks of the enemy. It will be remembered that the Roman writers describe with a sort of terror the appearance of the British and Gallic scythed chariots. Alone amongst the weapons of war used against them, this weaponed chariot seems to have inspired a real fear among the Roman soldiery. " The Gallic cavalry," says Livy, " charged the Roman legions by a method of fighting that was new to them, and which threw their ranks into confusion. A number of the enemy, mounted on chariots and cars, made towards them with such a prodigious clatter from the trampling of the horses and rolling of the wheels, as affrighted the horses of the Romans, unaccustomed to such tumultuous operations. Tearing their way through the ranks, the Roman soldiers were trampled and bruised to death." (Bk. x., ch. 26.)*

Beside the repeated descriptions by the Roman historians of the fear inspired by the Celtic chariots and of their furious onsets, accompanied by whoopings and songs, the shaking of the shields and brandishing of weapons, the Irish account of Cuchulain's scythed chariot seems but little exaggerated. ' Then Cuchulain said to Laegh, his charioteer, " O, my tutor, Laegh, canst thou tackle for me the scythed chariot, that is,

* cf. *ibid* Bk. xxi., ch. 25 ; Cæsar, Gallic War, Bk. iv., ch. 33 ; Tacitus, Life of Agricola, ch. 36 ; *ibid*, ch. 12.

if thou hast with thee the equipment and gear of the same ? " Then Laegh arose, and put on his charioteer's accoutrement, and he threw over the horses their iron coats of mail, adorned with gold, which covered them from the forehead down to the tail, defended with little blades, little spikes, little lances and hard-pointed spears, so that every movement of the chariot brought a spike near to one, so that every corner, every face, every point, every side of this chariot was a path of laceration for the flesh. . . .

' Then sprang Cuchulain of the weapon-feats into the scythed chariot with its iron sickles, with its thin-edged knives, its hooks, its hard spit-spikes, its hero's weapons, its contrivances for opening, its sharp nails that studded its axles and straps, and its curved sides and tackle. Then he delivered his thunder-feat of a hundred, of two hundred, of three hundred, until he rested at the thunder-feat of five hundred, because he felt that in this his first set-to and grappling with the hosts of the four provinces of Erin a number such as this must fall by his hand. With such impulse did he drive forward his chariot, that the ruts made by the wheels as he passed along might have served for earth-works or lines of defence, so high were the stones and earth flung up on either side. For he was resolved that on that day the men of Erin should not escape him ; therefore he charged round them in a circle, on either hand piling up a fence of the bodies of his enemy. Thrice on this wise he made a circuit of the host and he laid them, three lying upon three, all along his path.' This was, in fact, the first onset of the final struggle in which the whole of the hosts were at once engaged. Up to this moment the conflict had taken the aspect of a series of single combats, but from this time onward the final general engagement is heralded by the increasing seriousness and importance of the incidents. The increased energy of Cuchulain is expressed by the description of what was known as his *Riastradh*, or " Distortion," which so changed and magnified his bodily height and appearance that he was unrecognisable to his friends or enemies. This Distortion, which gained for him the title of the " Distorted One," came on always before any great display of energy. The description ends as follows :—

' The strong beatings of his heart against his breast were as the baying of a hound of war before the onset, or as a lion charging among bears. Above his head were seen the light of Badb and the rain-clouds of poison pouring forth sparks of ruddy fire, which the seething of his savage wrath thrust upwards in vapour to the heavens. Round his head his hair became twisted like the branches of a red-thorn bush thrust into the gap of a broken fence ; though a kingly apple-tree, bending beneath its load of royal fruit, had been shaken over it, scarce an apple of them all would have reached the ground, for on every single hair would an apple have been caught, from the turmoil of his wrath thrusting itself upward through his hair.

' From his forehead arose the " Hero's Light " in length and thickness like the whet-stone of a warrior. As high, as thick, as strong, as lengthy as the mast of a great ship, shot up the dusky stream of blood, straight out of the very centre of his head, whereof was formed a magic mist· of gloom like to the smoky

pall that drapes a regal dwelling what time a king at
nightfall of a winter's day draws near to it.'*

The Final Sections.—The final sections of the Táin
contain a varied and interesting series of episodes, but
its culminating point is the arousing of the hosts of
Ulster by Sualtam, the mortal father of Cuchulain, and
their gathering in clans upon the Hill of Slane, in Westmeath, each clan being distinct in appearance, dress, and
the character of its weapons. Ailell sees the mighty
host advancing, and gets Mac Roth, his herald, to describe the appearance, number, and leaders of each party
as they come swinging up the hill. This passage is
valuable for the details it gives of ancient weapons and
dress. Cuchulain is all this time lying upon a bed of sickness through the multitude and severity of his wounds.
When his own corps comes forward, his excitement
becomes so great that he has to be bound down with cords
and fetters to restrain him from joining the troop of
which he is the natural leader. At the report that King
Conor is in danger he can no longer be restrained, but
rushes into the fight. This general engagement, in
which the whole collected forces of Ulster are simul-
taneously engaged against the men of Erin, is known
as the battles of Gairech and Ilgairech. In their haste
the warriors of the north rush through the sides of their
tents without waiting to put on their clothes. They
simply grasp their weapons and pour forth naked into
the fray. This incident, taken in connection with the
fighting of the old grey warrior, Iliach, and of Ceithern,
who in frantic haste enter the battle " stark-naked,"

* cf. the blaze from the head of Achilles caused by Athene.
Iliad xviii.

bears out in an interesting way the observations of Diodorus Siculus, and of Tacitus, that the Celts and also the Germans frequently fought unclad.*

The final rout of Meave's host is brought about by a pretended flight of Fergus before Cuchulain, the result of a friendly compact between them ; seeing their leader turn his back, the hosts of Erin believe that all is lost and they fly in disorder towards Connaught, crossing the Shannon at Athlone (Ath-luain). Here Cuchulain covers the retreat of Meave's troops, while Fergus, watching the re-crossing of the ford by the broken host, sums up his view of the situation in the cynical words : " Verily and indeed, the upshot of this day, resulting as it does from following a woman's lead, is orthodox completely. To-day this host is cleared and swept away ; and even as without choice of path or forming of design, a brood mare preceding her foals wanders in a land unknown, such is the army's plight to-day." The Irish story-teller of ancient times never fails to direct the keen shaft of his wit against the actions of a woman.

The long but dramatic story ends appropriately by the Battle of the Bulls, and the death of both these terrific beasts.

* cf. Diodorus Siculus, Bk. v., ch. ii. ; Tacitus, Germania ch. vi.

CHAPTER V.

Introductory Tales to the Tain

The main story comes before us with a certain pomp and circumstance, accompanied by a number of shorter tales which explain the position of things at the time of the supposed raid, or prepare the way for it. They are variously counted in different manuscripts, certain tales but distantly connected with the subject, such as the " Wooing of Emer " being included in some lists but excluded in others, while in some instances we find the same incident related under different names. Thus the *Táin bó Regamna*, the *Táin bó Aingen*, and the Adventures of Nera have many features in common. Among the more important of these " Foretales," or *Remscéla*, are the following :

The Revealing of the Tain (*Fallsigad Tána bó Cuailnge*).—This piece is usually incorporated in a long wandering satire called the " Proceedings of the Great Bardic Institution " (*Imtheacht na Tromdhaimhe*). The portion that forms the true " Foretale " relates that as early as the seventh century the story of the Táin had been lost, nor could the united powers of the best poets of Erin, who were called together by Senchan Torpeist, the Chief Bard of Ireland, succeed in recalling the outline of the tale. It was known that it had been contained in an ancient book called the Cuilmenn, which was believed to have been carried out of Ireland to the

Continent. Two poets of eminence are deputed to go and seek the Táin, but before leaving the country they repair to the tomb of Fergus mac Roich in Connaught, and there, enveloped in mist and majestic in appearance, the spirit of Fergus appears before them, and in the course of three days he relates to them from first to last the tale of the raid, in which he himself had played so important a part.

A later version transfers the discovery of the Táin from the Pagan Poets to the Christian Saints of Ireland, to whom the story was revealed after a fortnight's prayer and fasting on the tomb of Fergus.

The Debility of the Ultonians (*Cess nóiden Ulad*). —This tale is written to account for the strange weakness and incapacity for exertion which fell upon the Ultonian warriors at the time of the attack of the forces of Ireland upon Uladh. Though a legend is invented as a solution, the real cause was probably some form of " tabu " or *geis*, such as are known to occur at stated periods among other primitive peoples.

Táin bó Regamna.—This is one of the wildest and least corrupted of the " Introductory Tales." It describes the coming of the Morrigan, or War-goddess, to Cuchulain before the opening of the raid, and her warnings of his early death and of her own intention to endeavour to destroy him. She is of terrifying appearance, and transforms herself into a black bird on a branch above his head. Connected with this tale are the *Táin bó Aingen*, and the piece called The Adventures of Nera (*Echtra Nerai*) which seems to be composed of two tales originally independent. The gist of the story is that the calf of a young cow, by which the goddess is accompanied, and which comes with her out of the *sidh* or fairy-mounds, is found fighting with the Findbennach, and threatening also to contend with its father, the Dond of Cuailnge ; but as this promising youngster does not play any part in the Táin, its importance to the central story seems unexplained. The early part of the adventures of Nera consists of a gruesome Hallow e'en yarn, to which the main incident is tacked on incongruously.

The Cattle Driving of Dartada, Flidais and Regamon (*Táin bó Dartada, Táin bó Flidais, and Táin bó Regamon*).—These short tales give an account, sometimes broken and confused in the form they have come down to us, of the efforts of Meave to collect cattle for her great war. The last of the three is a delightful and merry little episode of the elopement of seven young girls from Munster with the seven sons of Queen Meave, known as the seven Manes of Connaught. All three give us familiar glimpses of social life in ancient Erin.

The Cattle Driving of Fraech (*Táin bó Fraich*).— A longer tale, full of brilliant description and of fairy lore, which describes the wooing of Finnabair, daughter of Meave, by a young prince who is partly of supermortal or shee (*sidh*) birth. The wooing goes on for a long time, Meave only consenting to his suit on condition that he will aid her in the *Táin bó Cuailnge*. This Finnabair is made useful by her mother during the course of the war, being used as a bait to the warriors who undertake to go in single-handed combat against Cuchulain. She is successively offered in marriage to a number of these combatants, and finally dies of grief and shame because Rochaid, a young Prince of Ulster to whom she was attached, is set upon by the jealousy of twelve Munster chiefs, to each of whom, as to himself, Finnabair had been promised as " sole and only wife." Rochaid comes off none the worse. The history of this young girl of high rank illustrates painfully the social conditions of the time.

These tales, with the " Dispute of the Swineherds " (*De Chophur in dá muccida*), which relates the history of the previous existences and transformations of the Bulls as we have described them above, are the most important of the Introductory tales which bear upon the central story. The doctrine of re-birth, plainly insisted upon in the account of the Swineherds, and in several other tales of this cycle, forms part of a pagan system of belief common to the early Celt of Ireland, Britain and Gaul.

The same belief is taught in the curious and very ancient tales of the births of King Conor (*Compert Conchobhar*) and of Cuchulain (*Compert Conchulainn*), in which the mysterious supernatural origin of these personages is obscurely set forth. These tales are sometimes reckoned among the *remscéla*.

CHAPTER VI.

Tales subsequent to the Tain

With the close of the Táin the heroic feats of Cuchulain seem to be virtually over, but a series of tales relate in natural sequence the events immediately preceding and succeeding his tragical death. They are as follows :

The Battle of Rosnaree (*Cath Ruis na Rig*).— This long tale describes the humiliation and annoyance felt by King Conor that Meave has got away safe from his armies after the Táin, and that he has lost the Dond of Cuailnge out of his territories. He can neither eat nor sleep, and his followers fear that he will die. Cathbadh, his druid, advises him to await the spring season, and meanwhile to send for Conall *cernach*, who was out of the country in Scotland, and to collect a large force of hired mercenary troops for the campaign. This is done, and they meet the united armies of Find, King of Leinster, and Cairpre *niafer*, King of Tara, at Rosnaree, on the south-west bank of the Boyne, opposite the tumuli of New Grange and Knowth. Meave refuses her aid, but nevertheless the men of Ulster and their auxiliaries are nearly routed and are about to fly when Cuchulain enters the fight, seeks out the King of Tara, and slays him. Conor goes on to Tara, but Erc, Cairpre's son, makes submission to him and is seated by him on the throne of his father. In spite of Conor's advice to him not to fight against Ulstermen, and especially against Cuchulain, whose daughter he receives as his wife, it is in some tales said to be Erc who cut off Cuchulain's head.   The names of the foreign allies in this piece are borrowed from the historical " Wars of the Gael and Gall."   It is said that " from this battle originated the Battle of Findchora, and the great sea-voyage round among the men of Connaught and the Battle of the Youths."   These tales seem to be lost unless the tale we next mention be one of them.

The Great Rout of the Plain of Muirthemne (*Brislech mór Maige Muirthemne*).—This piece recounts the final events preceding the death of Cuchulain and the causes that conspired to his destruction.   A monstrous brood of ill-shapen beings, the Children of Calatin, whose father and brothers had been slain by Cuchulain during the Táin, are reared by Queen Meave and sent by her through the entire universe to learn wizard arts by which to accomplish the downfall of her enemy.   They attain at last to " Hell's fearful realm," where Vulcan forges for them three knives, three spears, and three swords of venomous quality for the destruction of Cuchulain, his charioteer Laegh, and his chariot-horse, the Grey of Macha.   The wiles by which he is held captive by them, and finally driven out to his death, are recounted.   The death of the hero usually forms a separate piece, but it is also included in this tale, which contains many connecting links necessary to the understanding of the history; it may possibly be the " Battle of the Youths " mentioned in the Battle of Rosnaree, for the three sons of the Princes slain by Cuchulain, namely, Lugaid, son of Curói mac Daire of Munster, Erc, son of Cairpre *niafer*, King of Tara, and

the six sons of Calatin were concerned in it.   It must
not be confused with Cuchulain's single-handed fight
in the Táin called by the same name.

Cuchulain's Death (*Aided   Conchulainn*).— This
piece follows directly upon or forms a part of the
Brislech mór, and recounts the death of the " Hound,"
as Cuchulain always calls himself, at the hand of Lugaid,
son of Curói mac Daire, King of Munster, who had
been treacherously murdered by Cuchulain in Curói's
own house, and of Erc, the young King of Tara.
Cuchulain's death is immediately preceded by that of
his charioteer, Laegh, and by the wounding of his steed,
the Grey of Macha, one of the two magic steeds caught
by the " Hound " in his youth, as they rose out of the
enchanted lake, and tamed by him in one night in a
three-fold course round the entire circuit of Ireland.
The incident of the Grey of Macha seeking the dead
body of its master and laying its head upon his breast
reminds us of the grief of Columcille's old white horse
at Iona for the approaching death of the Saint, as well
as of classical and Norse parallels.   Though the tale
as we have it in the Book of Leinster preserves the
archaic style of the earlier stories there are some
passages which are evidently later additions.   For
instance, the final paragraph seems to be adapted from
a late form of the death of King Arthur.   " But the
soul of Cuchulain appeared there to the thrice fifty
queens who had loved him, and they saw him floating
in his spirit-chariot over Emain Macha, and they
heard him chant a mystic song of the Coming of Christ
and the Day of Doom."   We give a brief extract
relating his death :—' Then Lugaid flung his spear

and struck Cuchulain, and his bowels came forth on the cushion of the chariot, and his only horse, the Black Sainglend, fled away, with half the yoke hanging to him, and left the chariot and his master, the King of the Heroes of Erin, dying alone upon the plain. Then said Cuchulain, " I would fain go as far as that lock to drink a drink thereout."   " We give thee leave," said they, " provided that thou come to us again."

' " I will bid you come for me," said Cuchulain, " unless I shall return to you myself."

' Then he gathered his bowels into his breast, and went on to the loch. And he drank his drink, and washed himself, and came forth to die, calling on his foes to come and meet him.

' Now a great mearing went westwards from the loch, and his eyes lit upon it, and he went to the pillar-stone that is in the plain, and he put his breast-girdle round it that he might not die seated nor lying down, but that he might die standing up.   Then came the men around him, but they durst not go to him, for they thought he was alive.'

The Red Rout of Conall Cernach and Lay of the Heads (*Dergruathar Chonaill ocus laoidh na g-ceann*).— The first of these pieces describes the terrible vengeance taken by Conall *cernach* for the death of his comrade. Each of these heroes had bound himself by an oath that the one who should survive the death of the other should avenge his loss.

In the second piece Conall is represented as returning from his " Red Rout," carrying on a withe the gory heads of the slain warriors.   He is accosted by Emer, Cuchulain's wife, who asks him the names of the dead champions whose heads he bears ; whereupon he recounts the names and exploits of each.   This barbaric custom of carrying the heads of the slain on a reed, dripping with blood, seems to have been an actual practice, for in the historical tract called *Caithreim Cellachain Caisil* describing the Irish and Norse wars of the south of Ireland in the middle of the tenth century, the heads of the slain chieftains of Munster are brought in the same manner to the green (now College Green) of the Fort of Dublin, and displayed before the Norse Prince.

This lay is usually followed by a brief prose account of the death of Emer.

The Phantom Chariot of Cuchulain (*Siabur Charpat Conculaind*).

—A curious piece, in which the pagan hero is brought up from the dead to witness before St. Patrick and King Laery (Laeghaire) to the truth of the Christian doctrine.   He appears before the King in his old form and splendour, performing his " champion feats," and beseeching the King to receive Christianity. This singular legend contains many ancient mythological allusions, and the poems which it introduces are interesting and archaic.

The Destruction of Bruidhen Dá Choga (*Togail Bruidne Dá Choga*).

—A tale relating events later than the death of King Conchobhar or Conor.   Two parties arose after his death, one in favour of giving the kingdom back to Fergus, son of Ros Ruadh, others saying that it should be bestowed upon Fergus mac Léide, King of Magh Line ; while Conall *cernach* sought to have it conferred on his own foster son, Cumhscraidh the Stammerer,

son of Conchobhar.   Cumhscraidh, fearing to plunge
Ulster into civil war, withdrew from the contest,
and by mutual assent another son of Conchobhar,
Cormac *conloinges*, was elected King.   Ambassadors
were sent to inform Meave of Connaught, with
whom, like other Ulster princes, Cormac was living
in exile, and he collected a body of troops and
proceeded across the Shannon to support his claim by
force of arms.

Like all princes of note in his day, Cormac had had
heavy *geasa* or prohibitions laid upon him on the day
of his birth, and the breaking of these bonds was a
certain foretelling of his death.   On this day, which
was to decide his fate, all these *geasa* were broken one
by one without his will or intention, and he knew from
this that he was foredoomed to die.   At first the
Ulstermen were triumphant, but Meave, fearing total
defeat, brought all her powers of persuasion to bear
upon Fergus mac Roich, and induced him to join his
forces with hers against his own people and to go out
against the men of Ulster.   They surround the house
of Dá Choga (one of the six great open houses of
hospitality and safety in Ireland, which are here described
in detail), in which Cormac and his host have taken
refuge for the night, and after a terrific contest the
house is set on fire, and all within, save two or three
persons, are burned to death.

This fine story contains a large element of the supernatural, and many details of great curiosity and interest
to the folk-lorist.

There remain one or two other tales belonging to the
cycle of such importance that they cannot be overlooked
even in a brief survey.

The Intoxication of the Ultonians (*Mesca Ulad*).—
This is one of those wild tales of adventure such as the
Irish story-teller seems to have delighted to tell. It
recounts a night raid of the heroes, who were all in-
toxicated after a feast, across the entire extent of the
country from Dun-dá-benn, near the present Coleraine,
in Ulster, to the fort of Curói mac Daire at Tara-
Luachra in Kerry. This Curói is represented in the
Feast of Bricriu as being, like Conall the Victorious
and Manannán mac Lir, constantly away in foreign lands.
He is said never to have passed a night at home, and
for safety during his absence he caused his fort to spin
round and round at nights, so that no one could find
the door by which to enter after sunset.

Early in the morning the fort was furiously attacked
by the Ulster heroes. Their coming had, however,
been counted upon by their foes ; they were induced to
enter an iron house concealed within wooden walls
under which in a hollow cellar enormous fires had been
lighted. These gradually heated the iron walls and
floors red-hot while the heroes were feasting within.
They managed to make their exit only just in time
to escape being roasted alive.*

The larger part of this tale is taken up with a
description of the heroes and their attendants as they
approached the fort. This is full of brilliant passages
invaluable for the information it gives as to the dress
and appearance of the groups of warriors, poets, druids,
etc.

* This unpleasant trick seems to have been a favourite
habit of disposing of enemies. See other examples in the " Tale
of the Destruction of Dind Righ," and the " Story of Branwen,
Daughter of Llyr," in the Welsh Mabinogion.

The Tragical Death of Conlaech (*Aided Conlaoich*).—This pathetic incident is found in numerous versions, verse and prose, both in Scotland and Ireland. It belongs to the early part of Cuchulain's career, and relates that on returning from Scotland, where he had been learning feats of championship with Scathach, Cuchulain left with her daughter Aiffe a ring to be placed on the hand of the son who should be born to her, with a proviso that he should not reveal his name to any stranger. Some years afterwards the youth Conlaech, or Connla, still a young boy, seeks his father in Ireland. Refusing to tell his name, he fights in mortal combat with his own father, and is killed by him by the deadly feat of the *gái bulga*, the only feat unknown to the lad. In his death he is recognised by Cuchulain, who pours out over the dead body of his son a pathetic lament. The story has a strong resemblance to the Persian tale of Sohrab and Rustem.

The Siege of Howth (*Forbais Etair*).—A rude tale, detailing the cruelties practised by Athairne, chief bard of Ulster, upon any who refused him the gifts he demanded. It is evidently intended as a satire upon the rapacity of the bardic community. On one occasion the Leinstermen rose to resist him, and he and the Ulstermen who were sent to his succour were shut off from the mainland on the Hill of Howth, and there cooped up without food and drink. The tale details their sufferings and their escape, with the subsequent adventures of Conall *cernach* and his combat with Mesgegra, King of Leinster. This is only one of several tales which dilate upon the cruel practices of Athairne.

The Feast of Bricriu (*Fled Bricrend*).—One of the longest and finest of the tales which have as their theme the carving of the "Champion's Portion," a special dish, assigned to the most valorous warrior to carve and distribute. It is a composite story, made up of a series of adventures, probably once independent. The main portion of the tale describes a feast provided by Bricriu, one of the Ultonian circle, known, from his love of bickering and stirring up strife, as Bricriu "of the Poisoned Tongue." The object of his feast is not to give pleasure to the king and champions, but to provide an opportunity for setting them by the ears. He builds a new house, to which he invites all the champions ; and on their arrival he converses in turn with the three prime heroes, Cuchulain, Conall the Victorious, and Laeghaire the Triumphant, inciting each of them, unknown to the others, to claim precedence over his fellows. On the arrival of the Champion's Portion the excitement rises to such a pitch that they all spring to arms, each of the three heroes contesting that the right to carve it is his. The same thing takes place with regard to the wives of the three champions; they also are stirred up by Bricriu to claim superiority over all the rest by virtue of their husbands' position. A curious scene, in which the ladies declaim in verse the deeds and status of their several spouses, is known as the "Women's War of Words."* The tale might well end here, but instead of this there succeeds a wild series of adventures in which, by a number of tests, the three champions prove their powers, Cuchulain always coming out first of the three. They visit the forts of Meave

*See page 81.

in Connaught, and of Curói in Munster (we seem to
have here two separate tales which the scribe of L.U.
endeavours to harmonise); and the piece ends with
a version of the incident known as the " beheading
incident," which forms also the subject of a separate
tale called the Bargain of the Strong Man (*Cennach
ind Rúanado*) and has the same theme as the North or
West of England Romance of " Sir Gawayne and the
Green Knight." In all these and some kindred tales
the central idea is that a knight consents to be beheaded
one day on condition that on the following day he may
return to behead his slayer. In the " Feast of Bricriu "
a ferocious being challenges all the heroes in turn to
have their heads cut off. Only Cuchulain will consent.
He first beheads the challenger, who returns alive and
whole the next day, and pretends to be about to behead
Cuchulain, but spares his life in respect for his bravery.

The Violent Deaths of Goll and Garbh (*Aided
Guill ocus Gairbh*).—This is evidently a post-Norse story
on the same subject. It describes the approach of a hero
of immense size to the shores of Ireland, which, he said,
had fallen to him by lot, and which he had come to
conquer. He calls himself *Mac rig na Germane tuas-
certaige don domun*, the son of the King of the Northern
Germany of the world." He is encountered by Cuchulain
who, after a fight in which he comes near to being
worsted, gives him a blow with his sword, the
" Cruadén Catutchend," or " Hardheaded Steel," which
severs his head from his body. This combat is succeeded by the death of the Giant Garbh, " the Rough."
In this story, which is evidently a composite one, we
have a fight between Cuchulain and a great hound,

here called Conbél, which repeats most of the circumstances of his boyish contest with the Hound of Culann
from which he took his name.   The whole story adopts
the tone and repeats the ordinary similies of the Irish,
but it is interesting as giving a double list of Cuchulain's
geasa or " tabus," which form the subject also of a
separate tract.

Mac Datho's Boar and Hound (*Scel mucci Maic Datho*).

—In this short but dramatic tale the contest for
the Champion's Portion lies between the Ulstermen
and the Connaughtmen, and chiefly between two heroes,
Conall *cernach* of Ulster and Cet mac Magach of Connaught.   This piece, with its abrupt songs and quick
dramatic movement reminds us of a northern saga.
The Champion's Portion is here a great boar, fed up for
many years on the milk of fifty cows and slain on the
occasion of a visit of the warriors of Ulster and Connacht
to the house of its owner, Mac Datho of Leinster.   A
long contention for the honour of carving the boar,
in which the heroes relate their various achievements,
ends on the entrance of Conall as follows :—

'"Rise, then, and depart from this boar," said Conall.

" What claim wilt thou advance why I should do
this ? " said Cet.

" I perceive," said Conall, " that thou art contending
in renown with me.   I will give thee one claim only,
O Cet !   I swear by the oath of my tribe that since the
day that I first received a spear into my hand I have
seldom slept without the head of a slain man of Connaught as my pillow ; and I have not let pass a day
or a night in which a man of Connaught hath not fallen
by my hand."

" 'Tis true, indeed," said Cet, " thou art a better warrior than I.   But were Anluan here, he could answer thee in another fashion ; alas, that he is not in this house "

" Aye, but Anluan is here ! " cried Conall, and therewith he plucked Anluan's head from his belt.   And he threw the head towards Cet, so that it smote him upon the chest, and a gulf of the blood was dashed over his lips.   And Cet came away from the boar, and Conall placed himself beside it.

" Now let men come to contend for renown with me ! " cried   Conall.   But   among   the   men   of   Connaught there   was   none   who   would   challenge   him.   And   they raised   a   wall   of   shields   like   a   great   vat   around   him, for in that house was evil wrangling, and men in their malice were making cowardly casts at him.'

CHAPTER VII.

The Love Tales

Among the miscellaneous contents of the Book of Leinster there occurs a valuable list of the stories known to the copyist as forming part of the répertoire of the fully-equipped poet or story-teller. This list is thrown into groups under separate headings, such as Battle-pieces, Expeditions, Voyages, Cattle-raids, Sieges, Plunderings, Events in Caves, Visions, Feasts, etc. One group is concerned with "Courtships" or "Wooings," and about this group we will say a few words separately. Stories about women play a large part in Irish Literature ; their elopements, their marriages, their griefs and tragedies form the subject of a large number of tales. The Irish may be said to be the inventors of the love-tale for modern Europe, and the great variety and beauty of these tales fits them for special mention. There are thirteen stories of Courtships and twelve of Elopements in the list in the Book of Leinster, besides a number of other tales in which women play a leading part. In the Arthurian cycle the women are deficient in colour and variety ; they lack distinctness and force of character, but in the Ulster stories there is a great variety of type, and the characters are drawn with individuality and fidelity to themselves throughout the different detached episodes which go to make up their life history.

We have the haughty amazonion Meave, and the

fairy-maiden, Etain; Emer, sprightly in youth and
high-souled in womanhood, the wife of Cuchulain;
Grainne, the vain and heartless coquette, who ruins
Dermot and afterwards marries his murderer, Fionn;
the gay girls in the Táin bó Regamon; the unfaithful
Blathnait, and the true and passionate Deirdre, with
many others beside.   Each is studied with the care of
a character in a modern novel and develops naturally
along the lines of the conception formed of her personality by the writer.   We are continually struck by
the wonderful power of character-painting shown in the
Irish tales.   We know each personage and all that
concerns him, down to the minutest detail of life and the
finest idiosyncrasy of temperament.   We know these
people so well that we can almost foretell what each
will do on any given emergency.

The Irish women belong to an heroic type. They are
often the counsellors of their husbands and the champions
of their cause; occasionally, as in Meave's case, their
masters.   They are frequently fierce and vindictive,
but they are also strong, forceful, and intelligent.   In
youth they possess often a charming gaiety; they are
full of clever repartee and waywardness and have a
delightful and careless self-confidence. Emer, especially,
has a great deal of the modern woman about her; she is
no love-lorn maid to be caught by the first words of a
wooer's tongue, even though her lover is Cuchulain;
she is gay, petulant, and not too readily satisfied.   He
thinks to win his cause simply by the fame of his name
and the splendour of his appearance, but she makes
larger demands; nor will she listen to his suit until she
has won from him respect and admiration as well as
affection.

The Wooing of Emer (*Tochmarc Emere*).—In this tale we learn that Emer was daughter of Forgall the Wily, of Lusk (Co. Dublin), a rich landowner in whose family, according to the universal custom of fosterage among the Irish, a number of young girls were being brought up with his daughter, and instructed by her in handiwork and womanly pursuits.   Emer is wooed by Cuchulain in the secret language studied only by the bards, but in which, among her other accomplishments, she is an expert.   After a year's waiting for her father's permission to marry, she is carried off with her own consent by the hero and wedded to him.   The tale includes an account of Cuchulain's instructions in feats of championship by Scathach, the Amazon of Alba (Scotland), who dwells in the Isle of Skye, which is called Scathach or Skye after her.   This expedition is also the subject of separate romances, and is of curious interest from the number of its mythological details, which are of great importance to the Folk-lorist.   As a specimen of the tale we give the charming picture of Emer and her maidens at the door of her father's dún when Cuchulain drives up in his splendid chariot.   It is drawn by the famous magic steeds which rose out of the grey lake of Slieve Fuad and the Loch of the Black Sainglenn, which were caught and tamed by Cuchulain.   This story seems to have been a popular one ; there are numerous copies of it, one of them being considered by Dr. Meyer to be pre-Norse.   'Then Cuchulain found the maiden on her playing field, with her foster sisters around her, daughters of the landowners that lived round the dún of Forgall.   They were learning needlework and fine handiwork from Emer.   Of all the maidens of Erin she was the one maiden whom he deigned to address and woo.   For she had the six gifts : the gift of beauty, the gift of singing, the gift of sweet speech, the gift of needle-work, the gifts of wisdom and chastity.   Cuchulain had said that no maiden should go with him but she who was his equal in age and form and race, in skill and deftness, and who was the best handiworker of the maidens of Erin, for that none but such as she were a fitting wife for him.   Now, as Emer was the one maiden who fulfilled all these conditions, Cuchulain went to woo her above all.

'It was in his festal array that Cuchulain went forth that day to address Emer, and to show his beauty to her.   As the maidens were sitting on the bench of gathering at the dún, they heard coming towards them the clatter of horses' hoofs, with the creaking of the chariot, the cracking of straps, the grating of wheels, the rush of the hero, the clanking of weapons.

'" Let one of you see," said Emer, " what it is that is coming towards us."

'" Truly, I see," said Fiall, daughter of Forgall, " two steeds alike in size, beauty, fierceness, and speed, bounding side by side.   Spirited they are and powerful, pricking their ears : their manes long and curling, and with curling tails, etc." '

The story goes on to describe the hero, and relates the conversation between Emer and himself, with the subsequent events.

Among the other tales in which Emer plays a con-spicuous part are the " Wasting Away," or " Sickbed of Cuchulain," " The Death of Conlaech," " The Feast of Bricriu," " The Great Rout of Magh Muirthemne," " The Lay of the Heads," and the piece entitled " Emer's Tragical Death."   She is always represented as a woman of fine powers and of great pride and spirit, devoted to Cuchulain and supporting him on all occasions. In her girlhood she is brilliant in her conversation and possessed of a delightful mingling of dignity and merriment.   Her superior intelligence is shown in her knowledge of the mystic language of the poets, a rare accomplishment for a woman.   His affection for Fand, one of the superior powers, is said to have been " her only jealousy " ; when she learns that Cuchulain and Fand have arranged to meet, she makes up her mind to destroy her rival, and prepares " fifty sharpened knives for her fifty maidens " with which to carry out her design.   But though Emer is jealous, she is not vindictive ; Fand's appeal to her leads to a very surprising and touching passage in which each of the two rivals declares her willingness to give up Cuchulain to the other.   Fand finally withdraws to the invisible world leaving her lover to his mortal wife.   The cause of Emer's jealousy on this occasion was clearly that Fand was her superior, one of the immortals.

The Women's War of Words (*Briatharcath na m-ban*).—This piece is part of the long story of Bricriu's Feast, but it occurs also in separate tracts.   When Bricriu had stirred up the heroes against each other by the insidious flattery of his " Poisoned Tongue," he practised the same methods upon Emer, wife of Cuchulain, Fedelm, wife of Laeghaire the Triumphant, and Lendabair, wife of Conall the Victorious, inciting each to claim precedence above the others on account both of her own beauty and accomplishments and the prowess of her husband.   These ladies set forth in turn their claims to priority of rank in long poetic pieces of

H

declamation recounting the feats of their several husbands and their own noble birth and appearance.
These rhetorical pieces are known as the Women's War
of Words, or the Battle-Speeches of the Women of
Ulster.

The Wasting Away of Cuchulain, called " The
Sickbed of Cuchulain " (*Serglige Conchulainn*).—One of
the longest and most artistic of the whole series of tales
about Cuchulain.   It describes the love of Fand, wife
of Manannán, one of the *sidh* or fairy goddesses, for the
hero, and her efforts to woo him away from mortal life
into the invisible land.   This she does by appealing,
not only to his love of pleasure and beauty, but more
especially to his romantic sense of honour and courage,
for she represents to him that Labraid " of the Swift
Sword-Strokes," a Chief in the invisible world, is in
great peril and prays the hero to come to his assistance.
Her appeals are made in a series of exquisite poems.
Cuchulain at first refuses the request, and twice sends
Laegh, his charioteer, in his place, but he finally is
persuaded to go, and after relieving Labraid he remains
some time with Fand in the blissful unseen world.   The
jealousy of Emer, Cuchulain's wife, and her attempts
to kill Fand, form the conclusion of the tale, which ends
in a beautiful and remarkable dialogue between the
mortal woman and her *sidh*-rival.   An incident loosely
inserted in the middle of the tale describes the election
of a pupil of Cuchulain's, Lugaid (Lewy) of the Red
Stripes, to the throne of Tara, and the instructions
delivered by the hero to him from his sick-bed on the
occasion.

Wooing of Ferb (*Tochmarc Ferbe*).—This long tale of the wooing of Ferb, daughter of Gerg, by Mane Mórgor, eldest of the seven Manes, sons of Ailell and Meave, is remarkable for the number and length of the poems it contains. The piece, of which the first few lines have been lost, opens with a picturesque description of the princely company of Mane as they set off in two-horsed chariots from Cruachan to the wedding. In the midst of the festivities, King Conor of Ulster, who is incited by Badb, one of the goddesses of war, to take this opportunity of destroying his Connaught foes, comes down with a troop of warriors, and the wedding-feast is broken up amid the tumult of strife. In a terrible hand-to-hand contest Gerg and Mane himself, with most of their followers, are killed, and the women are carried off captive to Ulster ; theré Ferb with her maidens die of grief for the loss of Mane.

The Courtship of Etain (*Tochmarc Etaine*).—There are several stories more or less connected with Etain, who is of *sidh*-birth but weds a mortal king. These stories have become confused in the course of repetition, so that it is difficult to piece them together in any connected order ; they overlap each other. Though the tales have to do with Dé Danann personages, their style is similar to that of the Cuchulain tales, and they seem to have been composed at the same period of literary activity. The chief of them is the " Wooing of Etain " or the " Story of Ailell and Etain " (MS. Egerton, 1782), an extract of which is found in L.U. Sometimes all the tales are thrown together. The introduction to the story of the Bruidhen Dá Derga incorporates part of the same tale. Etain is a *sidh*-maiden wedded to the god Midir of Brí-leith, but she becomes the wife of a king of Ireland, named Eochaid Airem, who sees her bathing her hair and hands when he is out riding and instantly falls in love with her.   One story relates that a brother of her husband's unwittingly becomes enamoured of her when she for the first time appears with the king at the Feis of Tara, and describes the means she took to cure him of his love.   Another very dramatic episode tells how Midir, her husband among the gods or *sidh*-folk, wins back Etain from Eochaid in a game of chess and carries her off to his fairy mound. A sort of introductory tale to these stories relates that in her former existence she had for a long time been carried about by Angus na Brugh in a house of crystal filled with flowers and sweet-scented shrubs.

The Story of Baile the Sweet-Spoken (*Scél Baili binnbérlaig*).—This seems to be a late but charming independent romance cf the deaths of two lovers for grief at the false tidings of each other's death.   It is said that out of their tombs grew an apple and a yew-tree bearing their likeness on the top.   In later days these trees were cut down and made into tablets on which were inscribed the "Loves and Wooings and Visions and Feasts of Ulster and Leinster," these tablets being laid up in the king's treasure-house at Tara.   Once when they were brought to the king and held in his two hands they sprang together and clasped each other "as a woodbine twines round a branch," so that they never again could be disunited.

CHAPTER VIII.

The Three Sorrows of Story-Telling
(*Trí truaighe na Sgéalaigheachta*).

There are three tales of which it may be well to say a few words, as they have been thrown together into a group under the title " The Three Sorrows of Story-telling," or " The Three Sorrowful Tales." The title is, however, a comparatively modern and a purely fanciful one, for the tales themselves have no natural connection with each other, their only link being that, like several other tales, they have a mournful complexion and ending. Two out of the three stories are connected with the earliest cycle of Irish mythology ; the third belongs to the Cuchulain series. They are :—

The Fate of the Children of Lir (*Aided Chloinne Lir*).—This tale, at least in the form in which we have it, does not appear to be ancient, although its theme connects it with the earliest mythology. Lir, or Ler, father of Manannán (called in Geoffrey of Monmouth and Shakespeare " King Lear ") was, as we have seen, the sea-god of the ancient Irish whose poetical name for the ocean was the " Plain of Lir." He has, however, no connection with the sea in this piece, but is king of a division of the Tuatha Dé Danann, and dwelt, after the Battle of Taillte, in which the gods were defeated by the Milesians, in the *sidh Fionnachaidh,* or the " shee-mound of the White Field," in the North of Ireland. The human character ascribed to Lir himself, the incident of the cruel stepmother, the use of the druidical wand to turn the children into swans, the thoroughly Christian purpose and complexion of the tale, mark

it as of late invention.   Even if the separate incidents
can be paralleled from early Irish sources, the general
tone of the story is that of the modern fairy-tale.   It
is not known to exist in any manuscript earlier than
the beginning of the eighteenth century ; and though,
no doubt, the basis of the legend is considerably older
than this, no allusion to or mention of the story is
known in any ancient manuscript.

It relates the sufferings of the four children of Lir
during a space of nine hundred painful years, first upon
the waters of Lake Derryveragh (*Dairbhreach*) in Co.
Westmeath, then upon the " Moyle " (*Sruth na Maoile*),
the narrow strip of water running between the north
of Ireland and Scotland ; and finally in the Western
Ocean off the coasts of Mayo and Galway.   They
have been changed into four swans by the cruelty of
their stepmother, who is jealous of the father's affection
for his children, by the stroke of a druidical wand.
Their sufferings are detailed in a picturesque manner
and at great length.   They are finally transformed
again, when the spell is over, into human beings, and
are instructed in the Christian faith by a saint named
Mochaomhog, who has built a cell and oratory on the
island of Inishglory (Inis Gluaire) in the Bay of Erris,
Co. Mayo.   They are, however, only aged and wizened
men and women, and they expire immediately after
baptism.   The piece is interspersed with songs which
appear to be older than the prose.   One of these has
been rendered familiar in Moore's " Silent, O Moyle,
be the roar of thy waters."

The Fate of the Children of Tuireann (*Aided
Chloinne Tuirenn*).—This story also belongs to the cycle

of the early mythology. It has a much more archaic tone than "The Fate of the Children of Lir." Being a less known tale it probably escaped changes which the companion story, if it existed in ancient times at all, has undergone. The Children of Tuireann are, however, mentioned in the Book of Lecan (1416), and in the ninth century work called Cormac's Glossary; though the actual story, as we have it, is derived from late manuscripts. The story is founded on the common Irish theme of a series of wild and prodigious adventures undertaken in order to gain or recover certain articles demanded by some being whose commands may not be disobeyed, usually in punishment for the committal of a crime.

In this instance the three sons of Tuireann, Brian, Iuchar, and Iucharba, have slain Cian the father of Lugh the Longhanded, and Lugh lays upon them a prodigious eric-fine. This triad of brothers, who were probably originally one, appear in the ancient poems of the mythological invasions of Ireland as sons of Breas the Fomorian, and Brigit, daughter of the Dagda. They are doublets of the Tuatha Dé Danann kings, Mac Cuill, Mac Cecht, and Mac Greine. Their position and splendour of person are acknowledged in the tale. Like Jason in search of the Golden Fleece, they set out to procure the enormous and varied demands laid on them by Lugh in eric for the murder they have committed, but the perils they go through are so severe that they only return to die. The harshness shown by Lugh in this tale is very unlike his usual character.

The Tragical Death of the Sons of Usnech (*Aided Chloinne Uisnig*).—This, one of the best-known

of the old tales, exists in an immense number of manu-scripts from the twelfth to the eighteenth century, and is still recited in a modernized folk-tale form in the Western Highlands. Its theme deals partly with Ireland and partly with Scotland, and the scene of the exile of the sons of Usnech on Loch Etive in Argyleshire still preserves the names of the wanderers.

The story relates that King Conor of Ulster, when an old man and a widower, reared up as his future wife the maiden Deirdre, a child of great beauty, but whose birth had been accompanied by portents of woe and desolation, in which the whole kingdom would be involved. The child was shut up in a lonely house with her tutor and nurse and never permitted to see the face of a man until she should be of age to marry Conor. This theme, a common one in the folk-tales of different countries, recurs in Ireland in the legend of Etain. On one occasion, however, Deirdre chanced to see Naisi, one of the three sons of Usnech, a noble youth, with whom she instantly fell in love. She induced him to carry her off to Alba (Scotland) where they took refuge for many years. The story of their return, their betrayal, and their death is told with much pathos. This is one of the tales which has undergone great variations in the course of centuries of recitation. In the earliest version in the Book of Leinster Deirdre is a barbarian woman, rude and passionate in her speech and savage in her actions. The portents of her birth are insisted upon, and the whole tale has a vigorous but ominous tone. Levarcham, her nurse, is a terrific and monstrous being, with abnormal powers and energies. As time goes on these savage features are softened down, and Deirdre and her nurse become gradually transformed into modern women of less formidable character. The mediæval recension is exceedingly beautiful, and is filled with exquisite songs, of which Deirdre's " Farewell to Alba " and her death-song over the graves of her husband and his brothers are well-known through Sir Samuel Ferguson's and Dr. Sigerson's English settings. The end of the tale varies in the different versions. In the oldest form, in keeping with its general rude and primitive character, King Conor forces Deirdre to return to him after the death of her spouse. A fine poem relates her sufferings in his house. Finally, in anger at her continued dislike of himself, Conor places her in a chariot between him and the tyrant Eoghan, the murderer of her husband. " She is," as he exultingly says, " like a ewe caught between two rams." In her despair she springs from the chariot and dashes out her brains against a rock.

In the mediæval version all this is changed ; after an appropriate lament she springs into the open grave beside Naisi, and dies upon his body.

A traditional addition says that King Conor was so incensed that even in death Deirdre and Naisi should dwell together in the mansion of the dead that he ordered them to be laid far apart in the burial-ground. Every morning the graves would be found open and the lovers be discovered lying side by side in one of them. Then he ordered stakes to be thrust through their bodies to keep them asunder, but two yew-trees sprang from these stakes and they grew to such a height that they finally embraced each other over the Cathedral of Armagh.*

* Cf., The Story of Baile the Sweet-spoken and the old border ballads of " Fair Margaret and Sweet William," or " The Douglas Tragedy."

CHAPTER IX.

Literary Summary of the Prose Romances

Having now gone through a considerable portion of the material belonging to the earlier Epic and Romance literature of Ireland, we are in a better position to estimate the literary character of the tales and to weigh their qualities and defects impartially.

Character of the Tales.—The tales of the Red Branch cycle are less courtly and sophisticated, simpler in style and conception, and totally deficient in the mystic religious flavour which gives a semi-ecclesiastical tone to much of the mediæval Arthurian romance. Though they differ greatly in character and literary finish among themselves, they have rarely undergone the late thirteenth to fifteenth century polishing which transformed the rude warriors of Arthur's Court into knights of the age of chivalry. The artificial tone and highly-wrought manners and moralities of the Arthurian Knights of the Round Table as we find them depicted in Mallory's " Morte d'Arthur " have not intruded themselves into the old Irish romance. We see the champions as we can actually conceive them to have lived in an early pre-Christian age ; their barbarities are described without a shade of disgust ; their chivalries are the outcome of a natural fairness and fineness of mind, and are not the product of a courtly attention to an exterior code of morals.

The tales are, moreover, purely and frankly pagan ; the Christian touches, where they do occur, are often later additions intended to convey a moral or a Christian termination to a story built up in an earlier age ; and they seldom interfere with the general tone of the romance.

The rudeness of the times in which they took their rise is shown by such customs as the carrying of the heads of slain warriors in the conqueror's belt, or the preservation of the same ghastly trophies in a hall specially built for the purpose in the Royal Palace ; in the brain-balls made from the heads of slaughtered foes and actually used in battle as sling-stones ; in the cruelties practised by bards and chiefs ; by the low condition of moral ideas and the universal custom of female slavery ; by the untrained tempers that made it impossible for warriors to sit down to a friendly feast without disposing of their arms in a separate hall, lest they should spring into a bloody affray before the close of the banquet, at some real or imagined insult.

Chivalry.—At the same time, with all this primitive savagery, the warriors show that they are conscious of a fine native code of honour. Conall *cernach* will not fight with an enemy who has lost his hand except with his own hand tied to his side, in order that they may combat on equal terms ; Cuchulain permits his antagonist, Loch Mór, to choose how he will fight and to fall with his face towards the enemy. When his deadliest foe, Queen Meave, is exhausted by leading her flying forces homeward over the Shannon and can no longer appear at their head, Cuchulain himself shelters her and takes her command ; when a youth, or charioteer, or one unarmed, attacks him, he will take no advantage of their helplessness. Throughout the cycle we feel in the presence of warriors who have formed a simple but strictly binding code of honour of their own. There is a spontaneousness in the exhibition of this romantic generosity quite unlike the conventional chivalries of Arthur's Knights or even of the more artificial tales of the Fenian cycle, which evidently date, in the form in which we have them, from the later self-conscious period. The heroes have about them something of the high spirits of the schoolboy, a delightful irrepressible buoyancy of mind and body that leads them alike into the most impossible adventures and into almost ridiculous excesses of benevolence.

Dramatic Force and Humour.—Another feature of the tales is their brilliant dramatic force and unexpectedness. Long and tedious as a story may be, taking it as a whole, the professional story-teller is seldom flat or uniform ; his fault is not that of dullness or want of variety. Rather, he is constantly surprising us by some sudden and unexpected turn in the narrative, some dramatic touch that stirs our latent interest to the highest point just when we least anticipate a change. Good examples of this are the tales of Mac Datho's Boar and Hound, the Sickbed of Cuchulain, and the Siege of Howth. Even in the lengthy narrative of the *Táin bó Cuailnge*, a great portion of which is occupied by the long series of hand to hand combats, there is little monotony. Each event has a special character of its own ; the writer's fertility and invention is everywhere equal to the strain laid upon it, and our interest and curiosity are kept throughout on the alert.

Connected with this dramatic quality, and largely contributing to it, is the strong sense of humour observable in the tales. This breaks out everywhere, not only in such wholly humorous productions as the " Exile of the Sons of the Doel Dermait," which is a conscious parody of the tale of the " Feast of Bricriu," but even in the non-farcical tales. Sometimes it is grim and weird, as in the appearances of the Morrigan and her kin, or when the dying Cuchulain, seeing his own blood trickling from his wound into a rivulet at his feet and a raven sipping it, " knowing that it was his last laugh, laughed aloud ; " frequently it is bombastic and exaggerated, as in some of the instances we have given from the Táin, and some of the purely humorous and satirical pieces of which we have hereafter to speak ; but everywhere it lightens and relieves the tedium of the recital. This quality is especially Irish ; the Arthurian romance is deficient in humour, hence a certain monotony of repetition which is conspicuously absent from the Irish tales.

Pathos.—Both Irish poetry and Irish prose exhibit, with all the roughness of manners, a wonderful tenderness and depth of feeling. We shall have to speak of this more at length in our study of the poetry, but it is present also in the prose pieces. The tenderness of the wife for her husband, of the father for his son, and the son for his father ; the heart-affection of friend for friend, the close kinship bred of fosterage, the abandonment of lovers lost to each other, are all the subjects of touching episodes in prose and verse. The splendid self-control of Macha in the tale of the " Debility of the Ultonians," the love-stories of Midir and Etain, of Emer and Cuchulain or of Deirdre and Naisi ; the lament of Cuchulain over his dead son Conlaech, or of Conall *cernach* for Cuchulain, or of Cuchulain over Ferdia, are all touched with the profoundest pain and affection.

Brilliancy.—The brilliancy of description in some of the later tales could hardly be surpassed. This is especially observable in the love stories or in those in which the high gods or fairy-folk appear ; here the artist lavishes a perfect wealth of minute description on the cavalcades, the appearance of the heroes, the trappings of the chariots, or the beauty of natural objects. The stories of the " Wooing of Fraech," or the " Wasting away of Cuchulain," or the " Wooing of Ferb," are examples. But this brilliant word-painting reaches its climax in the tales of the over-sea voyages to Magh-Mell, the pagan paradise. Here every lovely image is called up to describe the imaginary world of ideal beauty. The Voyage of Bran, the Adventures of Connla or of Teigue, son of Cian, or the Christian vision of Adamnan are among the most poetic productions of the Irish genius.

Varieties of Style.—It is not to be supposed that all these tales are formed upon a definite plan or partake of the same character. There is a great difference in style between the tales of the earliest period and those of the middle and later literary epochs. Indeed, the tales may be classed loosely into three great groups, the rough-hewn, abrupt, and archaic tales of the first period ; the more elaborated style of the second or best period of Irish prose, and the tedious narrations of the third or final period of development. No definite dates can be assigned to these periods ; but the first, in which the *seanchaidhe* or professional story-teller may be said to be feeling his way to a method of expression, may roughly be said to include tales which took shape in the seventh century or earlier, while the final stage, in which there are manifest signs of decay of style, may, perhaps, be dated from about the eleventh century. The best period of Irish prose would, therefore, lie between these dates, and may possibly be reckoned as belonging to the eighth, ninth, and tenth centuries, a period which was also productive of much fine poetry, whether we take into account the poems contained in the prose romances in the second or middle group of tales or those which occur independently.

Of the earliest style of composition the L.U. version of the *Táin bó Cuailnge* offers a good example. A comparison of this version with that in L.L., which belongs to the middle style of writing, will be found instructive. In the first stage the writing is abrupt and disconnected ; there are few poems, and these, where they do occur, are usually in the early declamatory style known as *rosg ;* there is no lingering over pathetic situations, even where these were evidently familiar to the writer ; the grotesque and weird play a large part in the stories. In the second style of writing every scene is carefully elaborated ; humorous and pathetic passages are introduced and made to yield their full share of dramatic expression ; long poems are frequent ; descriptions are enriched in every detail, and a certain fixed method of handling a subject is adopted. In the third period we get those turgid passages of description, filled with alliterative adjectives, of which much just complaint has been made. These occur chiefly, though by no means exclusively, in the semi-historical pieces, such as the Battles of Rosnaree,

of Moira (Magh Rath) and of Magh Léana, or the " Wars
of the Gall and Gael." It may, however, be hereafter
found that these differences of style are not altogether
dependent on the date of composition, but that they
are also due to provincial peculiarities. The redundant
style of writing is in any case a marked feature of much
work which undoubtedly hails from Munster. We are
not, however, as yet in a position to pronounce upon
this.

Literary Defects.—Thus, in spite of their fine
qualities, these tales are not without serious literary
defects. They are often wandering and wild, they
abound in repetitions and exaggerations, and in long
drawn-out descriptions of men and things which, though
invaluable as a record of social life, are tedious from an
artistic point of view. The sense of proportion and
balance is far better preserved in some stories than in
others, but the total effect sought after is often obscured
through the intrusion of these minute descriptions.
Such are the account of Conaire's host in the Bruidhen
Dá Derga, the reports of Mac Roth in the Táin, or of
the " Look-out man " in " Mesca Ulad." Though
these reports give us a wonderfully clear impression of
men and habits in ancient Ireland, they hamper and
delay the development of the plot.

Even less excusable is the wearisome repetition of
epithet and description. Certain given formula reappear with invariable regularity whenever the same
or similar conditions occur. No doubt this habit grew
out of the custom of recitation from an outline of the
story which was filled up from memory by the story-
teller as he went along. Nevertheless, though a

certain description may charm or impress us by its
fitness or beauty when we meet it for the first time,
its undeviating reappearance at a given place suggests
a lamentable lack of insight and invention on the part
of *seanchaidhe*.   Instead of obeying a spontaneous
inspiration, he is content to reiterate an old and well-
worn formula which has served the purpose of his
predecessors for centuries, and which has become fixed
through use as the one appropriate method of expression
for a certain kind of statement.   To take an instance :—
Of a fair youth or girl (for the same description is
applied to both), we are invariably told that " White
as the snow of one night were her hands ; red as a
fox-glove her cheeks ; blue as a hyacinth her eyes,
beneath eyebrows black as a beetle's wing ; red as
rowan-berries her lips.   You would think that between
her lips had fallen a shower of pearls, etc."

This pretty description, which the bard has so per-
fected in every detail that he can rarely imagine any
improving touch, stands equally well for Cuchulain
and Conall the Victorious, for Etain and Hector, for
Congal Claen, and Cormac mac Airt.   Charmed as we
are when first we meet with it, it becomes tiresome
when it recurs with the appearance of every fresh lad
or girl whom the poets desire to praise.   The same
observation applies to the description of a chariot and
its steeds, of a furious onset in battle and the inflation
of mind and body with which it was accompanied ;
to the manner of expressing the qualities of strength or
rapidity of movement, and to many other circumstances.
There is a fixed formula or system of simile for each
occasion which is rigidly adhered to.   This fault, a
common one in early literatures, including that of

I

Greece, is not in Ireland confined entirely to the older literature ; it is one of the most serious defects of all Irish writing, and we find it carried on into the work of the Jacobite poets and later bards of the seventeenth and eighteenth centuries.

The reappearance of the same similies is another form of the same defect ; these occur chiefly in the later literature, and in company with those adjectival passages which are one of the most serious blots upon the later style of writing.   Simile is frequently used in Irish writing with originality and effect, but there is a tendency to repeat the same stereotyped phrase just as a proverb might be repeated by an uninventive mind whenever an appropriate opportunity arose for its quotation.

But the gravest defect of Irish literature is undoubtedly its constant and frequently grotesque exaggerations. Chastity and conciseness of expression are the most difficult of all the attainments of the literary artist, and the Irish mind is especially prone to extravagant and hyperbolical expression of the emotions.   A multitude of examples might be offered to show that this exaggerated method of writing grew more marked as time went on, the earliest romances being far more terse and pure in expression than those of the later period.   In Irish literature, as in all literature, much depended upon the powers and capability of the individual writer ; some were stylists, others were not ; but though we find many stories that are moulded and polished with conscious art, and others that have a spontaneous and dramatic brevity, they show too frequently a fatal lack of the gift of self-criticism ; the Irish writer seems incapable of judging how to shape his material with a view to presenting it in its best form. The strict rules which he learned to apply to poetical composition fail him for the prose tale, and he is not able to supply the want from his own consciousness. Had he possessed this gift, his literature would have taken a foremost place among the romance cycles of the world. Yet, as it comes to us, and with full acknowledgment of its defects, it appears to us to have a claim upon the consideration not only of the nation which produced it, but also upon the general student of literary history, which has not hitherto been accorded to it. There is in it not only an element of fine and healthy optimism which is strangely at variance with the modern popular conception of the prevailing melancholy of Irish literature, but there is in it a stimulating force and energy which springs out of its own intense and human vitality, and which, wherever it is known, makes of it the fountain-head of a fresh creative inspiration.

This stimulating of the imagination is, perhaps, the best gift which a revived interest in the old native Romance has to bestow.

CHAPTER X.

Legends of the Kings

All history begins in legend ; and in Ireland, where so much attention was fixed upon the history of the race and on the central authority of the Kings of Tara, it was natural that there should spring up a large number of legends relating to the early settlements of the inhabitants in Ireland, and to the kings who ruled the country from ancient times. There exists, indeed, a whole series of stories which relate almost consecutively the supposed history of these rulers for over a thousand years before Christ and which carry the history down to the Danish invasions in the eighth century. The earlier dates are clearly imaginary ; it was the desire of the mediæval writers to make the native history stretch backward to the period of the Flood, and in order to accomplish this it was necessary to allow vast lapses of time, which were filled up by composing lengthy genealogies and annals of kings some of whom we may well believe to have been purely mythical. Yet it was from these ancient tales or poems that Keating and the later annalists were forced to draw their material, and for this reason they still have a certain historical interest as the fount of our ancient legendary history, while from the literary point of view they form a distinct section of early Irish romance. Putting aside for the present the Legends of the Settlements, which have, in fact, in the form in which they have been transmitted to us, whether as poems or prose legends, little literary value, we come to what were known as the " King-Stories " of Erin, or the legends of the Monarchs of Tara.   It was as much the business of the ancient story-teller to be able to recite the " King-Stories " of Ireland as it was his duty to have ready tales from the other cycles of romance. We may well believe that the " King-Stories " were much in favour at princely festivals in Tara and elsewhere, and to be a good teller of King-Stories was a mark of an accomplished minstrel.   These stories, as we have them now, show by their form and literary structure that they have been composed in very different periods. Some of them, like the fine romance of the Bruidhen Dá Derga, have all the peculiarities which mark the tales of the Cuchulain cycle : indeed, from one point of view it belongs to that series of tales, for it introduces several of the Red Branch heroes as well as some matter connected with purely mythological times ; others, such as the Battle of Moira (Magh Rath) and Magh Léana are evidently of much later origin in their present form, for they contain long redundant passages and elaborated details which, as we have said, are the mark of a style of writing common, especially in Munster, from the eleventh century onward.   This dissimilarity in the style and date of composition of the pieces as we now possess them must not however deceive us with regard to the actual origin of the legends themselves. That many of them are ancient we need not doubt, others were added by the ingenuity of the later poets as time went on to fill up gaps in the history or to explain the meaning of a place, or name, or of a personal title. To this topographical instinct we may trace the origin of

many of the ancient Irish legends, and we frequently
find two or more stories invented at different times to
explain a single name.   For example, two quite different
legends were invented to explain the origin of the name
of the ancient Capital of Ulster, Emain Macha, now
Navan Fort, two miles west of Armagh.   In the one,
Macha, an early Queen of great energy and power,
condemned five young princes, who were claimants to
the throne, to build a court or palace for her, the site of
which she marked out with her golden brooch or pin
unfastened from her neck, whence, according to this
story, it is called the " Emain of Macha " from *Eo*,
a pin, and *muin*, the neck.   The other story derives
the name from *emain*, twins ; because Macha, the
war-goddess of the Irish, gave birth, under peculiar
circumstances, to twin children at the spot so named.
In some such fashion many fine stories were invented
by the old romancers, and, like the pure romances, they
have no doubt undergone modifications from century
to century.   It is natural that tales should cluster
about the personages of such renowned princes as
Cormac mac Airt, Conn " of the Hundred Battles,"
Niall of the Nine Hostages, and King Guaire the Hospitable of Connaught.   A number of legends also arose
to explain the origin of the heavy tribute laid upon
Leinster by the Monarchs of Tara and exacted by them
during several centuries, called the Boromhean Tribute.
It is hardly possible that a tribute of this nature could
have been demanded year after year through eight or
perhaps twelve centuries merely to avenge a slight
placed, towards the close of the first century, upon the
daughters of a prince of Tara ; but the fact of the
existence of this tax would give rise to speculations

which these legends were invented to satisfy.   Into
these legendary accounts many historical facts were, no
doubt, woven.

There is a great deal of repetition in these " King-
Stories " ; the same incidents being related of different
kings.   For instance, the two greatest kings of ancient
Ireland, Cormac mac Airt and Niall of the Nine Hostages,
are both represented as being cast out of their rightful
position as infants, and reared up in secrecy, proving
their title to the throne on their arrival at manhood
by some special quality of mind or body.   Again,
two successive monarchs of Tara, Murtough mac Erca
and Dermot mac Cearbhal (Karval) meet their deaths
in the same manner and with much the same details,
both being burned alive in their own houses after an
attempt to escape into the great vat which stood in
every princely banqueting hall ; while the curious
" Legend of the Sovereignty " recurs in connection
with the various kings.   These repetitions are found
everywhere in the history ; there are two Crimthans who
perform much the same series of acts and carry on
foreign wars with the space of a century between them ;
two Kings Dermot (Dermaid mac Cearbhal and Dermaid
Ruadnaidh), and also two princes named Guaire of
Connaught, who lived in the sixth and seventh century
respectively, whose family history and whose legends
there is no possibility of disentangling.   Even characters
belonging properly to the mythology reappear again in
historic times.   Gods are revived as kings, and ancient
magicians as poets of a later day ; philosophers like
Morann, bards like Amergin or Ferceirtne, or gods like
Nuada seem to have no fixed date or place, but reappear
in a number of quite different connections which no

arrangement of the material can weld into a natural sequence. Partly this was accidental and unintentional, the result of a natural evolution which has taken place in many countries ; but partly it was the outcome of the necessity to fill up the long periods caused by the adoption by Christian scribes and genealogists of the Biblical chronology.

The historical reliability of these stories varies very much. In some, such as the tale of the Destruction of Dá Derga's Hospitable House, or the fairy-legend of Murtough mac Erca, although both the chief characters are probably historic, the legends about them are almost entirely fabulous ; in others, such as the Battle of Moira, or the tale of the Fall of Tara, though the tale has suffered expansions and accretions in accessories, we may regard the general substance of the tale as historic. We take these tales as examples of a large series.

The Destruction of the House of Dá Derga (*Togail Bruidne Dá Derga*).—This piece is formed on the lines of several of the tales of the Cuchulain cycle and evidently hails from the same period and is influenced by the same canons of writing. It is one of the most important of the tales relating the destruction by fire of the six large public places of entertainment or " Hospitable Houses " which in ancient times were built in various parts of Ireland, and which were presided over by wealthy landowners who were at once the chief farmers and tax-collectors of the provinces and the heads of these large open rest-houses for wayfarers. They were known as the Bruidhen or Hostal of Dá

Derga (Co. Dublin) ; the Bruidhen Dá Choga (Co. Westmeath) ; Bruidhen of Lusca or Lusk (Co. Dublin) ; Bruidhen of Mac Dareo (in Co. Leitrim) ; of Mac Datho (in Leinster) ; and of Blai the Hospitaller (in Ulster). Of the overthrow by fire of four out of the six there are fine tales remaining. They seem to have been composed of wooden dwelling-houses, kitchens, and halls built round a central court-yard, through which a stream ran or which had in it a well for the supply of the family. A garden and orchard lay round the house, and outside were lawns or playing-fields and outhouses for cattle, usually surrounded by three encircling raths or earthen ramparts as a protection against enemies. They were placed at the meeting of main roads leading in different directions. During an attack in time of war these large wooden houses were easily set on fire ; a few lighted brands flung upon the corners of the roof would speedily burn to the ground the whole edifice and all that it contained.

The Bruidhen of Dá Derga was situated on the River Dodder not far from the village of Donnybrook in the present County Dublin. The tale, as we have it, seems to have been added to from time to time, as it contains much mythological matter going back long prior to the time at which the main incident of the story is supposed to take place, and it includes part of the legend of the " Wooing of Etain," from whom King Conaire, the hero of the tale, was supposed to be descended. The fatality which overtook him is ascribed to the anger of the *sidh* or shee-folk at the marriage of the fairy-maid, Etain, to a mortal spouse ; but it is carried out through the agency of three wicked foster-brothers, who avenge themselves on Conaire for the check he sets upon their evil deeds, by

planning his destruction.   The main portion of the
tale opens with a curious account of the election of
Conaire to the throne of Tara through the prognostica-
tions of a sooth-sayer who, when thrown into a charmed
sleep by the singing over him of an incantation, utters
his prophecy as to the appointed king.   The sooth-
sayer partakes of a heavy feast and falls into a trance.
Whomsoever he should perceive coming towards him
in his sleep would, according to the notions of the
time, be received as the rightful king.   On this occasion
the magician perceived " a man stark-naked passing
along the road to Tara, with a stone in a sling " ;
and Conaire, forewarned by his fairy kin of the conditions to be fulfilled, set out on the road to Tara and
was presently elected to the monarchy.   But Conaire,
like all chiefs of ancient Ireland, is surrounded by
" tabus " or *geasa* which it forebodes evil to him to
break, and one after another these *geasa* of Conaire's
are broken through.   After a time he is forced into
a marauding expedition against his foster-brothers, and
on his way his " tabus " fail him.   There is a touch
of Northern weirdness in this part of the tale.   Among
his " tabus " was to " see the three Red Horsemen from
the *sidh* going before him," but as he proceeds on his
way along the road from the South towards the land of
Meath he marks before him three horsemen riding
onward towards the same place.   ' Three red garments had they and three red mantles ; three red
bucklers they bore, and three red spears were in their
hands ; they rode on three red steeds, and on the head
of each of them was ruddy hair.   Red were they all,
both body and hair and raiment, both steeds and men.
" Who are those who fare before us ? " asked the king.

" It was a ' tabu ' of mine for those three to go before
me, the three Red Ones to the House of Red.   Who
will follow them and bid them come towards me on my
road ? "   " I will follow them," said Conaire's son.
He rode after them, lashing his horse, but he could not
overtake them.   The length of a spear-cast was always
between them ; they did not come nearer to him, nor
did he gain on them.   He cried out to them that they
should not go before the king.   They halted not ; but
one of the three men sang to him over his shoulder,
" Alas, my son, great are the tidings, the tidings from
the Bruidhen ; a noble king's ardour consumes thee,
but through the enchantments of the ancient men
nine only will yield to him. Alas, my son ! " Thrice
King Conaire sent after them, offering them great
gifts if they would stay ; but still they only cried
behind them as they pursued their way, " Lo, O lad,
great are our tidings.   Weary the steeds we ride, the
steeds from the *sidh*-dwellings of Donn Tetscorach.
We are alive and yet we are not alive.   Terrible are
the portents ; lives will be lost, the carrion-birds be
filled ; sword-edges sharpened for the strife of slaughter ;
after sundown a field strewn with the broken bosses of
warriors' shields." '

Now, when the king heard that he knew that his *geasa*
had failed, and that these were the three Red Ones of
the *sidh*-mound, the false champions whom the *sidh*-
folk had banished from them and who were to revenge
themselves upon the king.

Conaire, seeing that his *geasa* are against him and
that, moreover, the whole country is in flame from the
war-bands of his foster-brothers raiding and destroying,
makes his way to the great house of Dá Derga.   A large

part of the story is taken up with a description of the king's host and followers as they sit at the feast. These descriptions are, as is usual in the Irish tales, supposed to be made by an onlooker, who reports the appearance of the warriors to the foster-brothers before they raid the house.   At length the assault is made and the house fired.   Conaire comes forth with his army, bravely defending the place, but is eventually overpowered and his followers killed.   A dramatic passage at the end of the story reminds us of the incident in the Alexander Saga in which water is brought to the thirsting conqueror in the helmet of one of his warriors, or of David before the gate of Bethlehem.   As is usual, however, the Irish tale, even if borrowing from classic or Biblical sources, retains distinctive features of its own.   It is said that "from the vehement ardour and the heat of the contests in which Conaire had fought he was attacked by a great thirst and he came nigh to perish by a consuming fever for lack of the drink he craved.   For the River Dodder which ran through the house had been licked up by the heat of the flames from the burning building and all the liquids in the house had been poured upon the fires."   But when Conaire appealed to his fosterer, a hardy warrior named Mac Cecht, he unwillingly undertook the task.   In the curiously exaggerated language into which the early writer always falls when he endeavours to describe a great feat of prowess, it is said that "Mac Cecht fared forth to seek a drink, bearing the king's son under his arm, and Conaire's golden cup, in which a whole ox with a pig might be boiled, in his hand, and he carried in his hand his shield and his two spears and sword and the spit of iron which held the cauldron."   With a terrific onset he bursts forth, dealing destruction as he goes, and " he went his way until he reached the Well of Casair which was hard by in the land of Cualann, but out of it he found not sufficient water to fill Conaire's golden cup that was in his hand.   Before morning he had gone round all the chief rivers of Erin, but in all of them he found not the full of his cup of water.   Then next day he visited the chief lakes of Erin, but though he sought in all the lakes he found not the full of his cup.   He went on again till he reached Uaran Garad on Magh Ai of Connacht.   It disappeared before him and sought to hide itself from him.   But a wild duck rose up before him from the water so that Mac Cecht rejoiced and he broke out into a lay and he brought therefrom the full of his cup and he went on till morning and reached Dá Derga's Hostel.   Then as he was going over the third rath towards the house he saw two warriors striking off the head of Conaire.   He smote one of the twain and struck off his head ; and at the other, as he was flying with the king's head in his hand, Mac Cecht cast a pillar-stone that was beneath his feet." Then he flung the water over the neck and headless body of the king.   With a touch of the grotesque never long absent from the Irish story, it is said that when it felt the water Conaire's head revived and began to praise the valour of Mac Cecht, regretting that he was not still alive in order duly to reward him. [*]

By way of contrast we may take next **the Battle of Moira or Magh Rath,** which gives us an example

---

[*] The tradition of talking heads which have been severed from their bodies is a common one both in Welsh and Irish Legend.   Compare the Wanderings of Bran's Head in Welsh, and the story of Donn Bó in the Battle of Allen in Irish Legend.

of the historic tale in its late development. The battle is historical; it is mentioned by Adamnan, in his life of St. Columcille, under the name of Bella Roth (Book III., ch. v.), and it was fought in 637 A.D. probably near a village of that name still existing in Co. Down. The belligerents were Donnell, King of Tara, and a young and light-minded prince of Ulster, named Congal Claen, who was discontented because Donnell had refused to place the whole of Ulster under his sway. Congal gathered a host of mercenaries from Alba (Scotland) and elsewhere to avenge his supposed injuries, and a severe battle was fought between him and the King of Ireland, in which Congal was himself slain by the chance shot of an idiot youth, and his army dispersed. The account has come down to us in a long and late version which is full of interesting and graphic details. The personal character of the rash and weak Northern Prince and of the noble and forgiving monarch of Ireland are drawn with much distinctness; and the curious description of the fierce appearance of the hosts of Erin "with their tufted moustaches and long beards hanging to their waists, their overhanging eyebrows and short-gathered vests beneath cloaks of black sheep-skin thrown over the shoulders" is only one out of many valuable details which this piece preserves of manners in mediæval times in Ireland. The fettering of the foreign soldiers, each of whom was manacled by the foot to his companion, lest he should turn and fly before the enemy, the rough test of their courage from the furious hound set to spring unexpectedly upon them, the exhortations of the Druid, the importance attached to the order of precedence at a feast, are among the interesting details here preserved to us.

The writer knew how to tell a story.   We give one example of the vividness with which the incidents are placed before us.   When Congal was gathering up his strength for a final onslaught before falling from the wound given him by the idiot, Cuanna, he meets the Prince of Desmond, a foster-brother of his own, brought up like himself at King Donnell's court.   ' " Wherefore," he cries, " does the large, soft youth of the men of Munster come among us ? "   " To send thee speedily to thy final destiny among the terrible people of the devil," the Prince replied.   Then Congal burst into a clear, tremendous laugh, and said, " Well do I remember the warlike feats of thy childhood, and the slow soft actions of thy boyhood, for thou wert ever clever at running away, even like thy foster-father, the king, whose dark mysterious ways and skill at battle-shunning we all know.   For the disposition of a foster-child is ever two-thirds that of its rearing and tutorage."   " Thy curses and thy lawlessness bind thee like a mighty fetter, O Congal, and the curses of hundreds greet thee every returning day."   Then they flew upon each other, and the sword of Congal was broken and his hand struck off by an upstroke into the air.   Congal cried, " It is the cutting of the thread of life to me, that the Prince ot Desmond should attack and mutilate me.   My sword and my right hand have failed me in battle." '

Yet, fine as this story is when the main incidents are set free from the mass of matter which encumbers them, it has the faults of much late Irish historical romance. It is filled with unnecessary and irrelevant material, it is long-winded and often prosaic ; above all, it is overlaid by those long alliterative passages which are the bane of the later literature.   A comparison of this story with the preceding tale we have been studying will enable the student to form a good idea of the two types of Irish story-telling, one of which is chiefly confined to the tales of the Ulster cycle and some other classical tales formed on the same model, the other includes a large number of the historical tales, with much late romance. The bulk of the Ossianic Literature stands apart from both. The essential differences between the two styles of writing have hitherto been ascribed entirely to the changed ideals of an earlier and later period of literary output. It is too soon to decide whether this explanation covers the whole of the ground; but it appears probable that more attention will have to be paid to the provincial element than has hitherto been observable if we are to arrive at a full explanation of the phenomenon. Though occasionally we get in a late version of an undoubtedly Ulster tale, such as the Battle of Rosnaree, the alliterative adjectives and prolix style which are found in much Southern writing, they are not characteristic of them as they are characteristic of a large number of historic pieces which undoubtedly hail from Munster. We can trace the special influence of Munster writing on this piece; for the Battle of Rosnaree incorporates whole passages from the Munster "Wars of the Gael and Gall." The question cannot be fully discussed here; but the very marked differences of style that we find seem to be more satis-factorily accounted for by supposing that the provincial element plays a part in them than in simply regarding them as the product of a different age.

The Battle of Magh Léana (*Cath Maigh Lemna*).—
From the later period of historic legend comes to us

the Battle of Magh Léana (Co. Westmeath) a piece also very valuable on account of its incidental notices of manners and customs, but containing much purely fairy-matter. Its purpose is to account for the ancient division of Ireland into North and South, or " Leth Chuinn " and " Leth Mhogha," with the circumstances that led up to this. The battle was fought about 137 A.D. during the reign of Conn of the Hundred Battles (*Conn Céad-cathach*) and relates to the warfare which existed between him and Eoghan or Owen Mór, prince of Munster, who had been exiled to Spain and had married the daughter of the King of Spain, returning with her to claim his kingdom and afterwards to dispute the monarchy of Ireland with Conn. In these wars the Fianna of Leinster and Connaught bear a part, the Fianna of Connaught siding with Conn, while Eoghan is found on the side of Cumhaill (Cool), father of Fionn, in the battle of Cnuca, in which battle Cumhaill was slain.

A good example of a battle piece is the account of the **Battle of Crinna,** one of the numerous battles fought between Cormac mac Airt (reigned 227-266 A.D.) and Ulster. The men of Ulster considered themselves insulted by Cormac, because when they assembled at the Triennial Assembly or Feis of Tara during his reign they found no proper preparation made for their entertainment. They immediately challenged Cormac, who, after gaining a promise of help from Lugaid (Lewy) his nephew, a Munster prince, set forth to meet them. The incidents in this battle do not place the character of the great King Cormac in a favourable light.

Other historic tales, such as the **Death of Muir-chertach or Murtough mac Erca** (King of Ireland

K

512 A.D.) and the **Fall of Tara** seem to be allegories of the struggle for mastery between the Church and State under the form of fairy legend, or satire. Yet both, no doubt, contain a germ of fact, however the material has been worked up by the fancy of the professional bard. The first relates the burning of King Murtough at Cletty, on the Boyne, by a witch-woman, whom he had taken into his confidence and who wrought spells against the king. The second and more important tale relates the supposed fall of the monarchy of Erin by the maledictions uttered against it by the twelve chief saints of Erin, who considered their rights infringed by the monarch. The defence of King Dermot, who was a Christian, is so fine that we insert it here. " Alas," he said to them, " this is an iniquitous war that ye have waged against me, seeing that it is Ireland's good that I seek after, to preserve her discipline and royal right ; but ye seek her disorder and ruin. For the Order of a Prince is conferred on such and such an one by God Himself, to the end that he shall by righteous rule and equitable judgment maintain his truthfulness, his princely quality, his place of governance. Now that to which a king is bound is to show mercy joined to stringent execution of justice ; to maintain peace in the tribal limits, to hold hostages in bonds ; to succour the wretched, but to overwhelm enemies ; and to banish falsehood from his realm. For unless on this hither side of death the King of Heaven's will be done no excuse will be accepted for us yonder."

It is difficult to know how much truth is contained in this story of the downfall of Tara. The central monarchy continued to exist until the coming of the Anglo-Normans to Ireland in the twelfth century, at all events as an official title, carrying with it a certain dignity and power.   But Tara itself as the seat of government seems to have been forsaken soon after the time of Dermot, and the monarchs chose other places of residence.   Fiach's Hymn to St. Patrick speaks of Tara as lying " silent " and " waste," and the Calendar of Angus compares the solitude and ruin of Tara with the busy life of the monastic schools of Armagh and other centres.   Therefore, even if we consider the story as we have it rather as an allegory describing a long-continued and slow struggle between the secular and ecclesiastical authority than as the record of an actual event, it preserves for us the memory of a change which certainly took place about this time.

The Destruction of Dind-Righ.—This is the legend that even in early times was reckoned as the first in the series of the " King Stories " of Erin, as is shown by the mention of it by Donn-Bó, the minstrel, in the piece called the Battle of Allen.   It is there said that Donn-Bó, " who was the best teller of King-Stories in the world, knew a tale of each King of Tara from the tale of the Destruction of Dind-Righ down to the kings who reigned in his own time."   It is a cruel story of the jealousy of one brother by another followed by a double murder and a seizure of the Kingdom of Leinster. The murdered prince left a son, Labhraidh, or Lowra the Wanderer, so named from the adventures he went through after he was driven out from the kingdom.   On his return he marched to Dind-Righ, the palace of the Kings of Bregia, now held by the troops of his usurping uncle, Cobthach (Coffey), sacked the fort, and slaughtered the troops.   He afterwards took a terrible revenge on

Cobthach by setting fire to the house to which he had
invited him in friendly banquet.   The inner walls were
of iron which were heated red-hot and all within perished.

Another tale, called LONGEAS LABHRADA, is connected
with this story.   It relates the wooing of Moriath,
daughter of the King of West Munster, by Labhraidh,
and his adventures during his absence from Erin.

**The Destruction of the Bruidhen of Mac Daréo
or Daire** gives an account of a rising among some
persons or clans called the Aithech-Tuatha (a word
which Keating takes to mean the unfree or servile tribes
of Ireland) against the Milesian nobles, whom they
slaughtered at a friendly feast at the Bruidhen of Mac
Daréo on the plains of Breifne in the present Co. Leitrim,
henceforth known as Magh Cró, or the " Plain of Blood."
The insurgents placed on the throne one Cairbre Cat-
Head, who held the sovereignty until the return of three
princes of the ancient line from exile and their subsequent
restitution to their rights.   The tradition seems to have
some mythological meaning and is not to be taken as
incorporating an actual historical event.   It is placed
in the first century of our era.

Tract on the **Expulsion of the Tribe of the Deisi**
in the reign of Cormac mac Airt from Meath and their
eventual settlement in Waterford and South Wales.—
This story, though containing some improbable incidents,
no doubt preserves the record of an actual emigration
of the sept.   The barony of Deece, in Co. Meath,
still retains the name in that locality ; and in Co.
Waterford, where the sept settled in the fifth century,
after many temporary resting-places, the two baronies

of " Decies without Drum " and " Decies within Drum " still bear witness to their final establishment in that district.

The Boromhean Tribute.—This piece gives the history of the causes out of which grew the laying of the heavy tribute upon Leinster known as the Boromhe (Boru) by the Kings of Ireland, a tribute seldom obtained without severe fighting.   Toole or Tuathal, monarch of Ireland 76-106 A.D., had two daughters, the younger of whom was sought in marriage by the reigning King of Leinster.   According to Irish marriage customs it was not permitted to a younger sister to marry before the elder, and the elder daughter was accordingly wedded to him.   He shortly afterwards gave out that she was dead, and gained the hand of the second girl while he held his first wife in concealment.   But the two sisters one day chanced to see each other and both of them died of grief and shame.   In revenge, an annual tribute of great severity was laid upon Leinster by the King of Tara, which continued to be exacted up to a late period. Several tales relate battles fought to secure it ; one of these, the Battle of Dunbolg, forms the main portion of this tale and recalls incidents in the Siege of Troy.   The piece also contains an account of the remission of the Tribute obtained by fraud by St. Molling from Finnachta, King of Ireland, in 674 A.D.   This part of the long tale is couched in a vein of cynicism and gives an unpleasant impression of saints like Adamnan and Molling.   It is probably related in the spirit of broad satire.

Battle of Magh Mucramha, the battle in which fell Art the Solitary, King of Ireland (166-196 A.D.).

Details of the battle, with much curious preliminary matter relating to events in Munster, are given, and the usurpation of the throne of Tara by Lugaid or Lewy Maccon is detailed.   In this piece, Cormac, son of Art, the hero of a number of stories and one of the most famous kings of ancient Ireland, first appears before his people.   He makes an award before the nobles of Tara which is so just that he is recognised by them as their rightful king.   Introductory to the Battle of Magh Mucramha may be considered a piece giving an account of the birth of Cormac, son of Art, which expands the incident of his first appearance at Tara. Other pieces, such as " The Panegyric of Conn's grandson, Cormac," " The Battle of Crinna," etc., are connected with the story of Cormac and with the period of his reign.

Adventures of the Sons of Eochaid Muighmedóin.

—This tale, which incorporates incidents found elsewhere in other forms, relates the means by which Niall of the Nine Hostages, Eochaid's youngest son, came to the throne instead of his elder brothers.   The story relates the cruel treatment of Cairenn, Niall's mother, by Monghfinn, Eochaid's first wife, who condemned her rival, the daughter of a Saxon king, to the most menial occupations.   Connected with this piece is one that relates the death of Crimthann, Monghfinn's brother, by the hand of his own sister, who poisoned him.

CHAPTER XI.

The Literature of Vision

Belief in Transmigration.—Cæsar tells us in the Gallic War (book vi., chap. xv.) that "one of the chief convictions which the Druids of Gaul desire to instil is that souls do not perish, but pass after death from one body to another; and they think this is the greatest incentive to valour, as it leads men to despise the fear of death."

We have already spoken of the belief in transmigration from form to form as being a part of the early mythology both of ancient Britain and Ireland; gods and goddesses being re-born as mortal men or women endowed with superhuman powers, or taking the forms of birds (especially swans), animals and insects, but always retaining their original individuality, and being capable of re-assuming at will their own form and powers. These beliefs belong to the very earliest stratum of Irish mythology, and are clearly outlined in such tales as the Wooing of Etain, the Dispute of the Swineherds, and the Birth-Stories of Conor and Cuchulain, or the Birth of Mongan. They may have undergone some modification in Christian times, but the essential idea remains unchanged.

It is to be understood that the Irish pagan belief does not exactly correspond with Cæsar's observations regarding the teaching of the Druids in Gaul.

In the pagan literature of Ireland we find no trace

of a belief in a life after death. The mortals who went into Magh Mell, or the Irish pagan Elysium, did not go there by means of, or after, death, they went as visitors, who could at will return again to earth. The distinction is essential. Until after the introduction of Christian teaching, the idea of a life after death seems to have been non-existant. It is quite different when we come to the late dialogues between Oisín and St. Patrick, which make up a large portion of the Ossianic poetical literature. Though anti-Christian in tone, Oisín had so far adopted the standpoint of the Saint that he admits the continued existence of Fionn and his warriors after death, the point of contention between them being where and under what circumstances this existence is carried on. Such a line of argument would have been impossible in pre-Christian times, when the idea of a future existence had not yet been conceived of. Both the re-incarnations of which we have now to speak, and the entrance into Magh Mell, were made during the continuance of mortal life; they have no reference to a life beyond the grave. It is important to bear this distinction in mind.

Outside the sphere of the ancient mythology the belief in transmigration is found also to persist; it re-appears in semi-historic times in such personages as Amergin the poet, or Tuan and Fintan, the survivors of the earliest settlers in Ireland, according to the statements of the chroniclers of the tenth and eleventh centuries.

These personages occupy the undefined border-land between the true mythology and the actual history. Amergin was said to be poet and magician to the Milesians at the time of their first landing in Ireland.

It is probable that at some time or other there was an actual poet of this name, to whom various ancient verses are ascribed ; but it is impossible to fix upon a date for his existence.   Like his fellow-poets Morann and Ferceirtne he belongs to several periods, and reappears as chief singer at the Court of Conor mac Nessa, and as one of the fosterers and tutors of Cuchulain. He is supposed, according to an ancient rune or incantation, ascribed to himself, to have passed through a long series of transformations both into animate and inanimate forms.   The opening of this poem or charm runs as follows :—

> I, the wind on the sea ;
> I, a powerful billow ;
> I, the sound of the ocean ;
> I, an infuriate ox ;
> I, a hawk on the cliff ;
> I, a flash of the sunshine ;
> I, a wild boar pursuing ;
> I, a river-salmon ;
> I, the lake of the low-lands ;
> I, the strength of song.

It is, of course, possible that these expressions may merely be similies meaning that the poet felt within himself the strength of the ox, the swiftness of the wild boar, and so on ; but it so closely resembles an ancient Welsh song ascribed to a bard named Taliesin, who in Welsh literature occupies exactly the position given to Amergin in Irish tradition as the ancient primeval poet of the race, that, taken in connection with the belief in re-incarnation which we know existed in Ireland in early times, it is more probable that it expresses that belief.   The poem of Taliesin is spoken also in the first person, and begins as follows :—

> " I have fled with vigour, I have fled as a frog,
> I have fled in the semblance of a crow, scarcely finding rest;
> I have fled as a roe into an entangled thicket ;
> I have fled as a wolf-cub, I have fled as a wolf in the wilderness.
> . . . I have fled as a fierce bull, bitterly fighting ;
> I have fled as a bristly boar below in a ravine ;
> I have fled as a white grain of pure wheat
> On the edge of a hempen sheet entangled, etc."

Some of these lines so closely resemble Amergin's poem that we might almost imagine them to be different forms of the same ancient rune.

The stories of Tuan and Fintan are late inventions, part of the pseudo-history created by the early official poets and chronologers to fill up the vast spaces of time that had to be accounted for somehow when, under Christian influences, it was desired to trace the history of the settlements in Ireland back to the time of the Flood.   The question of how the events of these remote times were supposed to be transmitted to the age in which they were chronicled in the early poems and genealogies seems to have perplexed the minds of the chroniclers, until they hit upon the happy expedient, suggested to them by the belief of their pagan ancestors, of making certain persons survive the Flood in which it was asserted that the first settlers had been swept away, and go through a sufficient number of re-incarnations to bring them down to within the historical period.   These two persons were Fintan and Tuan, who passed through a long series of animal shapes, and who were re-transformed into human beings in time to relate their experiences to Dermot mac Cearbhal, or Karval, in the sixth century.   Fintan was said to have been a brother of Cessair the daughter of Noah, who was supposed to have come to Ireland to escape the Flood.

These tales are as far away as it is possible to imagine from the simple belief and archaic tone of the ancient tales ; but they are curious as showing the invention of myths formed on the old belief at a time when the country had long been Christian.   These particular stories are, however, to be regarded not as survivals of an old tradition, but merely as convenient contrivances adopted for a special object.   The re-birth of Mongan, who is sometimes regarded as Fionn mac Cumhall under another name, and who is a re-birth of Manannán, is the story which of all the later tales comes closest to the older traditions.

Christian Modifications.—In many ways, however, the pagan system of ideas was too deeply rooted in the thought, the habits, and the social life of the people to be at once dispossessed when the outward form of religion was changed ; it held its place with persistant vitality, and only faded away slowly and, as it were, reluctantly before the introduction of the new doctrines and new methods of thought.

Nowhere can we so well trace this slow evolution of ideas as in the large body of literature that deals with the belief in the unseen world of Pagan and Christian tradition.   We find the Pagan tales at first under-going slight modifications when they are brought into contact with Christian teaching ; secondly, absorbing large portions of the new belief and dropping off at the same time many characteristic features of their own ; finally, we emerge into an atmosphere wholly controlled by Christian thought.   These tales, of which there has come down to us an unbroken series, provide us with a means of estimating a change that was doubtless extending itself over the whole sphere of mental activity.

(Sec. I.), The Pagan Conception.—The happy, careless nature of the Celt, always prone to believe the best rather than to fear the worst, conjured up for himself a very brilliant conception of the invisible world. It was to him Magh Mell, the "Plain of Honey;" Tír na n-Og, the "Country of Youth;" Tír Tairngiri, the "Country of Promise;" Magh Argatonél, the "Silver Cloud Plain."   These and many other beautiful names he applied to it, and he conceived it as a place of bliss and everlasting youth, where were to be found brave men and lovely women, palaces, music and pastimes, with the best of every sort of food and drink. Warfare and blood-shedding went on as in the old life, for to the Gael to fight was essential to happiness, and no Paradise would have been acceptable without it. The chosen mortal was usually tempted away into this lovely land by a fair maiden who offered an apple that supplied all wants or a branch of music that played melodiously and whose call was irresistible.   These features recur in almost every legend of the unseen world, but others vary.

The primitive idea seems to have been that the passage into the invisible world could be made without any actual means of transit.   The gods pass and repass over the border-land between the seen and unseen almost at will, as Etain and Midir did ; and even some mortals seem to have possessed this power, for Cormac mac Airt goes directly into the Land of Promise without any interruption or means of progression. But for mortals the idea of water to be crossed is usually present. The land of the unseen was usually separated from ordinary human life either by a belt of water, a lake or an ocean, which must by some means be traversed. Magh Mell is conceived of either as existant in an island, or sometimes in many islands, or as being a fair flowery plain visible only to opened eyes beneath the billows of the sea. Sometimes, as in the Voyage of Bran, these two different conceptions are found together.

The lord or ruler of this land is, most appropriately, Manannán mac Lir, the Ocean-god, whose dwelling is always supposed to be beyond the waves, and the passage is usually performed in a little skiff or boat of magic power, which is invisible to all eyes save those of the chosen mortal. It is thus that Cuchulain finds Magh Mell in an island in the lake ; that Connla of the Golden Hair and Bran mac Febail perform their journey. Not until far later times, when riding had become the ordinary mode of progression, do we find, as in the tale of Oisín in Tír na n-Og, that the boat has given place to a horse. Probably, had we the tale in its oldest form we should find that it, too, was framed on the original model ; but though it appears to be an old tale we possess it only in a modern poem written by Michael Comyn about 1750. As in the Voyage of Bran, the traveller returns from his magic voyage to find himself forgotten and a new race of men sprung up who remember his name only as the hero of " ancient stories," belonging to another age and cycle of things.

We will now examine some of these tales separately.

The Adventures of Connla the Fair (*Echtra Condla Ruadh*).—This charming little tale, one of the simplest of the series, tells how Connla, son of the Monarch Conn of the Hundred Battles, was one day seated beside his father on the summit of the Hill of Usnech when there appeared to him a lady, invisible to the rest, with whom he held converse.

When the king asks, " Whom art thou addressing, young lad ? " the lady herself replies : " He is conversing with a young and noble lady whom neither death nor age can touch.   Connla of the Golden Hair I loved, and I am inviting him to the Plain of Pleasures. There he shall be king for ever, and grief and woe shall touch him no more from the day he enters on his princedom.   Come with me, O Connla of the Golden Hair, the speckled neck and ruddy cheek ; until the awful day of Doom youth and beauty will not pass from thy person if thou wilt go with me."   Connla is sorely tempted to follow her, and the king, in despair at the unseen influence which he feels is being exercised over his son, calls on his Druid to drive away the lady by arts of wizardry.   As she is going, she throws an apple to Connla, and on this single fruit, which never diminished in size, he was nourished for a month, disdaining for it all other food.   At the end of a month the lady reappears, upbraiding Connla for being content " to await death amid the assemblies of short-lived mortals " rather than to become Prince in the Land of the Ever-living.   Connla does not reply ; he is torn between the desire to go with the damsel and his duty and love to his kin and race.   Again the lady sings of the land " which draws down the bright sun at eventide," a land of maidens and of all delight.   At length, with a single bound, the lad leaps into her Curach of Pearl, "the well-balanced gleaming skiff," and together they sail the sea, nor do men know to this day whither they went.

This tale, which is, except for an occasional expression, such as the "day of Doom," a purely pagan story, is a good example of this large class of tales in their simplest form. It contains all the essential elements: the maiden and the satisfying apple, the songs in praise of the unseen land, and the skiff to carry them across. Here Magh Mell seems to lie in the Western Ocean "which draws down the bright sun at eventide," but it may equally well be in a lake or in some unlocated place. Manannán was ever a wanderer, and there were many different avenues leading to his kingdom. Manannán is not always himself present in Magh Mell; in the Story of the Sickbed, or Wasting Away of Cuchulain, the unseen land is ruled by Labraid of the Swift Sword-strokes, and in this story Connla seems himself about to reign over it.

The Voyage of Bran, Son of Febal (*Imramh Brain*).—There is a group of seven tales among the valuable list of Bardic Stories given in the Book of Leinster called *Imramha** or Voyages, of which the Voyage of Bran is one. They are not, however, voyages in the ordinary sense of the word, but have the meaning of journeys into the invisible world. Out of the seven, two are still in existence, viz.: Maelduin and the Navigation of the Sons of O'Corra, while of

* The Imram was a voyage (lit. "rowing about") undertaken voluntarily or for pleasure; the Longes was usually a voyage of exile and penitence.

two or three others the substance is known though the separate tales are lost. The Voyage of Bran is one of the earliest of the *Imramha* and one of the simplest. It is largely composed of songs, and though it shows Christian influence, and is primarily intended as a prophecy of St. Columba, its poems preserve the antique flavour. Here we find the magic branch of melody and sustenance, the fair woman who tempts away the mortal from earth, and the double conception of Paradise as both beneath and beyond the ocean. It is full of brilliant word-painting and is one of the most joyous of all the Voyage tales.

Cormac's Adventure in the Land of Promise (*Echtra Cormaic i. Tir Tairngiri*).—This story has no boat in it. King Cormac mac Airt visits the Land of Promise in order to obtain a golden cup of truth by means of which ordeals were held. He is enticed thither by Manannán, who, in order to induce him to follow him, carries off in turn his daughter, his son, and his wife. The whole composition is devoted to praise of King Cormac and to detailing the virtues of the cup and the other magic gifts with which he is endowed.

(Sec. II.), Semi-Christian Visions.—If we pass over the LAY OF OISIN as belonging rather to the Ossianic legends than to the visions with which we are here dealing, we come to the second series of Voyages, those which, even if they have not always a Christian foundation, have a decidedly Christian flavour. It was impossible to wipe out of the people's mind dreams that had so strong a hold on their imagination ; the

happy deathless world was too beautiful and too firmly
fixed in the popular idea to be displaced.   It was
easier to infuse into ·these tales a Christian flavour.
By a not unnatural transference of thought the Magh
Mell of pagan vision became the "Land of Behest,"
or Christian Paradise.   From the Vision of Maelduin
to the purely ecclesiastical legend of St. Brendan we
find the gradual infusion of the new ideas going on;
the pagan form and groundwork remain, but the tale
assumes more and more a tone adopted from Christianity.
The most important changes of idea which they show
may be summed up briefly :—

(1) The semi-Christian vision is performed by real
    personages, and though a boat is still the
    means by which the voyage is carried out,
    it is no longer a magic barque hailing from
    the invisible world, but an ordinary curach
    or coracle built by human hands and sailing
    on an actual sea.

(2) The direction is always westward or north-west,
    out on to the Atlantic Ocean.   The "vast
    illimitable ocean" that girded their western
    shores was the natural land of wonder and
    mystery to the Irish monk or anchorite.
    Beyond it there lay he knew not what; but
    he dreamed, as in the "Voyage of Brendan,"
    of great rivers and fertile lands; and many
    a wandering monk set out to try and realise
    his dreams.   On the most remote rocks and
    islands of the coast these anchorite monks
    built their hermitages, wherever the tossing
    coracle might carry them; and they are found

L

in these legends grown old and hoary, with nails like claws and hair white as snow, perched through a long existence on some inaccessible cliff. The sailor-saint and the sons of O'Corra alike set forth in a spirit of investigation into the wonders of nature ; for to the mediæval mind the marvels of this world and those of the next were not far apart.

(3) The idea of the unseen world enlarges from that of a confined space or island in a lake, in which is a central fort or palace, into that of the open boundless ocean scattered over with innumerable islands in each of which some new marvel is to be found. The traveller in the Voyage of Maelduin and other similar tales passes from isle to isle finding ever fresh and greater wonders than before.

(4) But the really distinctive change is that gradually the conception of a perfectly happy land passes away and a note of penitence and punishment takes its place. The voyage itself is generally undertaken as an expiation for crime. Maelduin goes to discover the murderer of his father, and the Adventures of the Sons of O'Corra, of Snedgus and Mac Rialga, and of St. Columcille's Clerics, arise out of the commission and punishment of crime. They are penitential voyages, and this fact entirely revolutionizes the structure and tone of the tales. Gradually, but ever increasing in intensity as time goes on, the Happy Isles become places wherein joy and pain are mingled or counterbalanced. Along

with the "Isle of Laughter" we find the "Isle of Weeping," where the inhabitants, clothed in black and with fillets round their heads, "cease not from weeping and wailing continually." The sufferings endured by the inhabitants of the islands are each assigned as a punishment for some specific sin committed upon earth.

The final stage is reached when the voyage incident is omitted altogether and the whole Vision is concerned with the joys of paradise and heaven and the tortures of hell. Such purely Christian pieces are the Vision of Adamnan, a vision which is in parts of exceeding beauty, or the mournful and painful "Tidings of Doomsday," which dwells chiefly on the tortures of the lost. The link between the two is found in the Voyage of Brendan, in which a vision of Heaven and Hell is shown to the voyaging saint in some of the islands he visits. This voyage, however, has gathered into itself many foreign elements.

It may be well, as a specimen of this large class of semi-Christian Voyage Literature, to give a more detailed account of the typical "Voyage of Maelduin."

The Voyage of Maelduin (*Imramh Maelduin*).— This is the most famous of all the Irish visions, and is one of the few Irish tales that has been adapted by an English poet. In Tennyson's version of it, however, the distinctively Irish touches are hardly represented, and its wild flavour is modified to suit the taste of English readers. The story is later than the Vision of St. Brendan, whose voyage it mentions. It is of

great length, and seems to have incorporated oriental
ideas drawn from some such source as Sinbad the Sailor,
as well as Christian ideas.   In its groundwork as well
as in the brilliance of its imagination it is, however,
purely Irish and pagan.   The story is said to have
been remodelled or " arranged " by Aedh the Fair,
Chief Sage of Ireland, of whom nothing is known,
but who appears to have had a knowledge of Virgil,
as he quotes from the Æneid.   It was probably he
who gave it its Christian colouring.   The voyage
was undertaken by Maelduin to revenge the death of
his father, Ailell of the Edge of Battle, one of the
Eoganacht of the Aran Isles, who had been slain by
warriors of Leix.   Maelduin had been brought up in
ignorance of his parentage and only discovered the truth
through the remarks of some bystanders who upbraided
him for playing in childish heedlessness over his father's
grave.   The building of the boat and the number of
the crew (always an important point in these stories)
is determined for him by a wizard, but their luck is
broken by the persistence of his three foster-brothers
in joining themselves to the party, by which means
the charmed number is not adhered to.   Thus, though
they arrive in a single day at the island in which their
victims are to be found, they are not able to land upon it,
but are driven by a furious wind out of their course
all that night, and in the morning they have no knowledge whither they have come, for neither earth nor
land is to be seen.   Then, in the regular fashion of
these Christian stories, they lay aside their oars, saying :
" We will cease now to row and let the boat drift,
and whithersoever it shall please God to bring it, He
will bring," and they pass out into the great boundless

ocean.   The boat sails north-west, and in thirty
chapters the marvels they encounter are described.
Most of them come down direct from the fountainhead
of Irish inspiration ; such are the maiden who gives
them food which varied in flavour ; the apples which
satisfied all hunger and thirst ; the fair land beneath
the water ; the stream like a rainbow arching over
the island and salmon falling out of it, or the horse
performing feats with its own skin.   Some seem to be
derived from the later Christian circle of ideas, such
as the old man of the men of Ireland who went on
pilgrimage, and whose hair during his long sojourn in
the solitary island had grown to such a length that it
covered him like clothes.   He tells them that his boat
having split under him he " put under his feet a sod
of his own country and thereon set out to sea.   The
Lord had yearly added a foot to the breadth of the sod,
which had thus become an island, and every year a
fresh tree had grown up thereon.   The birds in the
trees were the souls of his kindred and spiritual children
therein awaiting Doomsday."

It is possible that there may be a reminiscence of
classical parallels in the incident of certain smiths
smiting their mass of iron on the anvil and hurling it after
the boat.   When the vessel draws near to this island the
wanderers hear one smith asking another " Are they
close at hand ? "   " Yea," saith the other.   " Who
are they who are coming here ? " he asks again.   " They
seem to be little boys in a little trough," he replies.
When they hear this, Maelduin advises the rowers to
retreat as rapidly as possible, but not to turn the boat,
in case the smiths should perceive that they were fleeing.
When at length the smith sees that they are flying from

him he rushes out with a great mass of molten iron in his tongs, and flings it after the boat, making all the ocean to boil, but Maelduin got away. (*cf.*, Odyssey ix., 539, 540).

Again, the description of the huge bird which spread out its wings in flying like a cloud over the heavens and carried in its talons a branch as big as an oak tree, with red berries on it, from which it and the travellers fed, reminds us of the Phœnix. It renews its youth by bathing in a lake which was reddened with the stones of the berries that had been eaten, and for three days it remains combing and preening its feathers and shaking its pinions. Then it rises up and flies thrice round the island before soaring away in full strength to the quarter whence it had come.

In Maelduin also the narrow Bridge of Difficulty first appears, a conception that belongs to Persian and Indian mythology, but which is found also in what seems to be a purely Irish form in the account of Cuchulain's training under Scathach, and which reappears in most of the later Irish visions, and the accounts of St. Patrick's Purgatory. The end of the Story of Maelduin recalls an incident in Adamnan's " Life of St. Columcille." The seafarers perceive a falcon on one of the islands. " The falcon is like the falcons of Ireland," said Maelduin. " That is true," said the others. " Watch it," said Maelduin, " and see which way the bird will fly." They do so, and notice that it is taking flight towards the south-east. Following it, they reach the island from which they had been originally driven by the wind into the wide ocean. They drove their vessel on the beach and approached a dún where the folk inside were feasting. They heard one saying to another : " We shall be all right if Maelduin does not come." " Maelduin is drowned," said another. " Nevertheless, it may chance that your sleep will be disturbed by him," said a third. " What should we do if he came now," said a fourth. " That I can tell you," said the chief. " Great welcome would be made before him, for he hath been for a long space of time in great tribulation." Thereupon Maelduin strikes upon the door. " Who is there ? " said the doorkeeper. " It is Maelduin," he replied. " Open," said the chief, " and welcome to you." They then enter the house and are warmly received and clad in new garments, and they declared the marvels they had seen, and that God had revealed to them, according to the words of the sacred poet: " Hæc olim meminisse iuvabit." (Æn. i. 203).

We need not linger over other voyages of the same class. In their general features and in many details they follow the same plan. The NAVIGATION OF THE SONS OF O'CORRA (*Imramh ua Corra*) was supposed to be made about the year 540 A.D., and the piece seems to have been written in Galway or the Aran Isles. It is found in the Book of Fermoy. The Litany of Angus Céile Dé invokes the Sons of O'Corra, who may, therefore, have been real men.

The incidents in the VOYAGE OF SNEDGUS AND MAC RIAGLA, found in prose and verse in the Yellow Book of Lecan, belong to the end of the sixth century, and concern the district of N. Meath, Louth, and Monaghan, where were the townlands of the men of Ross, who, according to this story, were reduced to a truly Egyptian servitude by two cruel chieftains. It is a curious wandering tale, of which a large part is taken up by the prologue, while some of the central portions unite so badly that we can only suppose that pieces have been omitted.

THE ADVENTURES OF ST. COLUMCILLE'S CLERICS.— This piece seems to be a later version of the Voyage of Snedgus and Mac Riagla with portions of the Vision of Adamnan woven into it. The epilogue is omitted. In both pieces St. Columcille is the adviser or " soul-friend," at whose command the voyage is undertaken.

The Legend of St. Brendan.—This, the most famous and widespread of any of the Irish mediæval visions, is found in Irish, French, Latin and German prose versions, and in two English metrical versions of the twelfth and fourteenth centuries. It is closely connected with the story of St. Malo of Brittany. The legend was very early known to the Bretons, and is mentioned in the *Roman du Renard* as one of the popular lays of the country. The English versions follow the Latin order in the main, but the construction of the German legends varies so widely from all the rest that we hardly recognise the romance of the Irish sailor-monk. The Irish versions differ essentially both from the Latin and European accounts. But all alike agree in inserting the incidents of the Whale island, Iasconius (Ir., *iasc*, a fish ?) on whose back they celebrate Easter ; the Visions of Heaven and Hell ; the Paradise into which they may not enter ; the isle of Singing-birds, and some other details. In the Irish version, which is confused and disconnected, St. Brendan makes two separate voyages ; the scribe seems to be trying awkwardly to fit floating traditions derived from outside into the Irish life he has before him.

The lurid description of Hell is built up by means of one of those interminable strings of adjectives similar to that in " Tidings of Doomsday," in which the later Irish scribes delighted ; the description of Paradise on the other hand is most poetic. Matthew Arnold's poem is adapted from the foreign versions and introduces the incident of Judas Iscariot seated on a rock, which is not found incorporated in the Irish life, though there exists a separate Irish piece containing the story. The Life of St. Brendan is one of the nine biographies of Irish saints found in the Book of Lismore.

The Adventure of Teigue, Son of Cian (*Echtra Thaidg mheic Chéin*).—This Munster tale, which is exceedingly picturesque and full of charm, forms a link between the earlier and later visions. It is purely Irish in tone, but, like the " Voyage of Brendan," it combines the island-wandering of the Maelduin story with the purely Christian vision of Paradise. In this tale Biblical ideas of Paradise are most curiously interwoven with the Irish pagan conception.

(Sec. III.), Visions of Heaven and Hell.—We now reach the third and final stage of this Vision Literature. In this stage the voyage incident has dropped out altogether, the older pagan elements are discarded, and we get visions whose only object is the recital of the joys of Paradise and the torments of Hell. These Irish Christian visions form an important part of that widespread mediæval literature out of which Dante's " Divine Comedy " was formed. THE VISION OF ADAMNAN (*Fis Adamnáin*) is without doubt the most beautiful of these visions. In it the soul of Adamnan,

conducted by an " Angel of Fellowship," as Dante
was led by Virgil, goes forth from the body and traverses
the realms of Heaven and Hell.   This vision, though
ascribed to the ninth Abbot of Iona (d. 704 A.D.), is
believed by Dr. Whitley Stokes to be at least three
centuries later than his time.   For this reason we have
not included it among Adamnan's writings.   This vision
appears never to have passed out of Ireland ; yet both
in form and spirit it resembles in so many points the
" Divine Comedy " that we might imagine that the
great Italian poet had studied it.   Especially striking
is the description of the painful and slow ascent to
heaven, attained, as was Dante's Purgatory, by a series
of toilsome stages, at the entrance gate to each of which
sits an Archangel who scourges the penitent across
the face and eyes as he admits him, thus gradually
accomplishing the soul's purification as it proceeds.
" The city wherein is the throne, thus it is, with seven
walls of glass of divers colours round about it, and
each wall loftier than the other.   A family very meek,
gentle, without lack of any good thing are they who
dwell in the city.   For none reach it and none dwell
in it save only pure saints and pilgrims devoted to
God. . . .   Hard it is to climb the seven heavens,
for none of them is a whit easier than the other.   For
there are six gates of protection which the human race
must pass before attaining to the kingdom.   A gate-
keeper and a guardian from the family of Heaven have
been set to protect each gate."

In the fiery river before the gate of heaven, which
" tries and washes the saints," and in the " shining well
with bloom and odour " we seem to foresee the river of
Lethe in the " Purgatorio " from which Dante, " being

bathed, returned regenerate." Still more striking is the Irish conception of Limbo, the place at " the hither side of the lightless land " appointed for those " whose good and evil have been equal." In the torments of the lost we find that effort to adapt each punishment to the crime it was intended to expatiate which became so marked a feature of the later literature. But there is a note of tenderness, pity and hope in this vision which is absent from most of the mediæval visions, and which make of many of them a mere catalogue of revolting and often grotesque tortures in the imagining of which the writers seem to take a horrible delight.

The later visions by Irish ecclesiastics and writers have much less of the Gaelic character and charm. Among them THE VISION OF FURSÆ or Fersius, a Galway monk who built a monastery in East Anglia and afterwards established the great monastery of Peronne in France, is the most suggestive. It is found both in Irish and in Latin (see Bede's *Eccle. Hist.*, Bk. III., chap. xix.). Later we get the legend of OWAIN MYLES, a Northumbrian knight of Irish extraction, who in the reign of Stephen made a descent into the afterwards famous place of pilgrimage called St. Patrick's Purgatory in Loch Derg, Co. Donegal, and wrote a report of his experiences. It is the first of many mediæval visions which took their theme from this spot. Of these the VISION OF TUNDALE is the most extravagant and grotesque. It borders on buffoonery, and, though Tundale was an Irish nobleman, hailing from Cashel in Munster, his legend is harsh as well as prosaic. The last of these St. Patrick's Purgatory recitals of importance found in Ireland is the long and tedious VISION OF COUNT RAMON, a Spanish noble who visited Ireland in the reign of Richard II. (1397 A.D.), and recounted his experiences in elaborate detail in Latin prose. From these late and degraded dreams or trances all the glamour and brilliance of the old world has passed away ; we are in a region of horror and gloom, with no touch of radiance or pure imagination to lighten it.

CHAPTER XII.

Early Ecclesiastical Writings

The introduction of Christianity into Ireland was accompanied by the establishment of large monasteries over the whole country, which not only provided religious centres for the Christianised inhabitants but which also formed schools for training in agricultural and general knowledge. While the chief object of these schools was doubtless to instruct the pupils in Latin with a view to prepare those who desired to enter ecclesiastical orders for their work, it would seem that they were open to all comers, both lay and clerical, irrespective of the profession which they might eventually adopt. They seem to have existed side by side with the lay schools of the poets, and probably the course of instruction in the two sets of schools, monastic and secular, was different, being designed for different purposes.

But the monastic schools must soon have eclipsed those of the poets, for we read of thousands of students attending instruction in some of the larger establishments, such as Bangor, Clonard, and Clonmacnois ; and in the seventh and eighth centuries pupils flocked over to these monastic schools in great numbers from England and France. In the oft-quoted phrase of Aldhelm, teacher of Malmesbury at the close of the seventh century, taken from a letter addressed by him to three young men just returned from Ireland : " Why," he exclaims, " does Ireland pride herself on a sort of priority, in that such numbers of students flock there from England, as if here upon this fruitful soil there were not an abundance of Argive and Roman masters to be found, fully capable of solving the deepest problems of religion and satisfying the most ambitious students ? " It became, indeed, a habit for those who wished to pursue a learned career or to fit themselves by contemplation and retirement for the life of religion, to repair to Ireland and spend some years attached to one of the great monastic foundations ; in connection with these he might have all the advantages of instruction and a life of communal interests, combined with the solitude which a hut or cell built by his own hands apart from the cells of his fellows could afford. " To live solitary " was the highest ideal which presented itself to the minds of thoughtful men in this period ; to pursue learning was their chief desire.

Catalogues of Irish Monastic Libraries.—From the catalogues of libraries belonging to the Irish-founded Continental monasteries of Bobio and St. Gall we may learn the curriculum pursued for the higher courses of study in Irish monastic schools from the seventh to the tenth century. It included, besides the study of the Scriptures and of the Fathers, a knowledge of geography and philosophy as they were then known, and an acquaintance with the classics.

We are fortunate in still possessing a tenth century catalogue of the manuscripts in the monastery founded by St. Columbanus about the close of the sixth century at Bobio on the slopes of the Apennines in North Italy. It contains a list of seven hundred volumes, some of

which had been bequeathed to the library by the learned
Irishman, Dungal, Principal and Teacher of Pavia Uni-
versity.   Besides large numbers of the works of the
Fathers of the Church and copies of portions of the
Scriptures, with commentaries upon them, we find both
Greek and Latin authors.   There are copies of Horace,
Virgil, Ovid, Juvenal, Martial and Persius mentioned in
the list, as well as portions of the works of Terence,
Cicero, Demosthenes and Aristotle.   Some of the lost
orations of Cicero and other classical works of import-
ance have been recovered from the Bobio manuscripts.
Those which have escaped the depredations caused
by time, fire, and thieves, now form part of the most
treasured possessions of the Public Libraries of Milan,
Turin, Vienna, and of the Vatican at Rome.   The great
Libraries of St. Gall, Würzburg and Reichenau, all
of them Irish foundations, owned manuscripts, both
sacred and secular, of no less interest and importance.
Valuable texts of Virgil, of Ovid's Metamorphoses,
and of Eutychius have been recovered from them.
Many of these ancient manuscripts contain commentaries and glosses in Irish, and fragments of Irish verse
are frequently found written on the margins.   These
glosses, or words and phrases explanatory of the text,
are in the most ancient form of Irish now known ; it
has been the work of such eminent scholars as Zeuss,
Ascoli, Zimmer, Stokes and Strachan to endeavour to
elucidate them.   Occasionally there are found among
them fragments of Ogham writing, which seems to show
that this form of caligraphy was not wholly confined
to memorial inscriptions or brief messages on stone or
wood, but was used also for ordinary purposes, and that
up to a comparatively late period.

Trained in Irish schools at home, there went out, between the eighth and tenth centuries, a number of learned men to occupy public positions abroad. Such are John Scotus Erigena or John the " Scot " or Irishman, the philosopher and Greek scholar who was tutor and companion of Charles the Bald and teacher in his schools (*circa* 840) ; Dungal, poet, theologian and astronomer, who became Lecturer to the Court of Charlemagne about 780 A.D., and afterwards founded and was first Principal of the School of Pavia in Italy ; Clemens, tutor to the future Emperor Lothaire, the successor of Dungal, as " Instructor to the Imperial Court " ; Virgilius, Bishop of Salzburg, formerly Bishop of Aghaboe, where he bore his Irish name of Fergal, afterwards Latinized Virgilius, geometrician and astronomer (d. 784), and Dicuil (*circa* 820), who wrote a very interesting geography of the world, containing much matter unknown before his time. Their work and learning belong rather to the history of mediæval European culture than to that of their native country ; but the position that these men took abroad and the anxiety of the reviving schools of the Court of France to secure Irish teachers, argues a system of education in Ireland in advance of that usually current in their day. It is a mistake to suppose that these men were driven out of Ireland simply by the disturbance of the monasteries in the Norse invasions ; their own energy and the need for trained teachers abroad forced them forwards to a wider field of action.

Knowledge of Greek in Ireland.—There has been much discussion as to whether a knowledge of Greek was possessed by the monastic teachers of ancient

Ireland.   The earliest ecclesiastical writings leave us
uncertain, for though writers like Philo, Eusebius and
Origen are quoted by early Irish monks, such as Aileran
of Clonard (d. 665, A.D.) and Cummian of Durrow
(*circa* 640), it is possible that they had read these
writers in translations, just as in the middle ages the
Tale of Troy and other classical pieces seem to have
been derived from Latin versions, rather than from
the originals.   But St. Columbanus (b. 543), who was
educated at Bangor Mòr (Co. Down), seems certainly
to have known Greek ; he says in his letter to Pope
Boniface that he knew both Greek and Hebrew; he
evidently understood Aristotle in the original.   In the
so-called *Instructiones Columbani* frequent Greek words
and expressions are used.   There is no doubt also
that John Scotus Erigena (*circa* 850) was a good Greek
scholar, for he translated the works of so-called Dionysius
the Areopagite for the newly-founded Abbey of St.
Denis at the request of Charles the Bald.   This work,
produced at a time when the knowledge of Greek
had almost died out in Europe, excited the greatest
astonishment among his contemporaries.   The learned
Librarian of the Vatican Library, Anastasius, exclaimed
when he read it : " It is wonderful that this uncivilized
man, dwelling on the confines of the world, should have
been able to understand such things and to translate
them into another tongue."

The best proof that Greek formed part of the
curriculum of Irish-founded monasteries is the fact
that copies of Greek as well as of Latin authors were
found in the great Libraries of Bobio in N. Italy, and
of Reichenau or Augia Regia on Lake Constance,
where copies of Aristotle, Demosthenes and other

Greek classics have been preserved. Several of them contain Irish glosses, showing that they were studied by Irish students. Among the manuscripts found in these monasteries are Greek vocabularies and Greek paradigms and declensions. They cannot be said to prove any very scholarly or wide acquaintance with the language, but they show that it formed part of the course of study. In Ireland also we have Greek derivations given in Cormac's Glossary (ninth century) in the Cóir Anmann, and elsewhere.

It is also worthy of remark that from very early Christian times a Greek text of the New Testament, or some otherwise unknown text formed directly on the Greek, was current in Ireland and Britain.

This is becoming more certain as the texts of the Biblical manuscripts are being examined and is a matter of very great interest. The remarkable group of Græco-Latin manuscripts of the Gospels and Epistles and of the Psalter found in St. Gall also bears out the familiar use of a Greek text of the Scriptures in Irish monasteries. Berger (" Histoire de la Vulgate ") draws special attention to these bi-lingual manuscripts, and says that St. Gall, more than any other single place, furnishes data for the history of the local texts of the Bible. The British St. Gildas (*circa* 520), who had great influence in Irish ecclesiastical affairs, corrects his old Latin version of the Scriptures by the Greek, and the influence of a Greek text is everywhere visible in the quotations of St. Columbanus. It is singular that one of the praises bestowed on Columcille in the *Amra* or Eulogy composed by Dallan Forgall is that he " spoke in Greek grammar "; whether this was true of Columcille himself or not it was evidently

considered a special but not unknown mark of learning
by the writer of the poem.

We must now speak briefly of the principal ecclesiastical and religious writings which came to us from
early Ireland. As most of them are in Latin they
need not detain us long.

Writings of St. Patrick.*—By far the most valuable
and interesting documents coming down from early
Christian times in Ireland are the writings of St. Patrick.
These probably authentic tracts are three in number,
the Confessio, the Epistle to Coroticus, and the Hymn
known as the Lorica or Breastplate of St. Patrick.
These writings are found in an ancient volume belonging
to the Cathedral archives of St. Patrick's primordial
See, and known as the " Book of Armagh." It contains
chiefly ecclesiastical and religious matter, as well as
the only complete copy of the New Testament which
remains to us in manuscript in Ireland.

The Confessio was evidently written in St. Patrick's
old age, as a defence against some attacks that had
been made upon himself personally and upon the
validity of his work. It is not an autobiography, but
incidentally it mentions several facts of interest regarding
his outward position and his birth and parentage, and
it gives us, and this is more important, an intimate
account of his manner of life in Ireland, his hopes,
temptations and encouragements, and the dangers that
he had passed through. Parts of the original document,

---

* St. Patrick probably came to Ireland 432 A.D., and may have
died 461 A.D., but these dates are uncertain.

said by the scribe who copied from it into the Book of Armagh to have been an autograph of St. Patrick's, seem to have been illegible to him ; and there are consequently occasional breaks and confusion in the narrative.   These sometimes occur at points on which we should most have wished for information.   It is nevertheless a document of the first importance for the life and times of the Saint.

The Epistle to Coroticus is a brief but earnest letter to a prince of Strathclyde, or some neighbouring part of Britain, named Coroticus, beseeching him to set free some young Christian youths and maidens whom he had taken captive in Ireland while the " holy oil of baptism was yet wet upon their brows," with the intention of selling them into slavery to the heathen Picts of Scotland.   This letter, full of a pastoral and affectionate interest in his young converts, appears from its vigorous tone to have been written while St. Patrick was yet in full vigour, and thus contrasts with the " Confessio," which seems to be the outpouring of the heart of an old man whose work is well-nigh done.   The Latinity of both is rude and unpolished, corresponding to Patrick's own statement that he was " not well-read as others who had studied law and sacred letters and who had always used one speech ; since he had been obliged to change his native speech (British or Welsh) for another tongue (Irish), so that it was plain to all in what a rough school he had been brought up."   Doubts as to the authenticity of the Coroticus letter have been expressed, but without much foundation.   It is difficult to imagine who else could so appropriately have penned it.

The Lorica or "Breastplate" of St. Patrick.—
This fine hymn is said to have been composed when
the Saint was approaching Tara (or Taillte, according
to some accounts) and felt himself to be in great peril
from the wrath of the King of Ireland. It is written in
Irish, and is by far the finest religious hymn composed
at this period in Ireland, being sung by him as a protection or Breastplate (Lorica) against danger.   In
the preface it is said to be a "lorica of faith for the
protection of body and soul against demons and men
and vices, and that whenever a person recited it
daily with pious meditation on God" he should be
safe from all these evils.   Many of the other religious
poems and hymns written by saints of the early Church
of Ireland had the same object.   They were protections
or charms intended to ward off disease or evil by their
recitation.   Thus the great poem of St. Columba, called
the *Altus Prosator*, was said to protect those who recited
it against every form of death "save death on the
pillow," that is to say, except in the natural course ;
and St. Colman's hymn was written by himself and his
students as a safeguard against the terrible pestilence
known as the Buide Conaill.   It is said that when
St. Patrick was blessing St. Sechnall he promised
that everyone who should recite his hymn in lying
down or rising up should go to heaven.   St. Sechnall
(Secundinus) complained that the hymn was so long
that few would be able to commit it to memory, whereupon Patrick promised that all its virtue should be
contained in the last three verses.

The form of this hymn, which consists in a repetition
of the same words or idea, is adopted from that of the
old pagan charms or incantations.   Many hymns formed

in the same manner are found in Irish manuscripts and are sung to this day in the western districts of Ireland and Scotland.*

The **Memoirs** by *Muirchu Maccu Mactheni*, written in Latin towards the end of the seventh century for Aedh, Bishop of Sletty (d. 698), and at his dictation, are found in the Book of Armagh and also in a manuscript at Brussels, which supplies some missing chapters. He complains of the difficulty that already existed in his own day of finding true details of the life of the Apostle of Ireland, and compares his venture to the launching of a frail skiff on a deep and dangerous sea. He says in his preface, " I shall undertake briefly and gravely to set forth these few among the many deeds of St. Patrick with slender skill, doubtful authors, forgetful memory, obscure text and mean speech ; but with most loving affection in obedience to the behest of your holiness and authority."

In spite of its modest preface this is undoubtedly the most reliable of the existing biographies of St. Patrick and represents faithfully the tradition current in the seventh century.   It contains few of the wild and often foolish and trivial legends which gathered like a fungus growth round the Saint's career in after times, and of which most of the later lives are made up.

Fiacc's Hymn.—This poem, which is written in Irish verse, and is ascribed to St. Fiacc of Sletty, a contemporary of St. Patrick, cannot be so ancient as the ascription would make it ; it is not an account

* Examples will be found in Mr. Alexander Carmichael's *Carmina Gadelica* and Dr. Hyde's " Religious Songs of Connacht."

given by an eye-witness, but is, as the poet says, composed from existing " histories and writings." It was evidently written some considerable time after the desertion of Tara (565 A.D.) ; it speaks of the Palace of the Kings as lying " silent and desert." It may possibly be earlier than Muirchu's life. It speaks of two Patricks, and gives two names to the subject of the poem, namely, Succat and Cothraige. This poem is very archaic in its language, and bald and vague in expression. It gives Patrick's birthplace as Nemthor.

Other documents concerning St. Patrick are :—

The Hymn of St. Sechnall or Secundinus in honour of Patrick. This hymn is written by a nephew of the Saint. The old prefaces to the hymn give St. Patrick's birthplace as " among the Britons of Ail-cluaide " ; the name of his father as Calpurn, and of his mother as Concess. It gives also his four names as Succat, the name given him by his parents ; Cothraige, his name when in slavery ; Magonius, the name given him by Germanus ; and Patricius, which was that bestowed on him by Pope Celestine. The hymn is in twenty-three stanzas, alphabetically arranged, and is in Latin. It is interesting as being a contemporary poem.

THE DICTA PATRICII.—Three brief sentences ascribed to the Saint himself, disconnected and in very rustic Latin, mentioning his journeys in Gaul and Italy.

A little later come " TIRECHÁN'S COLLECTIONS," or the " Annotations of Tirechán," also from the Book of Armagh. They also give four names to Patrick, and say that both Paladius and Patrick were commissioned by Pope Celestine. Both were named

Patrick according to this account, the first Patrick
or Paladius having been martyred in Ireland, " as holy
men of old testify." These notes are said to have been
copied by Bishop Tirechán from a book belonging to
his tutor, Bishop Ultán of Ardbreccan (d. 656). Tirechán
seems to have had a work before him, now lost, ascribed
to Patrick himself and entitled *Commemoratio Laborum.*

The Tripartite Life.—This, which is by far the
most elaborate and pretentious of the lives of St.
Patrick, is written under the form of three homilies
which, though each is complete in itself, treat the
subject in a fairly consecutive manner. The writers
have evidently been at pains to collect all the floating
material which had accumulated round the personality
of the Apostle of Ireland into their narrative. A Latin
version of it was printed by the learned Franciscan,
John Colgan, in 1647, and the Irish text with translation
by Dr. Whitley Stokes, in 1887. Colgan considered
that it was written as early as the middle of the sixth
century, but Dr. Stokes and Dr. Petrie show good
reasons for supposing that it was not composed earlier
than the tenth or eleventh centuries. It has all the
marks of the later saints' lives, of which a number
sprang up about the eleventh and twelfth centuries
for use in the church on Saints' days and festivals.

Lives of St. Columcille.—Next to St. Patrick,
the two Saints of early Ireland of whom we have the
most copious remains are St. Columcille or Columba,
and one of his successors in the monastery of Hi or
Iona, St. Adamnan.

Both were men of great energy and force of character,

and both impressed their spirit not only upon the church but upon the secular government of their day. Both, also, were literary men. To St. Columcille are ascribed a very large number of religious hymns and of poems on secular subjects, in Latin and in Irish. He was, indeed, a fine poet, and though we need not believe that all the numerous poems ascribed to him are really by his hand, the few of which there seems a reasonable certainty, such as his hymns "Altus Prosator," and "In te Christe," or his poems on leaving Ireland, on Derry, and on the Island of Aran, are sufficient to show that he had great poetic gifts. His whole mind was deeply imbued with the spirit of poetry, and his affection for the bards, by one of whom he had been educated before he passed on to the monastic schools, was shown in a practical manner by his efforts to save the order from extinction at the Convention of Drumceat. His poems will be dealt with elsewhere, but it may be useful here to notice together the chief documents relating to St. Columba, of which the most important is his Life, written by St. Adamnan, his ninth successor in the Abbacy of Hi or Iona.

Life of St. Columba (*Vita Sancti Columbæ*), by Adamnan. This lengthy Life of St. Columba by one of his successors at Iona is undoubtedly the most important Latin biography dealing with an Irish subject. Indeed, few of the Latin lives of Saints in any country throw so much light upon the social and religious conditions of the age with which they deal. It is from this "Life" that the greater part of our knowledge regarding the Saint is derived.

The work is divided into three portions containing (1)

the Prophecies ; (2) the Miracles ; and (3) the Visions of the Saint. It is thus not a direct biography, but it throws together under these headings an immense number of legends and stories relating to Columcille or Columba, out of which a fairly connected narrative can with patience be constructed. In compiling this Life at the earnest request of his brethren, as he tells us, Adamnan had at his command both information derived orally from those who had preserved traditions of the founder, and two earlier lives, one of which, that of St. Cummene the Fair, he has transferred almost word for word into his own pages.

The most important existing manuscript of this valuable text was accidentally discovered at the bottom of a book-chest in the town library of Schaffhausen in Switzerland by Dr. Ferdinand Keller in 1851. He says, "it lay there pêle mêle with some other MSS. and old books, totally neglected, bearing neither title nor number." It is the same copy that had been found by Stephen White, a learned Jesuit and native of Clonmel, in the Monastery of Reichenau, one of the Irish monastic foundations on the Continent, and published from his text in Colgan's *Trias Thaumaturga* in 1647. When it was removed to Schaffhausen is not known. It was undoubtedly written in the British Isles and was probably carried over to Germany in the ninth century.

Other lives of St. Columcille are that by CUMMENE, Seventh Abbot of Iona (d. 669), mentioned above as incorporated by Adamnan in his work.

AN OLD IRISH LIFE, found in the *Leabhar Breac* and in the Book of Lismore. This charming life is written in the form of a sermon or discourse on the text " Exi de terra tua et de domo patris tua, et vade in terram quam tibi monstravero." (Gen. xii. 1.) After describing pilgrimages of different sorts, it dilates on the " perfect pilgrimage " of Columba (to Iona) whereby both with his mind and body he left his fatherland and went forth to labour in Alba (Scotland).   This work was trans-ferred by O'Donnell into the collection of material for his copious digest.

O'Donnell's Life, finished in the Castle of Port-na-tri-namad or Lifford, Co. Donegal, in 1536, was compiled at the order of Manus O'Donnell, who ordered that all Latin lives already existing should be translated into the current Irish of his own day, and who gathered together all available material for his purpose.   St. Columcille was himself one of the O'Donnell clan, and this compilation was intended as a mark of affection and devotion to the memory of their great clansman. It was in the family of the O'Donnells that the " Cathach," a manuscript of the Psalter supposed to be written in St. Columcille's own hand and enclosed in a finely-chased silver cover or " Cumdach," was preserved.

But this life, though prolix and tedious by its length, adds nothing to our knowledge of the Saint, while it detracts from the actuality of his career and the dignity of his character by an interminable series of puerile and often unpleasant legends, the fruit of a diseased mediæval ingenuity.   There is a wide gap between the freshness of the " Old Irish Life " and this late sixteenth century compilation.

The " Amra " or Eulogy of Columcille.—This piece, now so obscure and fragmentary that it is difficult to make sense out of its detached phrases, is said to have been composed by the poet Dallan mac Forgall in honour of St. Columcille and as a mark of gratitude to him for having intervened to preserve the bardic order from destruction.   In the year 575 Aedh, son of Ainmere, King of Ireland, summoned the nobles and clergy of Ireland to a convention at Drumceat or Druim Cetta, in the North of Ireland, chiefly for the purpose of banishing out of Ireland the bards, who had made themselves intolerable by their demands and exactions.

St. Columcille came over from Scotland to plead for them and secured that the order should not be put down, although the bards were henceforth to be strictly limited in numbers, and in the prices to be paid for their poems. Thereupon Dallan, chief Ollamh or Poet, and head of the Order at this time, composed the Amra in praise of the Saint.   It is said in the preface that St. Columcille would not allow him to recite it farther than the prologue, because such lavish praise as it expressed " was only fitting for a man who was dead."   Dr. Stokes, its latest editor, does not think that it was intended as a metrical composition, but that it is " a complete piece of artificial alliterative prose, written probably in the ninth century and intentionally obscure."   Thus, in the form we have it, it may not have been written by Dallan at all, but it is probably founded on an earlier eulogy composed for the purpose mentioned in the preface.   The matter of the composition is glossed, and the glosses are explained, so that it is chiefly made up of scribal notes.   It was evidently as obscure to the mediæval scribe as it is to-day to us. It is unfortunate that the blessing which accompanies this incomprehensible piece is only bestowed on those who " understand it, both sense and sound."

Hymns of the Irish Church (*Liber Hymnorum*).—
There remain a large number of hymns belonging to the early Church of Ireland, some in Latin and some in Irish, preceded by prefaces which appear to have been copied and partly translated into Irish from a Latin original, for they are in a curious mixture of Latin and Irish.   These prefaces preserve the legendary account of the cause and place of composition of each hymn.   Among these hymns are three attributed to St. Columcille known as the *Altus Prosator*, the *In te Christe*, and *Noli Pater*.   The first of these is of great length and has a solemn splendour of metre and subject. After a confession of belief in the Trinity it describes the Creation and Fall of the Angels ; the Creation of the Earth and of Man ; the Praises of the Heavenly Host ; the Fall of Man ; and it passes on to the final judgment and general resurrection with the Second Coming of Christ.   This poem, which may be called The Paradise Lost of Early Ireland, was well-known in the Gallican Church, and it is found incorporated in a long poem by Hraban Maur (786-856).

Tradition says that the *Altus*, which is, like several other Irish poems, composed on the letters of the alphabet, each stanza beginning with the letter succeeding the last, was composed by St. Columcille in Iona while he ground a sack of oats in a mill in preparation for the coming of guests from Rome, and that the hymn was taken back to Rome by the visitors as a present to Pope Gregory.   The Pope approved the hymn, but said that in the praise of the Trinity it was scant, though praise was given through God's creatures; whereupon Columcille wrote the short hymn *In te Christe* to fulfil what the former poem lacked. It is, however, probable that the old tradition which says that only five lines in this hymn were actually written by St. Columcille is true, as it is not in the style of his usual writing but is made up largely of liturgical phrases. It was used as a hymn at the services of the Canonical Hours. It is remarkable to find St. Columcille writing poems both in Latin and in his native tongue; he evidently felt that Latin was more suited to religious poems; while those spontaneous poems on secular subjects to which he was moved in moments of great emotion are in Irish.

Among the most curious of these ancient hymns is St. Broccan's Hymn to St. Brigit, recounting her miracles; in one verse she is said to have been herding sheep on the Curragh in heavy rain, and on returning home she dried her upper garment by hanging it across a sunbeam.

A good number of Latin hymns, some of them the same as those found in the *Liber Hymnorum*, are also incorporated in a valuable service-book, called the *Antiphonary of Bangor*, which was taken from the great monastery of Bangor Mòr, in the North of Ireland, to Bobio, and was found among the Manuscripts belonging to that library. Among these hymns is one to "St. Comgal, Our Abbot," that is, St. Comgal of Bangor (Co. Down), the friend and companion of St. Columcille and the founder of the monastery. Among other hymns contained in this book is the beautiful hymn of St. Sechnall or Secundinus, intended to be sung during the Communion of Priests.   It begins :—

> " Sancti venite
> Christi Corpus sumite
> Sanctum bibentes
> Quo redempti sanguinem, etc."

There are also hymns for special festivals, for martyrs, and for particular hours of the day or night, as well as one in praise of the monastic family of Bangor Mòr.   Besides the hymns composed in Ireland, there are included a number of hymns and antiphons in general use in the church.

A few hymns written in the early period are in Irish and one or two of them are tender and beautiful.   Such are Mael-Isu's hymn to the Holy Spirit, three stanzas in rinnard metre, and St. Ita's hymn to the Infant Jesus, which are very simple and touching.   There are besides these several lengthy and more ambitious religious poems.   Of these the most widely known is the Christian Epic " Carmen Paschale," a Latin poem still used in the special services of the church.   It was composed in the fifth century by a poet named Sedulius, who seems to have been an Irishman.

Two lengthy compositions in Irish verse now claim our attention.   They are the " Calendar of Angus " and the " Saltair na Rann."

The Calendar of Ængus (*Félire Œngusa*).—This Calendar of Church festivals is ascribed to Angus the Culdee (*céile dé* or "Servant of God ") who lived about the end of the eighth and beginning of the ninth century, but its language would point to a later date (about the close of the tenth century).   St. Angus, to whom the

poem is ascribed, was a member of the Monastery of
Cluain Eidnech, or Clonenagh, in Queen's County, but
he left the place to escape the admiration which he had
gained by his eloquence and miracles, and for many
years worked as a slave at the Monastery of Tamlacht,
or Tallaght, near Dublin, until he was discovered and
obliged to confess his identity.   He is said to have
composed the Calendar after seeing a flight of angels
ascending and descending over the grave of an old
man whose goodness consisted, so far as he could
learn, solely in reciting the names of the Saints.   He
thereupon determined that he would compose a poem
commemorating all the Saints he had ever heard of.

In the prologue to the Calendar he invokes Christ,
whom he calls " King of the White Sun," and describes
the various martyrdoms cheerfully undergone by the
" Soldiers of Jesus."   He contrasts the nothingness
of earthly glory as compared with the love of Mary's
Son and with the happiness of " the lowly servants of
Jesus," and he compares the flourishing condition of
the monasteries in his own day and the crowd of students
or " champions of wisdom " attending Armagh Schools,
with the past glories and ruined forts and cities of the
pagan Irish, Rath Cruachan, Allen, Emain Macha,
and Tara, all of which had disappeared.

The Calendar consists of 365 quatrains, one for each
day of the year, each Saint being named under his
or her own date.   He tells us that the sources of his
compilation were the *Pairt* of Ambrose ; the *Sensus* of
Hilary ; the *Antigraph* of Jerome ; the *Martyrology* of
Eusebius, and " Ireland's host of books, the Calendars
(Martyrologies) of the men of the Gael."   The
entries are brief and uninteresting ; there is little

imagination or art in this long poem, in which substance is ruthlessly sacrificed to form.   The entries for each month are copiously explained in glosses and notes, which must have been written much later than the poem itself, as their authors are frequently unaware of the meanings of the words they try to explain.

The poem is written in the rare metre called *Rinnard*, and the first quatrain is as follows :—

Sén acrist molabra	Bless, O Christ, my speech ;
Achoimdi seacht nime	O Lord of the Seven Heavens !
Romberthar buaid lére	Let the guerdon of devotion be given me,
Ari greine gile	O King of the White Sun.

The Calendar of Angus is one out of several Martyrologies and lists of Saints compiled in Ireland. We may mention here (1) THE MARTYROLOGY OF TALLAGHT, a calendar founded on an ancient collection ascribed to Maelruain, Abbot of that Monastery in the eighth century (d. 792), but as it now comes to us, containing additions down to the year 900.   (2) THE MARTYROLOGY OF MAELMUIŔE (OR MARIANUS) O'GORMÁIN, Abbot of Cnoc (Knock, Co. Louth), *circa* 1166-74, a mere metrical list of names ; and (3) the much more important prose work, THE MARTYROLOGY OF DONEGAL, compiled by Michael O'Clery in 1630, of which we shall have to speak in its proper place.

The Saltair na Rann, or " Psalter of the Staves or Quatrains."—This is the longest religious composition extant in Irish.   The main body of it is made up of 150 poems, corresponding to the number of Psalms in the Psalter, from which it takes its name ; but twelve extra poems have been added, making 162 in all, or 2,098 quatrains.

N

It is an early middle-Irish poem and has also been attributed to Angus the Culdee, but it seems to have received additions as late as 998 A.D., as it mentions an Archbishop of Armagh who died in that year named Dub-dá-lethe.   It is written chiefly in *Deibhidhe* metre of seven syllables, but poem CLII. is in *Rannaigheacht Mhór*.   The scribe tells us that the poems fall into four divisions (*a*) The Psalter, thrice fifty poems ; (*b*) Poems on Repentance ; (*c*) Poems on Confession ; (*d*) Ten poems on the Resurrection.   But the poem itself does not bear out this opinion.   The first poem contains a description of the universe ; No. XI. relates the Penance of Adam and Eve ; Nos. XLII.-L. refer to the Life of Christ.   Other portions narrate the succession of events before the Last Judgment ; the Seven Resurrections ; the Coming of Demons out of Hell ; the Triumphs of Angels, rewards of the godly and punishment of the wicked.   These poems are interesting on account of the mediæval notions they preserve of the universe and of the history of Adam and Eve, etc. The firmament is conceived of as extending round the earth in five zones like a shell round an egg, having seventy-two windows with shutters on each window which open and close.   The seventh heaven revolves like a wheel.   The exact distances from the earth to the moon, from the firmament to heaven, and from the earth to the depths of hell are measured and set down.   There are curiously Irish ideas introduced into these poems, as where in the " Penance of Adam and Eve " Adam calls on the River Jordan " to fast with him upon God with all its beasts " that he may receive pardon for his transgression, in consequence of which the stream ceases to flow, and gathers its beasts together, and all supplicate the angelic host to unite in asking God to pardon Adam.

The Saltair na Rann incorporates in verse what were evidently well-known traditions (not all of purely Irish origin) formed upon the Old Testament stories ; many of the same legends are found in prose in the opening of the Brehon Laws, and in the *Leabhar Breac ;* or these may, on the other hand, be prose abstracts of the poems. They form part of the great collection of miscellaneous religious material of which this book is composed. Besides these legends, and some founded on New Testament subjects, the *Leabhar Breac* contains a great number of Passions or accounts of martyrdoms, under the form of sermons, and of homilies on various subjects partly in Latin and partly in Irish. They need not detain us here, but they are interesting as giving us an idea of the style and subjects used in religious teaching in Ireland about the twelfth or following centuries. From the same compilation, and sufficiently beautiful to demand a separate notice, are the—

Legends of the Childhood of Christ.—These charming tales, used probably as Christmas Eve readings, have all the freshness and simplicity of the mediæval Christmas miracle-play. Some of the incidents are found in the Protevangelion, but others seem to be the creation of the writer. The turn of expression and tone are throughout distinctively Irish. For instance, in the approach of the Magi to Bethlehem, we read, " As Joseph was standing in front of the house on a certain day he saw a great band of people coming towards him straight onwards from the East, and Joseph said to Simeon, " Who are those coming towards us, my son ?

Methinks it is from afar that they have come. I
fancy, my son," said he, "that it is the omen art of
Druids and it is soothsaying that they are practising,
for they take not a single step without looking up,
and they are communing with one another among
themselves ; and it seems to me that they are people
of a strange race . . . for white and wide are
their tunics, and purple and even-coloured are their
mantles, and they have long reddish hoods and speckled
and gapped shoes, like a king or chieftain, by their
appearance."   The story of the arrival of the tax-
gatherers to the cave which the Blessed Virgin was about
to enter, to take the implements of Joseph's trade in
place of the tax due by them, and their hesitation when
they find " no furniture save one little stool (and even
that not theirs, for it belonged to the master of the house)
and Joseph's implements of trade," is very naive and
charming ; as is also Joseph's visit to the city to buy
milk and cheese and his meeting with the shepherds
by the way.

Among the more important of the remaining portions
of the ecclesiastical writings are, from the literary point
of view, the old Irish lives of St. Patrick, St. Columcille,
St. Brigit, St. Senan, St. Findian of Clonard, St.
Findchua, St. Brendan, St. Ciaran, and St. Mochua,
which are found both in the *Leabhar Breac* and the
Book of Lismore.   They are written in the form of
homilies preceded by short general explanations of the
selected text.   The exceeding simplicity of style of
these early biographies, the intimate details they afford
of the lives and surroundings of the Saints, and the
picture they give of the social conditions of the period
make them documents of the utmost importance for

the historian of this period. Colgan has made use of some of these lives in his *Acta Sanctorum.*

Adamnan's Works.—We have spoken of the great life of St. Columcille composed by St. Adamnan, Ninth Abbot of Iona. There are one or two other works by the same author that must not be overlooked. Adamnan was born about 624 A.D. and died in 704. He was a man of great energy and one of the leading spirits both in the political and ecclesiastical world of his day. He was the personal friend of several crowned heads, especially of Finnachta, Monarch of Ireland, and Aldfrid or Alfrid, King of Northumbria, who had spent part of his youth in Ireland, where he seems to have concealed his name and position under the pseudonym of Flann Fina; while there he wrote a charming poem in praise of the country of his adoption. Adamnan travelled much between Hi or Iona, Northum-bria, and Ireland, and was everywhere consulted on national affairs and on matters connected with church organisation. The greatest national benefit conferred upon Ireland by Adamnan was the passing of a law through his efforts to exempt women from going forth into battle, which up to this time they had been forced to do. This beneficent law, called the *Cáin Adamnáin*, and the circumstances which led to it, form the subject of a separate tract, but it is also frequently alluded to with satisfaction by the annalists. St. Adamnan was as active with his pen as he was in other matters. He wrote a book on the Holy Land, *De Locis Sanctis*, which is highly praised by the Venerable Bede, who has incorporated some extracts from it in his Ecclesiastical History. (Bk. V., chaps. xvi., xvii.).

Adamnan had not himself visited the Holy Land ; his source of information was a French bishop named Arculf, who, after travelling in the East and visiting Palestine, Egypt and Constantinople, was cast by a storm upon British shores on his way home and forced to spend some time in these islands.   There he met Adamnan and related to him his travels, which the Saint wrote down from his narration.   He presented the book to his friend, King Alfrid of Northumbria, who rewarded him well for it.   There is also preserved a fragment called the PRAYER OF ST. ADAMNAN, but, like the Amra of Columcille, it is impossible to make much out of it.   These pieces seem to be intentionally obscure.

CHAPTER XIII.

The Official Poets

Primitive Verse.—The earliest literary expression of a primitive people is not, as a rule, couched in prose, but in a rude attempt at verse. Though this attempt may hardly rise above the sonorous repetition of a single phrase or set of phrases, the effect produced will satisfy the craving felt by the savage mind to impart dignity to his utterances. From the earliest times of which we have any knowledge in Ireland, all records of importance, whether legal, genealogical, historic, or even topographical, all matters, indeed, which were thought worthy of preservation at all, were committed to verse. The assistance to the memory at a time when all such records were retained by the memory only and were not written down was, no doubt, one reason of their versified form, but the stronger and, in itself, quite sufficient purpose gained was the additional dignity that was imparted to them by their sonorous recitation. Even around the brief legal decisions preserved in the ancient laws of Ireland there was, as we learn from the introduction, originally thrown " a thread of poetry," while the earlier portions of the annals and annalistic records still retain, scattered thickly throughout their pages of dry entries of local and tribal events, scraps of the poems in which the records of these events were originally made. Numbers also of long poems have come down to us preserving the early records of the kings, the early traditions of the successive settlements of the country, the succession of the Kings of Ireland, the names of the saints and their ancestry, the genealogies of personages of rank, and other matters of importance to the tribe or province.

A large number of them are contained either separately or in the annalistic records preserved in the great collections of material, such as the Book of Ballymote, the Book of the Dun, and (especially of those dealing with Leinster matters) in the Book of Leinster ; a large number are also found interspersed in such later seventeenth century compilations as O'Clery's " Book of Invasions," and " Succession of the Kings," and in the History of Keating, of all which indeed they form the basis and principal authority.   Though these poems are often composed in intricate measures, it would be most unfair to look upon them primarily as literary efforts, or to judge them as such.   Much false criticism has been bestowed upon these tribal poems, and they have been condemned as showing the poverty of invention and mechanical production of the Irish poets.   But to criticise them from the literary point of view as poems is entirely to misconceive their purpose and meaning. They do not even pretend to be poetry ; they are national and tribal records put for purposes of preservation and recitation into verse.   Their value as history is a separate question, and it does not fall within our province to examine it ; it is the business of the historian to test them by historical methods, and determine their importance as materials for the history of Ireland.   Here we have to deal with them purely as literature in order to explain how and for what purpose they were composed and in what regard they stand to the general literary output of the country.

Historical and Genealogical Poems.—A good example of this sort of provincial or tribal verse, incorporating traditions of great antiquity, is the Book of Rights, a chronicle of the stipends and tributes paid to the provincial kings, which formed part of a larger work entitled the Saltair or Psalter of Cashel,* drawn up at various times and frequently added to, and which contained matter of various kinds relating chiefly to the province and kings of Munster. It is variously attributed to St. Benan, the disciple of St. Patrick, to Cormac mac Cuileanan, and to Brian Boru. Probably each of them added to or revised portions of it, bringing it up to his own date.   It is evidently, in parts, as recent as the time of the Danish Kingdom of Dublin, for it relates the tributes exacted from the Danish Kings or paid to them by the Irish chiefs.

The Book of Rights is partly in prose and partly in verse, the prose occasionally adding some details or explanations not to be found in the verse.   The verse portions are, as we should expect, the oldest, the prose being added to make clear the circumstances and conditions under which the poems were written, and to incorporate remarks on historical points.   The lines rhyme in couplets, and the metre runs with remarkable smoothness, considering the very prosaic nature of the matter dealt with.   It shows a remarkable fertility and facility in versification to be able, without tedious repetition, to carry on through a lengthy poem a report of the tributes paid in kind or money to the

* For a full discussion of the age and contents of the Saltair of Cashel, see O'Donovan's edition of the *Leabhar na g-Ceart,* or " Book of Rights," Celtic Society's Publications, 1847.

various provincial kings.   The same may be said of
the tract on the Restrictions and Prerogatives of the
kings of Erin, which forms another part of the same
volume, and which is likewise in mixed prose and verse.
This piece is ascribed to the well-known CUAN O'LOCHAIN
who was chief poet in the reign of Maelseachlann II., the
Monarch of Ireland who was deposed by Brian Boromhe
or Boru.   He seems to have been a most prolific writer
of professional poetry incorporating the chronicles and
genealogies of the kingdom, and so highly was he thought
of in his own day that he became Regent of Ireland
after the death of Maelseachlann in conjunction with
a devout anchorite of Lismore, named Corcran Cleireach,
or "the Cleric."   It was probably while managing the
temporal affairs of the kingdom that he turned his
attention to the examination of the records of Ireland,
which he ordered to be "examined and ordered,"
after which he committed them to verse.   Many of the
long poems on Tara and its glories in the reign of Cormac
mac Airt, and on the origin of place-names, are ascribed
to him ; they exist both separately and incorporated
into the various recensions of the *Leabhar Gabhála*, or
so-called "Book of Invasions," which opens with an
account of the early settlements and legendary history of
Ireland.   He was unfortunately murdered by the men
of Teffia in 1024, but it can hardly be said that his
work was cut short, for more than 1,600 lines from his
hand have come down to us.   He was one of the most
famous of a group of famous men belonging to the
tenth and eleventh centuries, distinguished in their day
as genealogists, chroniclers, and poets, whose voluminous productions have survived to our own time.
It was probably the disorganisation of the country

through the perpetual Norse and Danish wars, and the consequent loss of many ancient records, that induced these men, who had the legends and traditions of their native land by heart, to enshrine them in verse and thus secure their preservation.   They are, in fact, the oldest historical documents left to us.   Their poetry is to be distinguished from that of the bards, who were attached to special families or clans, and who confined themselves to singing the praises or lamenting the deaths of their personal patrons and chiefs, while the verses of the official poets were usually national monuments dealing with traditions that affected the whole country, but in particular the central monarchy of Tara. Their thoughts have a wider range than those of the bards, and their attention is fixed rather on traditions that affect the whole kingdom, as viewed from the standpoint of the central monarchy, than on the interests of a special clan. · They are to the monarchy as a whole, in the time of its greatest importance, what each local bard became to his own chief when the central monarchy had fallen into decay.

Among the earliest of these national poets we may mention TORNA EIGEAS, or the "Learned," who is supposed to have lived in the time of Niall of the Nine Hostages, and to have died 405 A.D. (423 ?)   His title *Eigeas* or *Eces* was an official one, and many of the early poets bore it ; it denotes one of the three divisions of the rank of Ollamh, and those who gained it applied themselves to genealogy and official duties as distinguished from law or poetry proper.

Four poems are ascribed to Torna, three of them being addresses to his two foster-children, Corc, King of Munster, and Niall, the Northern Prince.   These two

young princes were rival claimants for the monarchy of
Ireland, and Torna endeavoured to soothe their animosity
and adjust their claims.   The chief interest of these old
poems is that long afterwards, at the close of the
sixteenth century, they suggested to the bards, Tadhg
mac Daire of Munster, and Lughaidh O'Clery of Ulster,
the famous poetical contest between the north and
south which is known as the " Contention of the
Bards," and to which these poems of Torna are generally
prefixed.   They are probably later, however, than
the fifth century, as they were written when Christianity
had been firmly established in the country.   Some of
them have been attributed to Torna O'Mulconry, chief
poet to the O'Conors (d. 1310).   The fourth poem
which bears the name of Torna describes the burial-
places of the pagan kings at Relig na Riogh, near
Cruachan, in Co. Roscommon.

Other prominent names drawn from the Norse period,
whose compositions occupy a surprisingly large place
in the literature of Ireland, are those of FOTHADH NA
CANÓINE (d. 876), MAOLMURA OF FAHAN (d. 884), FLANN
MAC LONAIN, murdered by the Decies of Munster in 918 ;
KENNETH OR CINEADH O'HARTIGAN (d. 975), MAC
GIOLLA CAOIMH or KEEFFE (d. 1016), and EOCHAIDH
O'FLOINN (d. 984).   A little earlier than this ninth
and tenth century group we find Cinnfaeladh (d. 678),
who wrote a poem on the Meadhall (*Miodhchuairta*)
or Banqueting Hall of Tara, and revised and improved
the teaching books of the poets, which were called
Uraicept.   A considerable part of the Law-tract
called the Book of Acaill is ascribed to him.   The
subjects that occupied the pens of all these men
were much the same.   In poems of immense length

they dwell on the early invasions of Ireland and the history of the country from Adam down to their own times ; but unfortunately it is the purely legendary history that interests them most.   When they approach the historical period they usually content themselves with lists of kings and genealogies ; the right of a certain king to reign was of more importance than the acts he performed during his term of office. The names of the monarchs of Ireland and the provincial kings, the genealogies of saints, the regal burial-places and similar subjects fill stanza after stanza.   In the eleventh century FLANN MAINISTREACH (d. 1056), who in spite of his title of Flann " of the Monastery " was a layman and Principal or " Fear-léighinn " of the School of Monasterboice, in Meath, and GIOLLA CAOIMHGHIN or KEEVIN (d. 1072) succeeded to the office and carried on the tradition of the earlier genealogists and writers of metre.

These two last-named scholars were most voluminous writers, a single one of Flann's poems totalling up to the incredible length of 1,220 verses, or 4,880 lines, while many others run to upwards of 200 verses.   His longest works are synchronisms of the Kings of Assyria, Persia, Greece, and Rome, with the Kings of Ireland reigning at the same time, and of the High Kings of Ireland with the Provincial Kings.   He wrote also poems on the territories and descendants of the O'Neills and O'Donnells of Ulster, and on the history of Aileach, and two poems on the succession of the Pagan and Christian Monarchs of Ireland respectively.   The writings of GIOLLA CAOIMHGHIN or KEEVIN are much in the same strain ; he deals with the origin of the Gaels and the colonisations of Ireland and gives chronological lists of kings and events from the Creation to his own date. Such feats of ingenuity and patience may well astonish us, while the annalistic learning to which they bear testimony witnesses to a certain interest in general history creditable in their day. But as literature in the strict sense such efforts cannot rank, nor were they ever intended to do so.

It is melancholy that two of these men, the foremost personages in Ireland in their day, should have been murdered by their own people. Cuan O'Lochain was, as we saw, Regent of Ireland 1022-1024, when he was murdered by the men of Teffia in Meath. Flann mac Lonain, who lived in the reign of Flann Sionna, is spoken of as the " Virgil of the race of the Scots (Irish) and the best poet that was in Ireland in his time " ; but in spite of the estimation in which his work was held, he fell a victim to the cruelty of the Decies of Munster.

This sort of composition went on continuously up to the beginning or middle of the fourteenth century, when it gave place to the family poems of the bards. The best-known writers of this genealogical verse after the eleventh century are TANAIDHE O'MULCONRY (d. 1136), GIOLLA MODHUDA O'CASSIDY, called "Dall Clairineach," Abbot of Ardbreccan (d. 1143) ; GIOLLA NA NAOMH O'DUNN, Chief Bard to the King of Leinster (d. 1160) ; and other members of the O'Mulconry family who lived in the early part of the fourteenth century.

Topographical Poems.—Along with these mental exercises in versified history, law, and genealogy we may class the topographical poems and the poems and prose tracts which concern themselves with rude guesses at the origin of names of persons and places and other pieces of like character. The composition of such poems had, we find, a definite place in the training of the file, or professional poet, the composition of Dindsenchus, or topographical poems (of which those on Tara form one section) forming one of the advanced subjects of study in the eighth year of the professional course. Along with magic and incantations it came near the end of their training, when all the simpler subjects had been mastered. Several of the authors of whom we have spoken above occupied themselves with this sort of composition, and in spite of the dryness of the subjects, and the exigencies of difficult metres, they are not entirely without literary merit.

There are prose as well as poetical forms of the Dindsenchus, as is usual in this sort of composition which is not inspired by any artistic necessity in the feeling of the writer, but by the duties of his official position. They give the legendary origin of Irish place-names, and thus preserve for us some old traditions which might otherwise have been lost. They are usually in *Deibhidhe* (pron. "Devvee") metre, but are not always strict in their adherence to its rules. In the Tara poems the metre is lax; but this carelessness about metre generally shows that later hands have altered the old forms. The general rules of this metre are that (1) each line of the quatrain should have seven syllables, the second and fourth lines having longer end words than the first and third; (2) alliteration and middle rhyme are frequent, and should be perfect in the last couplet. There are certain small variations in different pieces, but the rules are usually carefully observed.

This metre was well thought of and much practised

in Ireland for many centuries, and seems to have been the form of verse especially used for this professional poetry, for it is spoken of by a chief poet of the eleventh century, Ceallach O'Ruanadha, as the species in which history was accustomed to be written. Such poems continued to be composed up to comparatively late times. There are two topographical poems written by bards of the fourteenth and fifteenth centuries, JOHN MÒR O'DUB-HAGAIN or O'DUGAN (d. 1372), and GIOLLA-NA-NAOMH O'HUIDHRIN (d. 1420), which take us on circuit round the entire provinces of Ireland, giving an account of the chief families and their original territories " out of ancient books." Many of the families had died out in the time of the writers, but the poems remain as excellent authorities for the old conditions before the arrival of Henry II. The two poems, the latter of which was written to complete the former, are some-times united into one poem of 1,660 verses. O'Dugan's stanzas give an account of the chief tribes and territories of the northern half of Ireland, at the time of the Anglo-Norman invasion ; O'Huidhrin completes the account for Munster and Leinster. These are written in a form of poetry called *Dán Direach*, or " Straight Verse," a title that included several noted species of Irish poetry.

The importance of the topographical pieces to students at the present day consists in the large number of ancient traditions enshrined in them. A very interesting story relates the composition of one such piece in the time of Brian Boru " of the Tributes." Mac Liag, the king's poet and secretary, was one day seated on a hill between the present counties of Clare and Galway. Looking over the diversified country

before him he said, with a sigh, " Many a hill and lake
and fortress there lies in the range beneath us ; it would
be great topographical knowledge to know them all."
" If Mac Lonain were here," said his harper, referring
to Mac Liag's predecessor in his office of poet to the
king, " he could name them all and give the origin of
the names beside."   " Let this fellow be taken and
hanged," said Mac Liag.   The frightened harper begged
a day's respite, in order that he might send and tell
Mac Lonain what had befallen him through his too
warm partizanship.   Next morning Mac Lonain came
up the hill, and in return for the life of the unlucky
harper, he consented to recite a poem of thirty-three
stanzas, describing every natural feature of the district
and the origin of their names.

Closely connected with the Dindsenchus are such prose
pieces as the Cóir Anmann, or " Fitness of Names,"
a piece which does for the names of persons what the
topographical poems do for names of places.   It gives
explanations of the names of about three hundred Irish
persons of note, belonging both to the historical and
mythological periods.   Many of these derivations are
mere guess-work ; when the ingenious writer is uncertain
he gives a variety of possible derivations, leaving it
to the reader to decide which he will adopt.   For
instance, Conall *cernach's* cognomen he derives first
from *cern* " an angle," " because his head was angular " ;
or *cern* " a man," and *niadh* " valiant " ; or again, from
the Latin *cerno* " I see," " for he used to see equally
well by day and night " ; or finally, from *cern* " victory,"
" because he, above all others, was victorious."   The
chief value of such pieces is not in the derivation of
words that they contain, but in the scraps of curious

O

legendary matter that the explanations give occasion for.

Of much the same kind of value, from a literary point of view, are the numerous glossaries which have come down to us from various periods explaining and commenting upon Irish words that were considered difficult or obsolete at the time the glossaries were written. Of these one of the most important and ancient is known as CORMAC'S GLOSSARY (*Sanas Cormaic*), and is ascribed to the celebrated King-Archbishop of Cashel, Cormac mac Cuileanan, who died in 908 A.D. It contains, by way of illustration, much information about ancient customs and beliefs and some details about mythological personages not found elsewhere. It is, therefore, equally important to the philologist and to the student of folklore and social customs. Whether actually written by or for Cormac or not, it seems to date from near his time, and a universal and ancient tradition ascribes it to him.

Undoubtedly the most valuable and important work that comes down to us from the labours of the official poets and learned men of early Ireland is the remarkable collection of legal pronouncements with their commentaries known as THE ANCIENT LAWS OF IRELAND (*Senchus Mór*). These laws, sometimes called the Brehon Laws, from the fact that they were administered by the Irish Brehons or Judges, come down from pre-Christian times, and they continued to run in all parts of Ireland outside the English " Pale," that is, the district in and about Dublin, up to the time of Henry VIII. Their authority lasted in some independent portions of the country till the reign of James I., but the division of Ireland into counties and the general administration of the English laws throughout the land put an end to the native system, and by the close of the seventeenth century the professions of Brehon and Ollamh became extinct.   In the Introduction we learn that it was called the "Great" Senchus, or "Great Old Knowledge," on account of the number of learned men who assisted in its compilation.   Although the earliest decisions recorded are ascribed to ancient pagan lawgivers, such as Sencha, poet and ollamh of the Ultonians ; Amergin, the poet of the Milesian settlers in Ireland, and even Diancecht, the physician of the race of the Tuatha Dé Danann, the actual compilation is said to have been made in the time of St. Patrick, the older laws having been "purified and written down" by him. Certain portions which clashed with the "Word of God in the written law and the New Testament, and with the consciences of believers" were expunged, and the remainder was codified and probably for the first time recorded in writing by St. Patrick, with the assistance of three princes, two other bishops, and three brehons or poets.   These were the Kings Laeghaire (Laery), Corc and Dairi ; the bishops St. Benen and St. Cairnech, and the poets Rossa, Dubhthach, and Fergus.*   It was laboriously compiled at Tara during the summer and autumn months, and at a place called Rathguthaird,† a warmer residence, during the winter.   From the

---

* Laeghaire was Monarch of Ireland in the time of St. Patrick ; Corc was King of Cashel in Munster, and Dairi, or Daire, a prince of Ulster, so that a large part of Ireland was represented at this Conference.

† Supposed by the Editors to be an ancient fort where raths are still to be seen called Lisanawar, near the village of Nobber, about sixteen miles from Tara.

connection of St. Patrick with this work it is sometimes known as the *Cáin Patraic* or Law of Patrick.

The Ancient Laws which, even in their incomplete state, fill five large volumes, are composed of statements and decisions covering the entire field of social and private life in Ireland, with commentaries upon them. Though many of the details seem to us trivial and many of the explanations given absurd, these laws are yet invaluable for the minute and interesting light that they throw upon social customs. By their means we can reconstruct the whole system of society as it existed through many ages in Ireland in a more complete manner than the existing records enable us to do for any other country of Europe. It is not from this point of view, however, that they are to be taken into account in a literary history. Their chief interest from our present standpoint is that they were originally written in verse and that they still retain traces of their earlier form in several passages. Many of the judgments are stated to have been given in verse or to contain the recital of what " their predecessors had sung," and it is said that Dubhthach "put a thread of poetry round" the Senchus for Patrick. This takes us back to the original conditions under which the professional poets were also the law-givers and counsellors of the tribe. Some passages still run in that kind of rude declamatory rhythm which is the most ancient form of verse.

In their present form they seem to be arranged for convenience of oral instruction to pupils, and may be taken as illustrating the method employed in the schools of the Brehons ; that is, isolated phrases or portions of phrases are given, and commented on by the teacher ; these comments being further explained by the scribe who wrote it down, or by some later commentator. The Senchus Mór is the most important of all the Law Tracts, but others, such as the Book of Acaill, bear special titles of their own, and preserve the decisions made by eminent law-givers on cases belonging to some special class of criminal or social crime.

Position of the File.—As the verse of the File (pron. "filla") or Official Poet was something more than a mere exercise in metre, so the position of the file himself was higher than that which would have been claimed by the mere rhymster as such.   He was in the earliest times second only to the king himself, and his supposed possession of magical powers probably attracted to his person a dread and reverence which approached more nearly to that paid to the gods than to that ascribed to any human being.   The names of the earliest of the poets, Amergin, Ferceirtne, Morann, Dallan Forgaill, Senchan Torpeist, etc., come down to us from the dim mists of antiquity clothed in all the majesty of powers, not only of prophecy and foresight, but of miracle and incantation.   They have the power of raising storms, of calming the wind, or of covering their people in a magic mist to conceal them from view.   Their satires bring down death or disease upon the objects of their contempt or hatred.   They announce decisions, make laws, lay down precepts for kings.   When there is doubt about the succession, the file, as soothsayer, describes out of a sleep accompanied with special rites the appointed prince, whose claims may be otherwise unrecognisable to the people.   The file is, in fact, the spiritual leader of the people ; at once their Lawgiver, Magician, and Man of Wisdom.   In some cases the offices of chief and file seem to have been united, as in the person of Ollamh Fodhla, who was at once monarch of Ireland, poet and founder of the College of the Learned, and Law-giver. Usually the poet-magician must have been held, in the estimation of the people, as occupying a position of honour even above the king; he was possessed of greater powers, his very person conferring protection on the outlaw, and being regarded as sacred. The king could only act by his advice, and when disputes arose about the succession it was he who gave the decision.

The file is, then, to be regarded as in the earliest times combining in his person the functions of magician, law-giver, judge, counsellor to the chief, and poet. He was next to the king in rank, but above him in authority. His poetic gifts, such as they were, were exercised rather in uttering charms and incantations than in composing poetry for amusement; or else in putting into use the terrible faculty for satire of which the poets availed themselves freely, and which, when uttered by persons who were regarded as all-powerful, was dreaded as we should dread a visitation of the plague; it was indeed supposed to be attended with actual physical suffering, often with death, to the person satirised. In addition, the laws, genealogies, records of the tribes, and other matters belonging to the kingdom, were guarded and recited by the file. All these functions seem in the earliest stage to have been united in the hands of a single caste.

Division of Duties.—Later, but still at a very early time, the offices seem to have been divided, the brehons devoting themselves to the study of law and the giving of legal decisions, the druids arrogating to themselves the supernatural functions, with the addition possibly of some priestly offices, and the filí themselves being regarded henceforth principally as poets and philosophers. This division seems to have already existed in the time of St. Patrick, whose preaching brought him into constant opposition with the druids, who were evidently at that time regarded as the religious leaders of the nation, though there does not seem to be much sign that they were, as they undoubtedly were even at an earlier age in Gaul and Britain, sacrificing priests. Again, we find the bishops, filí, and law-givers or brehons represented as different classes in the conference held to purify the Ancient Laws from heathen customs.

A tradition ascribes this devolution of the functions of the official poets to the reign of Conor mac Nessa, King of Ulster in the first century, and it was necessitated, according to this story, by the obscurity of the language employed by the poets in their verse and legal decisions. On a certain occasion, when there was a contest between two noted poets for the position of chief poet of Ulster, the king expressed his intention of being present to hear the metrical contest which was to decide between the claims of the two applicants ; for a long time he listened eagerly to their trial of wit, but he found himself, along with all the uninitiated, unable to understand a word of what they were saying, so technical and obscure were their expressions. This he decided to be not for the benefit of the people, and he relieved the filí henceforth of their right. to give legal decisions, in the justice of which the people's welfare was concerned, and left them only the function of Court poets. The obscurity of the poets may

have arisen from their retention of an earlier form
of Irish gone out of use among the general mass
of the people ; we find these early poems accompanied
in most cases, like other ancient Irish writings, with
copious glosses added at a later time by copyists to
explain them ; the language of these copyists themselves being now often unintelligible to the student of
the modern tongue.   Or it may have been a sort of
poetic phrasing or " kenning," such as the Irish, in
common with the Norse and other peoples, indulged in,
the difficulty in this case arising from the obscurity of
the allusions employed.   We know that this allusive
form of speech was cultivated by the poets and the
learned with great assiduity and with a distinct poetic
effect.   Probably both causes combined to render the
language employed by the poets difficult to understand
by the common people ; and they, no doubt, retained
it through the pride of a fancied superiority which
they believed that it imparted to their utterances.
Changes in language are always more rapid before
the time of writing.

This ancient or bardic language was known as
" Béarla-Féine," and in it the laws and other matter
were originally written.   They seem to have persisted
in carrying on this obscure system of speech, and several
quaint satires survive which comment on the difficulty
that attended the comprehension of their compositions.
" That is, no doubt, a good poem if only we could
understand it," is the comment of many a bewildered
chief from whom the composer demands a heavy fee for
his effort ; the explanations that follow being frequently
more obscure than the original poem itself.   The conversation held between Cuchulain and Emer in " the

language of the bards," or the " Dialogue of the Two Sages "* which still exists, are good examples of the poets' speech, which draws largely for its allusions upon the ancient mythology. A long piece, called the " Proceedings of the great Bardic Institution "† affords an amusing satire upon this method of expression.

Knowledge of Writing.—The knowledge of writing on wooden tablets, on wax, and on parchment, was probably understood long before the time of St. Patrick, to whose coming it is generally attributed. The isolation of Ireland in the early centuries of the Christian era has been greatly exaggerated. A constant trade carried on with Spain, Gaul, and Britain could not have been unaccompanied by a knowledge of such matters as reading and writing, which were practised in all these countries. To the Romans, too, Ireland was well known. Already in the first century Agricola, looking across towards Ireland from the northern coasts of Britain, speaks of its ports and harbours as being " better known " than those of the sister isle, and he bewails his inability to carry his successful arms into Ireland, which would, he says, " have formed a very beneficial connexion between the most powerful parts of the empire." (Tacitus' Life of Agricola, Ch. xxiv.). The large number of Roman coins found all along the eastern portions of the country, dating from the first to the fifth century, proves that, though the Romans never conquered Ireland, there was continuous communication with parts of the Roman Empire from the

* Edited by Dr. Whitley Stokes in *Rev. Celt.* xxvi., p. 4.
† Edited by Prof. Connellan in Trans. of the Ossianic Soc. Vol. V. 1857.

earliest times. The foreign and British wars of the Irish and their constant intermarriages outside their own country, besides the hire of mercenary troops and the ordinary commercial intercourse with Britain and the Continent must all have combined to familiarize them with the current means of intercourse in their time. They travelled much, and it is impossible to suppose that they were quite cut off in the ordinary matters of a simple education.

Perhaps the earliest actual proof we have that they were possessed of books and writings, which seem to have been in the native tongue, is from the writings of Orosius, who early in the fifth century gives an account of an Itinerary of the writer and traveller Æthicus of Istria, who had some time before this visited Spain, Britain, and Ireland. In the latter country he says that he remained a considerable time " examining their volumes," and though he calls the writers of these works " unskilled toilers and uncultivated teachers," he at least proves that writings existed in some sort of large manuscript books before the date of St. Patrick's coming to this country. If they were tribal genealogies, law tracts, and annals in Gaelic verse it is little wonder that he could make nothing of them.

Retention of the old System.—But it is probable that long after the knowledge of the art of writing had come to Ireland, the lore of the schools was still preserved almost entirely by memory, and was seldom committed to writing. Cæsar tells us that in the similar schools of the Druids in Gaul, " they are said to learn a great number of verses, and some remain in their course of study as long as twenty years ; nor do they

think it right to commit these things to writing, although
in other business, both private and public, they make
use of Greek letters." (Gallic War, Bk. VI., ch. xiv.).
He thinks that they do this in order to keep their lore
secret, but it is more probable that they preferred the
retention of the ancient system, and were suspicious of
book-learning, which would be associated in their minds
with foreign influences, and later with the antagonistic
teaching of the Christian monastic schools, in which
instruction in the reading and writing of Latin formed the
foundation of the course of study. It is, to my mind,
probable that the study and use of reading and writing,
the latter being executed on wax tablets, and confined
at first to the study of portions of the Psalms and the
Gospels and of Books of the Hours, Lectionaries and
hymns, was confined for perhaps a very considerable
length of time to the monastic schools, and that the
ancient method of oral recitation was continued in
the secular establishments. In modern days, when
the use of printed matter has to a large extent
weakened our powers of memory, the retentiveness
of the unlettered or bookless man is a thing that we
find it difficult to conceive of. The whole system
of training in the pagan schools tended to develop the
memory to what to us seems an abnormal extent. The
student was obliged from the beginning of his course to
learn by heart a number of tales and poems and to recite
them without the loss of a single word. Each year
during his course a larger number of tales and poems
had to be acquired, until he had at command, for recitation at any moment, some three hundred and fifty tales,
besides a vast quantity of poetry. His education lasted
twelve years, by which time he had acquired, besides the

subjects already spoken of, a knowledge of grammar and prosody, of law and legal decisions, of composition in the innumerable metres employed in Irish verse, of history and genealogies, and of the older tongue in which much of this knowledge was enshrined. He was, indeed, at the time of taking his degree as Ollamh (equivalent to our doctor's degree) a master of the prose and poetical literature of his native land, of its history, mythology, and geography, and of the various forms and developments of the Gaelic tongue. Besides all this, he studied, in the higher branches of his course, divination and soothsaying, acquiring a knowledge of incantations and magical powers over nature. When we consider the immense range and difficulty of the studies imposed on these men, we are not surprised that, even apart from the obscurity of their style, which no doubt formed a convenient excuse for a change in the old system, it was found necessary to break up the branches of study and to confine special departments to special classes of men, such as divination and sorcery to the druids, law and justice to the brehons, and literature to the filí. Yet the entire course seems to have been still pursued up to quite late times.

Now, it would appear that all, or nearly all, this instruction was acquired by word of mouth, was conveyed in large part in poetry, and was retained in the memory. It is usually taken for granted that once the knowledge of writing extended itself to Ireland all current literature would begin to be written down. Nothing is more unlikely ; the very fact of the changed conditions, though it would gradually modify existing methods, would tend to make the special depositories and carefully-trained masters of the national literary inheritance the more jealous of the preservation apart of their own peculiar knowledge, and the more anxious, by the rarity and mystery of their acquirements, to preserve their position of importance.   It was only gradually, as the authority belonging to the filé and druid came to be claimed by the Christian teacher, that their power faded away.   The gradual combination of the secular and monastic schools, and the occasional appointment of a secular Principal to a monastic school, as in the case of Flann Mainistrech or " Flann of the Monastery " (d. 1056), who was Principal of the monastic school of Monasterboice, would tend to equalise the system of teaching, and to detract from the special prerogatives of the old secular establishments.   But this process would be only gradual and reluctantly acquiesced in by the heads of the secular schools ; it would probably become necessary for them, in order to retain their position, to introduce those subjects which made the monastic teaching so popular.   The aim of the two systems remained, however, different ; the old schools aimed at the production of a limited number of learned men, who usually adopted the learned professions because their fathers and grandfathers had been filí or brehons before them (for the professions were largely hereditary), while the monastic schools sought to provide a general secular and religious instruction which, though it was primarily intended to fit men for the clerical or monastic life, included for some period of their lives almost the whole Christian population.

Course of Instruction.—The instruction in the schools of the learned comprised a seven years' course for the bard and a twelve years' course for the ollamh or file ; that is to say, a student could not receive his practising qualifications in a less time than this. The first years were occupied chiefly in acquiring by rote certain poems and prose tales, with easy lessons in philosophy and grammar, and a certain number of " oghams " and of " drecht " (perhaps law-forms or metrical forms for composition) ; these were continued in gradually increasing number and difficulty up to the end of the sixth year, by which time the student had at his command the goodly number of one hundred chief stories and one hundred and seventy-five secondary stories; had learned to compose in simple metres, and was well grounded in law, grammar and philosophy. Each year as he advanced step by step he gained a fresh and more settled position in the school, shown by the title of the stage to which he had advanced. He had by this time passed through the primary stages of Fochloc, Mac Fuirmid, Dos, Cana, and Cli ; he was now about to enter on the more advanced courses special to an Anruth, and to those who intended to proceed to the highest branches of their profession as Magicians or Druids, Doctors or Men of Law, or Chief Poets.

By this time the student had begun to practise the exceedingly complicated forms of poetical composition reserved for the higher grades, and with which the lower grades were never permitted to meddle, each grade having its own special metres in which composition was permitted, but being restricted to these and the metres previously acquired ; for a Dos, whose metre was called " Laid," to attempt to write verse in " Nath mór," or for a Cli, whose metre was " Anair," to attempt to write in " Anamain," the metre reserved for the ollamh, would have been the gravest breach of professional etiquette, and would, no doubt, have been visited with the most serious consequences. Nor do these rigorous laws appear to us without meaning when the extreme difficulty of the higher forms of composition is taken into account; for unpractised hands to have undertaken them would have tended to bring them into contempt. Besides, the rewards for composition in the higher forms were very large indeed, each form of verse having its fixed price; and it could not be permitted to an inferior poet to contend for the rewards of the highest professionals. A chief poet of the O'Neills in Ulster, in bewailing the death of his patron about 1240-50, remarks that he had received from him as much as twenty cows for a single poem, while the demands of the poets in earlier times became so oppressive that they were more than once threatened with total suppression, and were, in the days of St. Columcille, restricted by law both as to their numbers, retinue and rewards.

But to return to the courses of instruction. From his sixth year, as Anruth, if he desired to go further, his education became more advanced and embraced the higher branches of professional knowledge. He had then qualified as bard or ordinary poet, and could practise in that capacity. He had now to study the "Poet's Speech," that mystical language which was the special medium of bardic communication. The eighth year of the file's education was an important one. To his other studies were added the composition of Dindsenchus, or topographical poems and prose pieces, the Legends of the Kings, and the study of magic and incantation. Those who passed on to this stage aimed at becoming fully-equipped magicians, or Men of Wisdom, the advisers and soothsayers of Princes. The ninth year was chiefly devoted to the acquiring of incantations or charms, by the recitation of which, accompanied by certain magic rites, the magician was able to recognise and track a thief, to bring luck to a new house, to prevent a horse stumbling or throwing its rider, or to secure long life to the person for whom the charm was made.   This latter incantation is addressed among others to " the Seven Daughters of the Sea, who weave the threads of the sons of long life," an interesting instance of the meeting of Northern and Irish mythology. His final years were given to the study of the highest forms of metrical art, by which time he had mastered the whole range of mediæval learning as recognised in Ireland, and had gained his degree of ollamh, with the right to wear the mantle of crimson birds' feathers, which was the symbol of his profession ; to carry the golden musical branch or wand of office, and to fill the highest posts in the kingdom next to the king himself.   His privileges were so great that there was every inducement to a young man of special ability to undergo the rigorous course of study demanded for the education of a file or ollamh, in order to attain the fine position of dignity and wealth opened out before him.   He was both Judge, Counsellor, Poet, and Magician, and the latter office placed at his command, in the opinion of the people, the power of life and death, for his satire or curse was attended with the direst results.   He could raise storms and mists, interpret dreams and foretell lucky days ; he was called upon to pronounce in all matters of difficulty. His fees and emoluments were princely and to be had for the asking, and he had no personal expenses, He went about attended by a numerous retinue, and if he desired to fix his abode in any particular place, or to establish himself and his community upon any province at any particular time, it was a dangerous thing to refuse him the best hospitality the district could provide. These exactions became extremely oppressive, and the pride and overbearing behaviour of the Bardic Companies was a constant subject of just complaint.*

* We have used in the above accounts of the training of the File or Chief Poet, and the Ollamh or Chief Brehon, the information contained in the tracts published by Thurneysen from the Book of Ballymote. Other manuscripts give a slightly different account; these probably show the modifications made in the original curriculum as time went on.

P

CHAPTER XIV.

The Bards

Distinction between the File and Bard.—The order of bard was in every way an inferior one to the order of file. The bard was looked down upon by the fully equipped file as a man of a lower order of education, much as a medical man might look down upon a doctor practising with inferior qualifications. The bard could claim none of the high positions open to the file; he was a " mere rhymster," whose business it was to spin off inferior verse, but whose up-bringing had never led him into the broader paths of a wide and specialised education. The " Metres of the Bards " formed part of the seventh year's study of the fully-trained file; but it was merely one out of his wide series of subjects, a single incident in his extended course, whereas it concluded the training of the ordinary bard. Nevertheless even the bardic metres seemed to have comprised fifty different species of verse. There were two classes of bards, the Saor-bhárd and Daor-bhárd, or free and unfree bards, divided again into eight grades. The last of the eight, the " Bárd-áine," was not a practising bard, but merely inherited the profession from his forefathers, the caste of bard being passed on from grandfather to grandson in the same family. Each class of bards had his own fixed class of metres, in which it was lawful for him to compose; the King-bard (Riogh-bhárd) had for his special use Nath-bhairdne with its divisions;

the Ansruth-bairdne had two kinds of metres called
Ollbhairdne, and so on.   The rewards of the bards were,
like his honour-price, only half those of the file.   For
instance, for a poem in the two kinds of Nath-bhairdne,
he got five milch cows (not after all a prize to be despised
for a single poem), while for a poem in Ollbhairdne
he could claim two milch cows and a heifer of the third
year.

It is very difficult to tell when the distinction between
the file and the bard fell into disuse and the file himself
ceased to exist.   We find the line between the two orders
still clearly drawn at the time of the compilation of
the " Book of Rights," that is to say, in the tenth
century or later ; for we read in the Epilogue to the
stipends and rights of the King of Tara :—

> This is the history of the King of Tara ;
> It is not known to every loud-mouthed bard ;
> It is not the right of a bard, but the right of a file,
> To have a knowledge of each king and his law."
> (O'Donovan's Ed., p. 183).

This verse well expresses the contempt felt for the
bardic office by the superior file, and it confirms the
accuracy of the old teaching-books of the poets, which
make the acquisition of national and provincial records
and law a part of the higher specialised study of the
officials who aimed at posts of honour in the State.

Extinction of the Fili.—It is usual to ascribe the
extinction of the official poets to the Norse invasions
and the supposed disorganisation of social, artistic, and
literary life that is attributed to them.   The verse
that we have quoted above might alone have sufficed

to correct such loose and inaccurate deductions, for it evidently describes a condition of things that was by no means forgotten at a late period of the Norse settlements, when the tributes to and from the Danes and Norsemen, which are described in the tract from which the quatrain is taken, were regularly enforced.   It was very late in what is distinctively known as the Norse period, which begins about the close of the eighth century and may be said to terminate as a distinct epoch shortly after the time of the battle of Clontarf, in 1014, about which time the foreigners became absorbed in the general population, that the most prominent of the official poets lived and wrote.   Mac Giolla Keeffe, Eochy O'Flynn and Kenneth O'Hartigan lived during the last ten years of the tenth century ; Mac Liag, Cuan O'Lochain, Flann of the Monastery, and Giolla Keevin flourished during the eleventh century.   They were at the very height of their power and influence during the whole of the Norse period, and it is from this time that the great body of the official poetry comes to us, though it continued to be produced till a much later period.   The gradual extinction of the office of file is to be ascribed to natural causes.   His occupation was, in fact, gone.   Long before the close of the period of his greatest activity the necessity for his existence had passed away ; he was but singing of conditions and glories which were to him, as they were to the people, merely a memory and old tradition. The office of the file became limited to gathering up and enshrining in verse the ancient traditions of his native land.   He was no longer regarded as a magician, capable of raising the wind, charming off disease, or striking an enemy to death by his satire ; his religious functions had ceased, and poetical effusions could be obtained from the bard at a less costly rate. Nor were his tenacious powers of memory so greatly needed in days when writing was the common acquirement of layman and priest alike. The recording of the tribal annals, the ancient tales and early poems, in large provincial or family documents, such as those which have come down to us, made the old versified method of oral recitation needless and out of date. It is from the twelfth century that the great collections, the Book of Leinster and the Book of the Dun, date ; and it was probably about this time that the metrical form of preserving the national and tribal records was given up. The brehon had absorbed part of the file's duties ; the druid first, and afterwards the saint and priest, had superseded him in other directions ; while as a recorder and transmitter of intelligence, the scribe and the family bard could supply all that the clan or chief required.

Thus gradually the official poet became extinct, part of a system of things that had passed away, and the scribe and the despised bard took his place. The Norse and Normans had little to do with the change, except in so far as their coming had helped to change the social condition of the whole country. The true cause was the gradual evolution of the later conditions, the spread of education, and the fall of the central monarchy. The bard or genealogist attached to each family, the scribe attached to each monastery, amply supplied the wants of the chiefs and of the church, while it devolved upon the trained story-teller to recite those ancient tales at feasts to which it was the pleasure of the guests to listen in the twelfth century as it had been the pleasure of their forefathers in the sixth or seventh.   The devolution of duties was the natural result of a changing condition of things.

Rise of the Bard.—From about the thirteenth century to the close of the sixteenth the hitherto despised family bard became the most important literary man in Ireland.   We are not to think of the bards simply as makers of verse, or singers of elegies.   They were much more than this.   They were personages of considerable political power, who made it their business to enflame the ardour or soothe the passions of their chiefs. By their songs, reciting the deeds of the ancestors of their lords, they stirred them up to wars ; by persuasion, they averted displeasure from some personage or clan in whom they felt an interest.   It was they who advised, warned, threatened, or encouraged ;   their praise was as much sought after as their blame was dreaded. Moreover, they wandered about the country, welcomed and feasted wherever they went, and the acquaintance that they thus formed with tribal affairs and with the trend of events was of service to their own chiefs and available for the guidance of the tribe at large.   They were trained from birth for their office, and, as Dr. O'Donovan says, " they discharged the functions and wielded the influence of the modern newspaper and periodical press."   They formed a guild apart, and for substantial rewards they gave information and encouragement useful to their patrons, sang their praises and deplored their deaths.

The influence wielded by the bards is best shown by the anxiety of the English Government to suppress an order which they felt to be dangerous to their power in Ireland, or failing this, to buy their services for their own use. A great number of laws were passed with the object of limiting their power, and occasionally regular raids were made upon them, as, for example, when in 1415 Lord Justice Talbot " harried a large contingent of Ireland's poets, as O'Daly of Meath, Hugh Oge Magrath, Duffach, son of the learned Eochy, and Maurice O'Daly. In the ensuing summer he raided O'Daly of Corcomrua (Co. Clare), that is, Fergal mac Teigue mac Angus Rua." (Four Masters).

Nor did they always succeed in pleasing their own patrons. For instance, about 1213, the poet Murdoch O'Daly, of Lisadill, had a quarrel with a steward of O'Donnell's, a vulgar loon who fell to wrangling with him about a cess to be paid to the chief. " The man of verse," say the Four Masters, " lost his temper with him, and, having taken into his hand an extraordinary sharp axe, dealt him a stroke whereby he left him dead, lifeless." The bard flew to Clanrickard, whither the Northern Chief, more to avenge the insult to himself than to punish the breach made upon his steward, marched in chase of the offending bard, ravaged Clare and laid siege to Limerick, whence the culprit was passed on from house to house till he reached Dublin. Thither again O'Donnell pursued him, and the bard was finally banished to Scotland, from which circumstance he is known as " Scottish Murray" (Muireadhach Albanach), under which name he wrote several good poems, found both in Scottish and Irish collections. He seems to have travelled, for one of them mentions a visit made by him to the Mediterranean, and he frequently expresses the joy that it would be to him to find himself off the Scottish coast or to breathe the breath of Ireland. He seems, however, to have slipped back to Ireland and to his old home more than once, and finally he gained O'Donnell's pardon and a grant of land by the production of three poems in his honour. " Scottish Murray's " own comment on his deeds and their punishment is pithy and quaint. In one of his poems he says, " Trifling is our difference with the man (O'Donnell) ; that a bumpkin was abusing me and that I killed a serf—O God, doth this constitute a misdemeanour ? "

It was easy, too, to fall into disgrace if a chief did not consider himself sufficiently praised by his bard. An amusing instance of this is the story of Mac Curtin, hereditary poet of North Munster in Elizabeth's reign. Hearing that Donogh, Earl of Thomond, President of Munster, had been prevailed upon to desert to Elizabeth's forces, he wrote a long poem recounting the noble deeds of the ancestors of the Earl, but holding up to reprobation the name of his own chief, whose varying allegiance had proved satisfactory neither to the one party or to the other. " How am I afflicted," he exclaims, " that a descendant of the great Brian Boru cannot furnish me with a theme worthy of his exalted race ! " The Earl was so angry that Mac Curtin was obliged hastily to fly from his vengeance ; he bitterly repented his words, and one day perceiving Lord Thomond's troop of horsemen coming towards him along the road, he got up an elaborate device with the object of reinstating himself in his favour. He flung himself on the ground, apparently in the agonies of death, his wife hanging over him weeping. When the Earl approached he bade her appeal to him for mercy as a dying favour. As soon as this was granted, the bard's agonies ceased, and the Earl, probably amused at the whole incident, received him again among his attendants.

A similar story is told of a troop of bards who visited Turlogh Luineach O'Neill, a chief of Tyrone. On their arrival he sent to enquire what they had brought him. They reply that they have brought him " a gift that must shed on him the highest honour ; poems that show his descent from ancestors the worthiest this kingdom has ever produced ! " When O'Neill heard this he exclaimed : " What, so much said of my fore-fathers, and nothing of myself ? Inform these gentlemen that while they are here they shall not lack any accom-modation that Tyrone can afford ; but me they shall not see. Assure them that I would prefer to throw lustre back upon my family rather than to receive renown from it."

Historical Summary.—Before speaking of the bards in order, it will be well to go back to the beginning of the history and sum up briefly those more personal and unofficial poems which, though they were composed by the official poets, are of a different character from the productions of which we have hitherto spoken.

It is impossible during the early period to distinguish accurately between the file and the bard. Both at times wrote pieces that may be termed national in the sense that they deal with traditions and genealogies that belong rather to the race than to any particular clan or sept ; but both also wrote poems to the chiefs in whose families they were brought up and supported, or threw off verses for special occasions which cannot be reckoned among the official poems. Thus Mac Liag was chief poet of Ireland during King Brian's brief rule as monarch, but he was first and essentially the family bard of the O'Brian family, whose praises he sang on all occasions, whose histories he wrote, and whose deaths he bewailed.   In this sense he performed the duties of the bard of later days, and we have, therefore, included him here.   For the same reason Cormacan or Cormac, of Aileach in Donegal, who was chief poet in his day and occupied the highest rank, that of "Eigeas" or "Eces," is mentioned in this chapter, because he was exclusively attached to the family of the O'Neills, and is known only by his poem relating the deeds of Murtough mac Neill.

Archaic Verse.—A small group of very archaic verses in the form of runes or incantations, and bearing the names of the semi-legendary poet Amergin, who is said to have accompanied the Milesian settlers to Ireland, takes us back to the beginning of Irish literary history.   The poem of which we have already spoken,* and in which Amergin describes the transformations he has gone through, is written in what is called " Rosg," a sort of declamatory blank verse much used in later times for war-odes and other extemporaneous effusions intended to incite ardour or military enthusiasm among troops going into battle.   Here it is distinguished by the emphasis laid on the repetition of the " Am " or " I am," at the beginning of each line, which imparts dignity to the verse.   Though unrhymed, the short poem is so broken up that there is no monotony, a sudden change in the metre being made to correspond to the change of idea.   Of the two other short poems ascribed

---

* See Chap. XI., p. 121.

to Amergin one is written in what is known as Conchlann or Conachlon verse, in which the last word of the very short lines is repeated at the beginning of the next line or rhymes with it.   The poem is also alliterative.*

These poems are rather charms or incantations than poems ; they are descriptive of the beauties of the coast of Ireland as first seen by the invaders.   They are very ancient, and nearly every word is glossed by later copyists.

The other poets of this ancient group, Roigne, son of Ugaine Mòr, Adhna, Ferceirtne, Morann, and their compeers were, if they ever existed at all, rather the forerunners of the filí than poets in the true sense of the word.   To them is ascribed the composition of laws, precepts, teaching books for the schools of the poets, poems on the early settlements and topographical pieces. There is an archaic poem by Ferceirtne in praise of Ollamh Fodhla, in which the establishment of the *Feis* or Triennial gathering at Tara and the founding of a College of the Learned for the instruction of those pre-paring for the offices of file or ollamh, are ascribed to that monarch.

A few brief lines of real beauty, however, are said to be written by Lugadh, son of Ith, a contemporary of Amergin, called in the Book of Invasions the " Primeval Bard of Erin."   It is a poem of lament for the loss

---

* Conachlon is sometimes used in later poetry, but not precisely in the same sense.   The first word of a stanza is frequently made to correspond with the last word of the previous stanza, thus linking together the whole poem, and this is also called Conachlon.   It is found in the Calendar of Angus and other poems.

of his wife, Fial, who died of shame because she saw her husband bathing and thought him to be a stranger. This early elegy of twelve lines is most skilfully wrought and is touching from its brevity and simplicity. Some ancient fragments, such as the address of the Morrigan, or Goddess of War, to the Rude Forces of Nature after the Battle of Moytura, or the description of the Bulls in the " Dispute of the Swineherds," may be mentioned as examples of archaic verse ; they are declamations without rhyme, but possess either Conachlon or alliteration. The early pagan and Christian charms come next to these in the primitive character of their composition.

A very remarkable piece of great length is the " Dialogue between the Two Sages " (*Immacallam in da Thuarad*), that very remarkable poetic dialogue supposed to have taken place between Ferceirtne and Neidhe, an elder and younger applicant for the position of ollamh or chief poet of Ulster on the death of Adhna. This series of poems is not only valuable for the ancient mythological traditions that it contains and the notices of charms and other folk-beliefs, but as the first of those poetic contests which were always much in favour in Ireland and which culminated and closed in the sixteenth century in the " Contention of the Bards." The beautiful spirit of deference shown to the elder poet by the younger, and the readiness of the elder to acknowledge the brilliant attainments of his young antagonist are alike charming, while their choice expressions show that the " Language of the Bards " meant something more than mere intentional obscurity of dicton and aimed at preserving a noble and chaste form of expression among the learned classes.

In a second group we get the poets belonging to early Christian times.   They are—

Dallan Forgaill (otherwise called Eochadh Dallan) (d. 596 ?), the contemporary and friend of St. Columcille and his attendant at the Council of Drumceat in 588, on which occasion he wrote the eulogy called the *Amhra Choluimcille* in gratitude for the saint's intervention on behalf of the bards.   Besides this, there exist two odes written by him on the weapons of Aodh mac Duach, King of Oirgaill, who, as it appears, refused to give up his shield called the Dubhgiolla to Aodh Finn, Prince of Breifne.   These poems are preserved in a tract called " The Reformation of the Bards."

Senchan Torpeist (d. 647) was a Connaught poet who is connected with the reign of King Guaire the Hospitable.   It is to his efforts that the recovery of the Tale of the *Táin bó Cuailnge* is said to be due. Besides a poem on Fergus mac Roich, there is ascribed to him a lament over the dead body of his predecessor, Dallan Forgaill, which still exists.

Flann Fionn.—This young Northumbrian Prince, who came over to Ireland for his education during a period of exile from his native land, has paid a graceful tribute to the country which gave him hospitality in a sweet poem which is well known from Mangan's setting of it, beginning—" I found in Innisfail the Fair. . . ." The name of Flann Fionn was merely an adopted title probably intended to conceal his princely birth while he was studying in the schools of Ireland.   His real name was Aldfred or Alfrid ; he was recalled to Northumbria

in 685, and reigned till 705.   He was a great friend of
St. Adamnan, whom he probably first met in Ireland,
and he seems to have been one of the most enlightened
princes of his day.   To him Adamnan presented his
"Book on the Holy Places."   Some of these poems
have a claim to remembrance ; though they never rise
to the fine freedom of the occasional poems we have
to speak of elsewhere, there is a certain quiet stateliness
in their diction which renders them not unworthy of
the occasions for which they were compiled.

One of the most vigorous and attractive poems that
comes down from Norse times is that which contains
the account of the proud journey of the great Prince
Murtough, son of Niall *glundubh*, or "Black-Knee," and
his followers from Aileach in Ulster round the whole of
Ireland, taking hostages from every prince and province
on the route.   They journey through the deep snow of
a bitter winter, and from the thick sheepskin capes or
hoods that the soldiers wore or used for tents at night
the journey is called the Circuit of Murtough "of the
Leather Cloaks " (*Muirchertach na g-cochall g-croicenn*).
The poem describes the departure of Murtough from
Aileach in Donegal with a thousand followers, their
march through Eastern Ulster and the warm reception
given them by the neighbouring princes, their arrival
in Ath Cliath, or Dublin, and the submission to him of
the Norse Prince Sitric, who paid him a great eric
in "fine good wheat, food, bacon and red gold, with
meat and cheese given by the Queen " for the slaying
of his father Niall by the Norsemen.   In Munster he
would accept no hostage for the traitorous and turbulent
Prince of Cashel, Cellachan, but carried him off in chains.
On his return to Aileach he sent on messengers to his

wife, Queen Dubhdaire of the Black Hair, bidding her
" to send out her women to cut rushes " in preparation
for his arrival.   For five months the hostages are nobly
entertained at Aileach, the Queen herself waiting upon
them, and then Murtough in a proud humility hands
them all over to the reigning monarch of Ireland,
Donnchadh, son of Flann, who was, as he said, greater
in position than he.   The account of this high-minded
and generous prince, the Irish counterpart of Edward
the Black Prince, is the most refreshing incident that
comes to us from these dark and stormy times.   It is
a relief to turn from the dreary wastes of metrical
officialism to a poem so strong and fresh, presenting us
with a noble picture of family and clan life.   The
author is **Cormacan**, son of Maelbrigid, chief poet to
the O'Neills, who accompanied his chief on his famous
circuit.   He died in 946 A.D.   The poem rhymes in
couplets and has alliteration.

While Cormacan Eigeas was singing the praises of a
Northern Prince, a young man in the south of Ireland
was preparing himself for a still more exalted position.
Mac Liag, the bard or file attached to the family of
Brian Boru (Boroimhe), or Brian of the Tributes, was
destined to see the sudden rise of his master's house
to supreme power and to lament its overthrow.   Liag
is not a family name, but the name of a saint who lived
in the fourth century, as whose servant he styled himself Giolla mhic Liag.   He is supposed to have been
of the family of the O'Conchertaighs of Mayo and Sligo.

Mac Liag was attached to the family of Brian as
secretary or scribe, and accompanied him when he
ascended the throne of Tara as arch-Ollamh or Chief
Poet of Ireland.   To him are ascribed a number of

poems dealing with the events of his own day, and bewailing the downfall of the house with which he was connected after the Battle of Clontarf.   Among the best-known of these is the fine Lament over Kincora, the palace of Brian on the Shannon, in which he enumerates and bewails in turn the members of his master's house fallen in battle, Brian himself and his sons Murrough and Donough, with the Scottish and southern allies of their clan.   Mac Liag lived at the height of the Norse supremacy in Ireland, when Dublin, Limerick and Waterford were ruled by Danish Princes, and when the admixture of Norse and Irish blood through three or more centuries had resulted in a solid and beneficial union between the two nations.   Large portions of the country, especially in the south, were, to a great extent, Danish communities, living in friendly intimacy with the people among whom they had settled, and taking sides with one party of the Irish or the other in the tribal feuds, besides being themselves divided into two usually antagonistic parties as Danes and Norsemen.   Their power in Munster had become so great in Brian's time that he and his elder brother, Mahon, exerted all their efforts to dislodge them from the south, and having met with some successes, Brian further pushed his ambition towards dethroning the reigning monarch of Ireland and seizing the central monarchy.   His prowess and successes raised around him a crowd of eulogists who sang, in lavish fashion, the glories of his house and of his deeds.   The Munster tongue was ever sweet and apt to praise ; and Brian, as the first of the southern monarchs to sit upon the throne of Tara, after centuries of Northern supremacy, reaped the full benefit of their melliferous eulogies.   Of these poets the chief was undoubtedly Mac Liag, several of whose poems are preserved. They seem to have been great favourites, for they exist in a number of different copies.

To him are also frequently ascribed the annals which deal with the reign of Brian and with the previous history of the south during the period of Danish influence. There seems to have been a group of historians and poets attached to the court of Brian, who was a liberal patron of learning, and it is very probable that Mac Liag took an important part in the work of arranging and compiling the existing annals of Munster and bringing them up to his own date. Perhaps he himself added the portions relating to his patron and to the wars which he himself witnessed ; the details of this contemporary period are in all the annals of the south particularly full, and bear the stamp of having been written by poets attached to Brian's person. It would be natural that at the moment of the expansion and supremacy of the southern province, an effort should be made to collect and bring into prominence the annals of the Munster tribes. The larger part of these southern annals is occupied with the Danish wars, which obtained a special importance owing to the part taken in them by Brian and his family. There exist a large number of isolated tracts on the Battle of Clontarf (1014) and the events that led up to it ; they contain certain variations as to the history and causes of the battle which it will be interesting, when a larger number of them are published, to consider side by side. Dealing with the same period, but including a summary of the preceding events and containing later additions, are the important annals called the " Wars of the Gael and Gall," the " Annals

of Munster," and the Leabhar Oiris, or Book of Chronology and Annals on the Wars and Battles of Ireland,
all dealing chiefly, though not exclusively, with affairs
in the south.   In all these works Mac Liag is supposed
to have had a hand, and to have been for his own and
the preceding periods one of the chief compilers. This
is probably the case with regard to the " Wars of the
Gael and Gall," though large use has been made of
earlier annals ; these have not been very skilfully
interwoven and frequently overlap, causing repetition
and confusion in the narrative.

Our poet lived for some time among the Norse in
Dublin, receiving, with other bards of Brian's house,
hospitality at the court of the Norse king.   The
powerful alliance of the Norse kings of Northumbria
and of the Western Isles and Man with Dublin, made
that city during a great part of the tenth century one
of the most important headquarters of the Northern
races, and of the religion, art, and literature which
flourished under their later rule.   The frequent visits of
the poets of Norway and Iceland to Ireland, and the
welcome given to Irish bards at the courts of the Norse
kings, brought about developments of great importance
to the literature of both countries.

Mac Liag did not long survive his master, Brian,
who was slain at the close of the Battle of Clontarf,
though not actually fighting in it, for he was then an aged
man of over seventy years.   The poet took refuge in
the island of the Danes or Dark Gall (*Innse Gaill Duibh*)
in the Shannon, probably King's Island near Limerick,*
then chiefly inhabited by Danes, and died there in 1015.

---

* It is often said that Mac Liag went to the Hebrides (*Innse
Gaill*), but this is a mistake.

Several of the poems which occur in the *Leabhar Oiris* were written in his old age and from this spot ; but the compilation itself is in part, at all events, later than his time, and written after his death.   It is impossible to over-estimate the importance of Mac Liag's poems in any study of the history of his own day.

Closely associated with Mac Liag in many of his historical and literary undertakings was the bard **Erard,** or **Urard mac Coise,** secretary and historian to Maelseachlann II., the monarch of Ireland who was deposed by Brian.   Mac Liag was not himself present at the Battle of Clontarf, near Dublin, in which Brian fell (1014), but Mac Coise was present in the train of Maelseachlann, or Malachy, as he is usually called, and witnessed in safety (for a poet's person was inviolable) the whole contest.   Maelseachlann had entered the battle on the side of Brian, but he had no reason to feel gratitude or fidelity to the man who had unseated him from the throne of Ireland, and when the fight began he withdrew his troops and remained idly watching the progress of the combat from a place of safety.   All that Mac Coise witnessed he related afterwards to Mac Liag in a poem still remaining, and Mac Liag was induced by the interest of the recital to visit the scene of the battle before the interment of the slain had been concluded.   The details recorded by these two intelligent annalists and poets no doubt form the basis of the annalistic accounts in the Histories of Munster.

Mac Coise wrote several other poems.   O'Curry numbers four, and mentions also a most singular prose piece in which, under the form of an extemporized allegory, he shames one of the Ulster O'Neills into giving him redress for having plundered the poet's castle at Clartha (Clara, in Westmeath), and demolished the building.* His remaining poems are historical.

O'Reilly mentions two poets of the name, one of whom died in 990 and the other in 1023, but they are evidently one and the same person. Mac Coise died at Clonmacnois in the latter year.†

Among the minstrels gathered round Brian was **Mac Giolla Caoimh** or Keeffe, who wrote two or more poems still preserved to us in the *Leabhar Oiris*. They are, like Mac Liag's effusions, laments on the downfall of Brian and members of his house. He seems to have been a great traveller, for he says that he had visited Greece and had passed through Palestine, going thence eastward to try and find the site of Paradise. Such long pilgrimages seem not to have been uncommon in Ireland about this period.

A very beautiful anonymous poem has also been preserved from the close of the Norse period, urging Randal, son of Godfrey, King of Dublin and the Hebrides (who died of plague in Dublin in 1095), to lay claim to the throne of Ireland. The author speaks of the Lia Fáil, or "Stone of Destiny," as being still at Tara when he wrote. The poem speaks of the royal residence of Randal as being at Emhain Abhlach, or "Emain of the Apples," in the Isle of Mull. Thus a place often mentioned in early Irish mythology as the home of Manannán or the Land of Promise is for the first time identified in this eleventh century poem as an island

---

* O'Curry, *Mans. Cust.* II., pp. 127-135.
† O'Reilly's *Irish Writers* at these dates.

off the western coast of Scotland.* It is here called
" Emain of the Apples," " The Tara of Manannán,"
and the " Emain of the son of Lir, son of Midir," so
that its old mythological traditions were still preserved.

Deferring to a later chapter the history of the rise
of the great families of the hereditary bards, the O'Dalys,
the Mac Wards, the O'Higgins, the Mac Brodys, the
Mac Daires and others ; or of the scribal and annalistic
families, such as the O'Mulconrys, the Mac Firbises,
and the O'Clerys, we will here single out a few names
of the best-known among the bards who wrote up to
the beginning of the sixteenth century. Any general
criticism of the contents and character of the work of
the bards will be more usefully made when the individual
contributions of each have been passed under review.

Muireadhach Albanach, " Murray or Murdoch
the Scotchman " (c. 1214-1240).—We have already
given an outline of the career of this turbulent bard,
whose real name was O'Daly, and who belonged to the
famous bardic family of that name. He was fourth
of the seven sons of Angus O'Daly, the grandson of
Cuchonacht O'Daly, named Cuchonacht " of the school,"
who was chief professor of poetry at Clonard and first
poet of the race (d. 1139). He thus belonged to the
O'Dalys of Meath. Murray wrote several poems
addressed to Donough Cairbreach, one of the O'Brien
family, and the first to drop the title of " king " and
use the style of O'Brien of Thomond (about 1208) ;
and to Murrough O'Brien, another of the same family.

---

* Here the Island would seem to be the Island of Mull, but in a
tract in the Yellow Book of Lecan it is said that the I. of Arran
was Manannán's land and " Emhain Abhlach."

These chiefs shielded Murray from the wrath of O'Donnell and furthered his escape out of the country to Scotland.   He also sent a poem to Cathal O'Conor, " the redhanded " of Connaught, written on ship-board on the Adriatic during one of the wanderings, possibly in the Holy Land, by means of which he filled up the period of his exile.

In his old age, after his return to Ireland and reconcilement with O'Donnell, he wrote religious poems, some of which are preserved in the Scottish " Book of the Dean of Lismore." It would seem that after their tempestuous careers he and King Cathal Redhand (*cródhearg*) made up their minds together to embrace the religious life ; and there is a curious dialogue extant supposed to be carried on between them while they are submitting their heads to be shorn.   From this time we hear no more of Murdoch O'Daly, and the date of his death is uncertain.   In Scotland, where his poems are well known, he bears the title Murray Albanach, and Skene calls him the first of the great race of Macvurrichs, bards to Macdonald of Clanranald.   He entered their service after his exile from Ireland and he became chief poet of Scotland.

Giolla Brighde Mac Conmidhe, or Gilbride Mac Namee, chief poet of Ulster in the time of Brian O'Neill, King of the Cineal Eoghan, who was killed in the battle of Downpatrick in 1260, and his head carried to London and buried under " a white flag stone " of some London church, while the body was laid near the tomb of Brian Boru in Armagh.   Over this prince Mac Namee sang a fine lament relating the triumphs of the clan and bewailing the indignities and loss that

had befallen himself since his chief's decease.   He
was accustomed, he says, to receive as much as
twenty cows for a single poem.   These heavy prices
for poetic compositions seem to have been common ;
a poem by Teigue Og O'Higgin, who flourished in
the early part of the fifteenth century, mentions the
same price as his ordinary reward.   The poet devoted
his talents to the praise of the O'Donnells, in whose
house he was a retainer, and a large number of the
poems attributed by O'Reilly to Flann Mainistrech are
believed by O'Curry to be the work of this poet.*   There
is no doubt that the date given by O'Reilly (1350) is
quite incorrect.   He was a contemporary of Scottish
Murray, and wrote two of his poems to the same Donough
Cairbreach O'Brien, Lord of Thomond, in 1208, who
was Murray's friend.   He also wrote a poem to Maelseachlann O'Donnell, Lord of Tir-Conaill, between
1241-1247, and several of his poems are earlier than
this.   Besides his historical poems on the families of
the O'Neills and O'Donnells there are other effusions
from his hand.   A poem in the British Museum describes
a vision seen by him within the ancient raths of Emain
Macha, in which the Northern O'Neills and other
divisions of that wide-spread tribe meet and congre-
gate from north and east and south, while from the
west come up the Tuatha Dé Danann, weaponless,
but carrying in their hands the wands of bards.   By
acclaim, Rolfe mac Mahon of Oriel, to whom the poem

* See O'Curry's notes and corrections to the remarks of
O'Reilly (" Irish Writers," *Circa* 1350 A.D.), in *Mans. Cust.* II.,
pp. 162-166, and III., 270 ; and *cf.* O'Grady's Catalogue of MSS.
in the British Museum at *Add.* 19,995 (arts. 12, 15) ; *Eg.* 111
(arts. 14, 15, 16, 17, 79), with the notes on these passages.

is addressed, is chosen as their leader, but the chief is warned to beware the manœuvres of " maidens of the lightsome countenance," who must be guarded against " as a house is protected against fire," and is implored to apply himself strictly to his duties as a chief.   Another poem, written during a three-months' tossing about at sea in the Levant, appeals to the incompetent helmsman and captain to "take a hardy course and strive to make Damietta."

To Gilbride also is often applied the epithet Albanach, " of Scotland," with which country the O'Donnells of the North of Ireland were in constant communication.

One of his two poems to Donough O'Brien (d. 1242) describes a vision in which he was carried in a ship to Limerick where he saw Donough seated upon a chieftain's throne.   The second, a poem of peculiar beauty, was composed when he was sent by the prince on a mission to Scotland to try and bring back "a jewel" of O'Brien's which had been carried away to that country.   He seems to have been unsuccessful in his effort.   O'Curry, by a curious and plausible chain of reasoning, considered that this " jewel " was the harp presented by Henry VIII. to the Earl of Clanrickard, which is now in Trinity College, Dublin, and is commonly, but erroneously, called the Harp of Brian Boru.*   It would appear, however, that this harp belonged to the O'Neills.

Donogh mor O'Daly (d. 1244).—This poet, who wrote exclusively religious poems, and who has been called the Ovid of Ireland from the sweetness of his verse, lived at Finnyvarra, Co. Clare.   He was buried at the monastery of Boyle, in Co. Roscommon, and is called

---

* O'Curry, *Mans. Cust.,* Vol. III., p. 271.

by O'Reilly and others Abbot of Boyle, but there is no
evidence that he was an ecclesiastic or that he ever
occupied that position.   He wrote an immense number
of poems (O'Reilly names over thirty known to himself),
some of which seem to be well known all over Ireland.
They are gentle and tender compositions, many of them
addressed to the Blessed Virgin Mary, or containing
reflections on the hollowness of life, and appeals to
repentance and self-examination.   Most of them are
written in a frame of profound self-depreciation and
humility.   Donogh Mór is undoubtedly the greatest
religious poet that Ireland has produced, and the most
famous member of his gifted family.   Other members
of the O'Daly family who wrote in the fourteenth
and fifteenth centuries are :—

Angus Roe O'Daly (d. 1350), of Meath, poet to
Rory O'Mulloy, a chief in King's Co.   One of his poems
was written to appease the wrath of a patron whom
he had offended.   He begs him to turn his attention
to attacking the English and to leave his own poet
alone.*

Geoffrey Fionn O'Daly (d. 1387), chief poet of
Munster, who wrote a poem to the young heir apparent
of the Mac Carthys, urging him by valiant deeds to

---

* O'Reilly gives poems by two poets named Angus O'Daly
fionn " the Fair," both called *na diadhacta* or " The Divine,"
and living before 1430 and 1570 respectively.   The poems of
both are religious and on similar subjects.   This seems obviously
to be a mistake.   The date 1570 seems to be the right one ;
and the single political poem ascribed to this O'Daly, written in
1409 to Donald M'Carthy, Prince of Desmond, is probably
wrongly attributed.

sustain the reputation of his ancestors.   He also left a
religious poem on the vanity of the world (MS. *Eg.* 111).
There are poems existing by many other members of
this prolific bardic family written before the sixteenth
century.

Of the great family of the O'Higgins (*Ui h-Uiginn*),
of whom there are no less than thirty-three entries
in the Four Masters between 1315-1336, two must be
mentioned :—

Tadhg mor O'Higgin (d. 1315), who wrote a long
poem in praise of the prowess of Manus O'Conor, whose
wars and raids, usually directed against his own brother
Cathal, occupied the minds of Connaughtmen pretty
continuously from 1285 to 1293.   Teigue, who, as the
poem states, was the tutor of the prince, takes
great credit to himself for the horsemanship and hardi-
hood of his pupil, and records with satisfaction the
liberal rewards bestowed by Manus in return for his
instructions.

Tadhg Og O'Higgin (d. 1448).—A more voluminous
writer, whose verses are addressed to the representatives
of the O'Neill, O'Conor-Sligo and O'Kelly families living
in his day.   He is called "the Arch-instructor of
Ireland's and Scotland's poets."

From this time, and for near a hundred years, the
schools of the bards sank into comparative obscurity,
producing few men of rank and power ; but they rose
again into prominence about the middle of the sixteenth
century, and continued to produce poetry that has both
an historic and a literary value for another hundred
years.

CHAPTER XV.

Poetry of Nature

The Spontaneous Poetry.—The finest poetry of ancient Ireland does not, however, come to us as the output of the professional file, or of the family bard. The official nature of their positions and of the work that was expected of them, was in itself sufficient to deaden the spontaneousness of their compositions. The habit of producing poems for the sake of reward on public occasions, and the demands on the filí for the production of genealogical and historical verse for the honour of the tribe, must have had a prejudicial effect upon their art as such. It was being constantly directed to ends not purely artistic. But Ireland possesses, besides these professional efforts, a great body of verse which seems to be the spontaneous poetic output of unknown and, in some cases, non-professional poets. We find this verse either standing alone or else interspersed in the prose romances. As a rule, it is anonymous ; but occasionally an introductory passage introduces the writer and explains the circumstances under which the poems were written. They are on different subjects, often being pure poems of nature, or love-songs, or laments on the death of some personal friend. In the prose romances they spring naturally out of the story, being fitly introduced at points of special pathos or passion, and frequently taking the form of a dialogue between two of the personages in the tale.   Such are the beautiful descriptive poems on Magh Mell in the "Voyage of Bran" or the "Sickbed of Cuchulain"; the laments of Deirdre, of Cuchulain, or of Crede, or the love-songs scattered everywhere throughout the tales.   They occur chiefly in the middle or best period of Irish story-telling, and some of the romances are to a considerable extent made up of a succession of poems in a large variety of different metres.   But besides those verses, which form an integral part of the tales, there exist a good number of separate poems of the most exquisite finish and loveliness scattered here and there through the manuscripts, sometimes preserved in only one particular copy.   These poems preserve for us the essence of all that is purest and best in Irish art.   Their swift and subtle observation of the changing aspects of nature, their delicate sensibility, their freshness, and the chasteness of their expression set them apart from almost any poetry in any language that we could name.   "There is in them," says Dr. Kuno Meyer, who has set many of them before the public, "such delicate art, so subtle a charm, so deep and true a note, that with the exception of the masterpieces of Welsh poetry, I know nothing to place by their side." *   Many of them, too, are curiously modern in their tone ; the "Song of the Old Woman of Beare," the quaint lines written by some Irish student in the monastery of Carinthia in the ninth century to his cat, on the border of a copy of the Epistles of St. Paul, which he was supposed to be studying; the lines written by Cormac mac Cuileanan in the same century, which Dr. Sigerson aptly compares to Tennyson's "Crossing

* King and Hermit, edited by Kuno Meyer, 1901.

the Bar," might have been written yesterday ; old though they are in actual date of composition, they have nothing archaic in their tone or sentiment.

The scope of a text-book does not admit of lengthy quotations, and without a knowledge of the verse the criticism of poetry is useless. We prefer to give a single example which will serve for some remarks on the structure and age of these poems.

Poems of Nature.—The example we choose is the singularly beautiful poem of Marbhan, the hermit swineherd, composed in reply to the surprised demand of his princely half-brother, Guaire the Hospitable of Connaught, why he preferred to live in a retired hut in the forest, keeping the herds and swine of the king, rather than to dwell, as his birth and position entitled him to do, in the king's palace.

"O Marbhan, O Hermit," exclaims Guaire during a visit to his brother's hermitage, " Why dost thou sleep abroad, thy head upon a floor of pine, rather than upon a quilted couch ? "

The question calls forth a poem that cannot well be surpassed for delicacy in the swift and varying impressions it sums up of the allurements and charms of sylvan nature.

> " I have a shieling in the wood,
>   None knows it save my God ;
>   An ash-tree on the hither side, a hazelbush beyond,
>   A huge old tree encompasses it.
>
>   Two heath-clad door-posts for support,
>   And a lintel of honey-suckle ;
>   The forest around its narrowness sheds
>   Its mast upon fat swine.

> The size of the shieling tiny, not too tiny,
> Many its familiar paths,
> From its gable a sweet strain sings
> My lady in her cloak of the ousel's hue . . ."

Then turning suddenly from the contemplation of
his cell, and from the memory of the old companions
which occupies his mind for a moment, he with an
abrupt change of metre appropriately befitting the
change of thought, breaks out into praise of the
forest scenery and of the teeming forest life.   He
speaks of the leafy head of the green-barked yew,
which, like Hood's fir-tree, seems to him to " support
the sky " ; of the bounty of the wood and moor-lands,
which, in their rich store of apples, berries, herbs, and
cresses, provide him with a banquet better than that
of any prince ; of the company of goats, wild deer,
badgers, foxes and pigs which gathers around him in
friendly curiosity and shares his solitude, and of the
exquisite sounds of waving branches and twittering
birds, which make music far sweeter and more lovely
than that which Guaire has at his command.   So
persuasive is his eloquence, that Guaire acknowledges
that the possession of a crown is not to be weighed
against this reposeful quiet.   We give a few stanzas,
in Dr. Kuno Meyer's translation, from the close of the
poem, in which he speaks of the rustling of the leaves
and the song of the birds :

> " The voice of the wind against the branchy wood
> Upon the deep-blue sky ;
> Cascades of the river, the note of the swan,
> Delightful music.
> The melody of the bright red-breasted men,
> A lovely movement ;
> The strain of the thrush, familiar cuckoos,
> Above my house.

Swarms of bees and chafers, the little musicians of the world
A gentle chorus ;
Wild geese and ducks, shortly before summer's end ;
The music of the dark torrent.
The bravest band makes music to me,
A band who have not been hired ;
In the eyes of Christ, the ever-young, I am no worse off
　　than thou art　.　.　."

The metre of the second part of this poem is the same as that used by the writer of the poem ascribed to St. Columba, and possibly written by him, when leaving the shores of Ireland, but it is employed with even more extraordinary attention to the intricate rules of old Irish verse.　The short second and fourth lines rhyme.　There are three alliterative words or syllables in each of the first and third lines, while the intermediate lines are also alliterative ; the word beginning the second and fourth lines corresponds to and begins with the same letter as the final word of the first and third lines.　When the brevity of the lines, which have in them only four and two beats respectively, is taken into consideration, the mastery of language and the ingenuity of the writer in forming a lovely poem in spite of the stringent exigences of his craft is almost incredible.

We give as a specimen the first of the verses quoted above :—

Fogur gāithi *f*rie *f*iod *f*lescach
*f*orglas *n*ēol,
*E*ssa abhai, *e*ssnad *e*alao,
ālaind *c*ēoul.

It is to be remarked that in Irish poetry there is an elaborately thought out and perfectly intelligible law governing the use of the vowels and consonants in versification.   All broad vowels rhyme together, and all slender vowels, while the consonants are divided into six groups, the members of each of which rhyme together, but none of which will rhyme with a consonant from another group.   Thus, for instance, in the two next stanzas to that which we have quoted, the words " dil " and " tigh " make perfect rhyme (comhárda), and in the third, the words " seimh," and " ceir " do so. A glance at the footnote will explain this.*   The effect upon the ear is at first strange and surprising, as all new sound effects either in music or in poetry must appear, but it permits of a variety of combinations which could not be attained by absolute rhyme, such as that to which we are accustomed, and it has, when once the ear is trained to listen for it, a chastity and purity of effect beside which exact rhyme sounds poor and cheap.   It was no chance, but the requirements of ears trained to the delicacies and the precise values of sound, that led to the evolution

---

* The six divisions or groups into which the Irish poet arranged the consonants are as follows :—

> p, c, t—hard consonants.
> b, g, d—soft consonants.
> ch, ph, f, th, sh—rough consonants.
> ll, nn, rr, m, ng—strong consonants.
> bh, gh, dh, mh, l, n, r—light consonants.
> s—queen of consonants.

The sound of ch is a deep guttural, as c in loch ; bh, mh become v or w according to their connexion in a word ; ph has the sound of f ; dh and gh approach to the sound of y, or at the end of a word are silent ; sh, th, become obscured.

The division is, therefore, a natural one into labials and gutturals ; the group of letters in each set having a natural kinship with each other.

of this beautiful law of poetic correspondence.   The careful arrangement of the succession of open or closed vowels in Irish verse should also be noted.   It adds much to the harmony of the sound.

King Guaire the Hospitable, of Connaught, and his brother Marbhan lived in the seventh century ; the poem, as we have it, is ascribed by the editor to the tenth century.   It is to the eighth, ninth and tenth centuries that several of the most perfect of these songs are, by the test of language, to be ascribed.   At this early date it would appear that the system of Irish verse structure was fully developed and was used with the greatest freedom and mastery by the native writers. They were at this time perfectly conversant with the use of rhyme, which they called *Comhárda*, alliteration, called *Uaim*, and a very beautiful poetic grace, which was called *Uaithne*, and which is found, if not in the earliest, at least very early in the native verse.   This was the introduction of a middle assonance, or a correspondence between the end word of the first and third lines and the middle words of the intermediate lines. This is too important a feature in Irish poetry to be passed by without a full understanding of the method and effect of its employment ; its use adds a peculiar beauty to much of the best Irish verse.   It can be made quite cbvious to the English reader.   As an example, we may take a stanza from the famous song of Fionn mac Cumhaill in praise of May, the second stanza of which runs thus :—

> Gairid cāi crūaid *den*,
> is fo*chen* sam sāir ;
> suidid sīne *serb*,
> imme *cerb* caill crāib.

R

Here we have not only alliteration and terminal rhyme but the added internal rhyming of the alternate end words with a middle word in the following line. In English the stanzas might be rendered thus :—

> Dust-coloured cuckoo cries
> Welcome ! Sweet summer breeze !
> Sad, surly winter *dies*,
> Green *lies* the growth on the trees.
>
> Seeks the swift herd the *pool*
> Dabbling *cool* as it passes,
> Soft spreads the loose heather's *hair*,
> *Fair* spring the bog-cotton grasses.

This poetic device seems, in the manner in which it is used in Ireland, to be an invention of the native poets. In such a song as the Lament of Gelges (called elsewhere Crede) over the body of her young warrior-husband after the Battle of Ventry Harbour, it would be almost impossible to reproduce in English the delicate and intricate melody, the lovely lilt of the verses, which this effect of *Uaithne* or internal rhyme helps to produce.

The familiar " Farewell of Deirdre to Alba " in the tale of the Tragical Death of the Sons of Usnech has many features in common with the Lay of Gelges. The short broken line at the beginning, which is very frequently and effectively used in Irish Laments gives here the effect of the gentle swing of the boat as it passes down the smooth waters of Lake Etive.

Out of various good renderings of this poem Dr. Sigerson's is to be preferred on account of the care with which he has preserved the original metre.

> Glen Massin !
> Fair the ferns, green the grass in !
> We slept with moving *pillows*
> On *billows* in Glen Massin.

> Glen Dá Roe !
> Love to all who thither go,
> Cuckoos call from bending *bough*
> O'er the *brow* of Glen Dá Roe.

A large number of poems are ascribed to Fionn mac Cumhaill, who was looked upon as equally famous as a warrior and poet.   The latter portions of the poem of which we have just spoken are full of lovely images expressive of the busy life of reviving nature in the spring-time, the bees carrying with their puny strength the harvest of the blossoms, the shrill song of the lark " a timorous persistent little fellow, who sings at the top of his voice," the " sounding harp of the forest-trees making music," and the talking of the rushes.

A fine poem also contains the response of Fionn to a lazy lad who refuses to draw water on the bleak sides of Slieve Gullion, because he said it was too cold, and the streams were perilous after the heavy rains.

The boy sings :—

> Cold till Doom !
> Glowers more fearfully the Gloom !
> Each gleaming furrow is a river
> A loch in each ford's room.
>
> Each pool is deepened to a perilous pit,
> A standing-stone each plain ; a wood each moor ;
> The clamouring flight of birds no shelter finds
> White snow winds towards the door.*

Fionn, in reply, bursts forth into a song in praise of the coming spring.   This poem of the winter's cold uttered by the lazy lad is also found in other connections,

> *Fuitt co bráth !
> Is mō in donenn ar cách
> is ob cach etrice ān,
> (ocus) is loch lān cach āth.

and seems to have been a well-known song, which was fitted into different legends as occasion required. Other songs ascribed to Fionn or to members of the group of poets around him are the Blackbird of Derrycarn, the song to Arran of the Stags, which was a favourite hunting-place of the Fianna, and a number of other fine poems in the Colloquy of the ancient men. Some of these poems in the form we have them are later than those we are here discussing, and must be dealt with elsewhere. We need not suppose that Fionn wrote all the poems that appear under his name ; when a poet's name became famous many poems of a similar sort whose authors were unknown gathered round it. The same thing has happened in the case of St. Columcille, to whom over a hundred and fifty poems are ascribed, many of which must be later than his day. But this saint was a true poet, as may be gathered from the few poems that seem almost certainly to be from his hands, and the very ascription of the poems to him shows the reputation in which his gifts were held. St. Columcille may be called the first patriotic poet of Ireland. His affection for his country is shown in many charming legends, as well as in the depth of his remorse which caused him, as the most severe privation that he could inflict upon himself, to exile himself from his native land. This passionate love of home and country comes out especially in the well-known poems supposed to be written from his coracle on the way to Alba.

"How rapid the speed of my coracle ; its stern, alas ! turned Derrywards !
I grieve at the errand over the proud sea, voyaging to Alba of the ravens !

There is a grey eye, that looks backward to Erin,
Through life henceforth it shall not see, the men of Erin or
    their wives.
From the ample planks of oak, I stretch my vision o'er the
    brine,
From my moist grey eye a large tear falls, when it turns
    back to Erin's shores.
Take back my blessing to the West—my heart is broken in
    my bosom ;
Should I be smitten with sudden death, 'tis for love of the
    Gael that I am smitten.*

Another beautiful song attributed to the saint and supposed to be written by him when tossed on the waters of the Moyle, between Ireland and Scotland, expresses his regret at leaving his fatherland for the barren wastes of Iona, and his envy of an old fellow-disciple, still remaining amid the pleasant slopes and woods of Durrow.   This poem has been so well transposed into English verse by Dr. Douglas Hyde that we take the liberty of quoting from it.   Though the accent in the Irish falls upon the first syllable rather than the second, imparting to the verse a crispness that is not quite conveyed in the translation, the version keeps otherwise exceedingly close to the original, introducing no new idea of the translator's own fancy.

" O Son of my God, what a pride and a pleasure—To plough
    the blue sea,
  The waves of the fountains of deluge to measure—Dear
    Eire, to thee ;
  The host of the gulls, with their joyous commotion—And
    screaming and sport,
  Will welcome my own " Dewy Red " from the ocean—
    Arriving in port.

* Adamnán's Life of Columba, edited by Wm. Reeves.

> Oh ! Erin, were wealth my desire, what a wealth were—
>   To gain far from thee,
> In the land of the stranger ; but there even health were—
>   A sickness to me.
> How happy the son is of Dima ! no sorrow—For him is
>   designed,
> He is having, this hour, round his own cell in Durrow
>   The wish of his mind ;
> The sound of the wind in the elms, like the strings of
>   A harp being played,
> The note of the blackbird that claps with the wings of
>   Delight in the glade.
> With him in Rosgrencha the cattle are lowing—At earliest
>   dawn,
> On the brink of the summer the pigeons are cooing—And
>   doves on his lawn."*

Many of these poems have been modernised in
language and rhythm as time went on, but it is
probable that the poems themselves are old.   A poem
whose author is known to us is the splendid " Song of
the Sea," composed by Ruman mac Colmain, who must
have been renowned in his day, for he is called " the
Homer and Virgil of Ireland."   This song, the only
one of his known to have been preserved, proves that
he was a genuine poet of nature.   He died in 747.   It
is said that this poem was written in response to a
demand from his own people for a test poem, that they
might prove whether he was a great poet or no.   He
had, it is said, written a fine set of verses for the Vikings
of Dublin.   Ungratefully and ungraciously, they
declined to give him the price he asked for his poem,

---

* Hyde's Literary History of Ireland, p. 172.   The original
of the last stanza runs as follows :—

> Estecht co moch i Rosgrenchai
> risin damhraidh
> Coicceattal na ccuach don fiodbaidh
> as bruach samhraidh.

whereupon he composed one of those satirical quatrains so dreaded by the people, threatening that, unless the sum he asked were given him, he would "carry off the honour" of the man who refused him. The effect was instantaneous, for they offered him whatever he asked. His demand showed shrewdness; he asked for "a penny from every bad Viking, and twopence from every good Viking." Money poured in, for no man wished to be thought a bad Viking, and he collected so large a reward for this single poem that he was not only himself provided for during the rest of his life, but he endowed the Church of Cell Belaig, in which place, we learn, there were seven streets inhabited entirely by Norsemen, and gave another third of the gathered wealth to the school in that place.

Thus he magnanimously restored two-thirds of his gainings to the people from whom he had received them. Still, he did not get off without some return for their generosity, for the Vikings demanded that he should make them a poem in praise of the sea (a most appropriate topic for the Norsemen to choose) "in order that they might know whether he possessed original poetry or not." Then he wrote the fine poem which we still possess in praise of the ocean. It is quoted in the Metrical Treatises as a specimen of the *Laid Luascach,* or "Sea-saw" song, but in spite of its evident popularity only one copy has come down to us. The reflection is a melancholy one; it suggests to us how much fine poetry is for ever lost. It begins as follows :—

> A great tempest on the Plain of Lir ;
> Wildly across its high borders
> The wind has risen, the hurricane has reached us,
> We are slain by the fierce winter,
> Flung upon us across the main.

> Deeds of the Plain, the swelling Plain of Lir
> Trouble and destruction on our hosts,
> Greater than all tales, less, indeed, than none,
> This tale of the terrible, ship-breaking tempest,
> The incomparable, great story.

And it goes on to describe the movement of the waters as the wind from north and south, from east and west, urges them on. It has all the full, strong freshness of the billows rushing forward at spring-tide, just as on the other hand the " Song of the Old Woman of Beare " is instinct with the mournful, restless, downward curling of the slowly ebbing tide.

> Ebb-tide to me,
> For with the ebbing sea my life runs out,
> Old age has caught and compassed me about,
> I mourn the glad youth passed away from me.
>
> The flood-wave thine
> Mine, but the swift back-flowing ebb-tide's call ;
> Out of my hand the ebb-wave carries all,
> Towards thee the flood-wave foams across the strand.

These artists have expressed the very spirit of the ocean.*

Love Songs.—Of the immense number of fine love-songs and laments we can only mention one. It is the love-tale of Liadain and Curithir, a poem ascribed by its editor to the ninth century. It relates the meeting and parting of a young poet and poetess, who,

---

* The Irish of the second of these stanzas is as follows :—

> Tonn tuli
> ocus in dī athbe āin :
> in tabair tonn tuli dīt
> berid tonn athfe as do lāim.

after plighting their troth, are separated for ever by
the over-hasty act of Liadain in taking the veil.   It
thus represents the conflict between the natural and
the religious ideal of life.   The final lament is full of
the tenderest emotion and the most passionate regret.
The form of the lament, three short lines, in which the
first has only two beats, the others four, is singularly
fitted to express the urgency of grief, and the repetition
of the beloved name at the end of the second line in
verse after verse adds to the intensity of the feeling
expressed.

> I am Liadain,
> Who loved Curithir ;
> It is true as they say
>
> The music of the forest
> Would sing to me when Curithir was here,
> Together with the voice of the purple sea.*

There is a fine freedom in these spontaneous poems,
both as regards the sentiment and the metre, that is
very surprising, a mastery of form that argues the
highest cultivation, not only of the special art of poetry,
but of the whole intellectual faculties of the writers.   If
we are to consider that these poems represent the
general standard of education, it must have been very
high indeed in the eighth, ninth and tenth centuries,
and even supposing that it represents only the standard
of the schools of the poets, it shows a refinement of
mind which proves that alongside the fighting and
raiding conditions of life there was also another side

* The Irish is—

> Ceol *caille*
> fomchanad la Curithir,
> la *fogur faicre flainne.*
> —Edited by Dr. Kuno Meyer, 1902.

tending towards a true ideal of culture and taste.   As several of the poems of which we have been speaking are mentioned in the teaching books of the poets as examples of metre, and in other places, we may conclude that they were not all by unknown poets, but were familiar verses, held to be good poetry in their own day.

Metres in Irish Verse.—The distinguishing feature in old Irish poetry is that each verse is confined to a strict number of syllables ; a rule from which there is no deviation.   But as time went on, this strict attention to the counting of the syllables gradually gave way to the more general method of word-accents and stress of the voice.   This change in the method of writing poetry had an effect even on the older verse. Attempts were made to bring the old poems which were still recited among the people, or which were found in the romances, up to the later standard of poetic usage.   The later scribes, instead of copying the old poems exactly as they found them, recast them on the principle of accents and stress of the voice, thus radically changing their form.   We have examples in such poems as those interspersed in the story of the " Fate of the Children of Lir," of which some existing versions are older than others, showing how these changes were made.   A very large number of the poems ascribed to early saints and poets conform, not to the old system of counting the syllables, but to the later manner. These changes in the verse make it very difficult indeed to date a large number of the poems that are supposed to be ancient.   Both the language and the form has been modernised.   The change was gradual, and Irish poetry falls into two classes, that in which the counting of the syllables is rigidly adhered to, and that in which the accentuating principle is adopted. The precise limits of time to which these changes may be assigned are not at present clearly defined. The chief metres employed in ancient Irish verse were called Deibhidhe, Seadhna, Rannaigheacht mhór, Rannaigheacht bheg, and Casbhairn. These were all species of Dán Díreach, or Straight Verse, in which certain rules had to be followed in every form, while others varied with the particular species chosen. The technical difficulty of these metres was very great indeed.

Early Use of Rhyme.—It is noteworthy that the names of the different metres and of the degrees of the poets, as well as the technical terms of their craft, are purely Irish. They show that the whole system was formed and in vogue before the introduction of the Latin language into Ireland, and that it is a native product which outside influences did not largely modify. The exact balance of indebtedness of Irish poetry to Latin poetry, and of Latin poetry to Irish example, has not yet been struck. Scholars like Zeuss, with some later writers contend that it was the Celts who invented rhyme and taught it to the Latins. There seems to be solid reason, at least, for believing that the Irish used rhyme which they called *Comhárda*, *Uaithne*, or middle assonance, and *Uaim* or alliteration, at a very early period. The general system of sound values on which these rules of metre were founded must, for such perfection to have been attained in the use of them in the ninth or tenth century, have been understood and practised throughout a long preceding period. There are traces of

the use of these same poetic graces in some Latin
poems composed by Irish writers towards the end of
the seventh century, such as the Latin hymn of
Cuchuimne in praise of the Virgin, but we cannot go
much beyond this ; for even if the earlier poems
ascribed to St. Columba and the other saints, whose
dates are known, are by the men to whom they are
ascribed, they have undergone much corruption and
change in their language and possibly also in their
structure during the course of centuries of repetition.
They have evidently been modernised as time went on.*

However this may be, the fact that the terms employed
are all Irish shows that the forms themselves were not
consciously or deliberately adopted from without into
Irish poetry, but that they were of native development
and the invention of the poets themselves.   It is said
in the second text published by Thurneysen, which
formed a teaching book for the filí, that there are
sixteen portions of poetical knowledge which the filí
must know.   Such are (1) the last word (iarcomarc)
of a poem must accord with the first word of the first
verse, either the whole, the half, or the beginning of
the word being in agreement ; (2) the binding of the
keyword of a verse with the beginning word of the next
by alliteration, called *uaim do rinn ;* (3) the union of
the whole strophie as conveying a single connected
idea (*Cobfige celle*) ; (4) the equality of the strophie
within itself (*Brosna suad*), etc.

* For a full discussion of these matters see Zeuss, Gram. Celt.,
edited by Ebel, p. 977, 946-8 ; Sigerson, " Bards of the Gael
and Gall," Intro. pp. 3-5, 29-39 ; Hyde's Mac Ternan Prize
Essay, pp. 41-53 ; Thurneysen, Mittelirische Verslehen, Ir.
Texte. iii., heft i.

Many of the titles have very poetical significations. For example, the Fochloc is so called because his art is slender as a sprig of brooklime (fochlocán) ; the Dos or Doss, a student of the third year, is so called because he resembles a *dos* or young tree ; the Cli means a pillar (*cleith*) of a house, for " as a pillar elevates and supports a house so is the *Cli* elevated by his judgment and art ; " the Anruth means a " noble stream," because his poetry is as a stream of pleasant praise, and to him there returns for it a stream of riches.   So in the ecclesiastical schools the students were, in different grades of advance, styled by terms meaning " the Interrogator ; " the " Illuminator," " the Stream of a Cliff," etc.

Literature of the Norse Period.—We must draw attention to the fact that the period of which we have been speaking as the best period of early Irish verse, that is, the eighth to the tenth or eleventh centuries, is the very period during which, if we are to credit the repeated assertions of early Munster annalists and modern historians, the literature of Ireland was being stamped out, the schools destroyed, and the books dispersed by the Northmen.   To the Dane is attributed not only the burning of churches and monasteries, but the extinction of all social, artistic, and literary life among the people.   But the witness of facts points exactly in the opposite direction.   The meeting and intermingling of the two nationalities, in many ways so dissimilar, yet so fitted to supplement each other, was accompanied with a great outburst of activity, not only in the practical directions of building and mercantile industry, but in artistic and intellectual advance. Even in the worst period of Norse raids and destruction

of churches, the internal life of the monasteries seems
to have been little disturbed ; it is from the seventh
to the ninth centuries that the most perfect of the
existing illuminated manuscripts date.   The Book of
Durrow dates from the seventh or the eighth century,
the Book of Kells from the eighth or the ninth century ;
the most important of the other illuminated copies of the
Gospels from this and the following centuries.   Yet
the work of illumination demanded the most undisturbed
repose and freedom from anxious care.   It is to the
same period and the tenth century that the most
beautiful of the poems of which we have been speaking
are ascribed, while the ninth and tenth century appear,
so far as we have the means of judging, to be the culminating point of Irish prose romance.   It was also the
prime period of the schools of the poets, and the age
from which the larger number of the historical and
topographical poems and a fair number of the bardic
efforts come down.   It was during this time that
Maolmura of Fathan, Flann mac Lonain, Kenneth
O'Hartigan, Eochaidh O'Floinn, Urard mac Coise, Mac
Liag, Cuan O'Lochain and Flann of the Monastery
flourished.   It was thus during this very period that
the schools of the poets were at the height of their
prosperity, and were producing the men whose fame
in their own day has carried on the memory of their
tradition to the present age.   In ecclesiastical metal
work, in church architecture, in the sculptured crosses,
we find the same advance during the tenth to the
twelfth centuries.   The coming of the Anglo-Normans
in no way impeded this steady progress in purely native
art, which continued along a line of expansion up to the
beginning of the thirteenth century, from which time

it seems to have declined before the influx of foreign ideals.   We hear of no Irish poet of repute falling a victim to the savagery of the Norsemen, though two of the foremost of the filí were slain by their own countrymen. On the contrary, we hear of many of them being made welcome, not only to the Danish Court in Dublin, but at the courts of the Northern Kings across the sea.   The bard or skald was as great a favourite in the Northern courts as he was in Ireland ; he accompanied his master on his foreign expeditions as part of his train of household dependents, and the frequent interchange of kindly hospitalities between the Norse skald and Gaelic bard produced interesting modifications in the literature alike of Iceland and of Ireland.   To Norse literature, especially to the Edda, which is believed to have been developed under Gaelic influences in the Hebrides or Western Isles, which were largely peopled by Northmen, it added a sweetness, an observation of nature and a delicacy of feeling in which it had been before deficient, while it also probably influenced the northern metres ; while Ireland on its side owes to the connection the material for many a fine poem and heroic tale.   To the incursions of the Northmen, and the new and wider outlook on life opened up by them, the saga of Fionn mac Cumhaill, in particular, owes a large part of its interest.   It reached a new and expanding development after the intercourse with the Norse.   It is to be remembered also that the home of the Icelandic sagas was that south-western portion of the Island of Iceland which was to a large extent peopled in the ninth century from Ireland.   As we read the Land-namabók, which gives the history and settlements of the early inhabitants of Iceland, we almost feel at home, so frequent are the Irish names of Konel (Conall), Njal (Niall), Kjarval (Cearbhal), or Meldun (Maelduin). The saga of the death of Njal (Niall) which contains the Norse account of the Battle of Clontarf, and the saga of Kormak (Cormac) show us that these names continued in the Island to the close of the tenth century. Two well-known Northern poets, Cormac and Hallfred, travelling in what they felt to be friendly countries, spent much of their time in the Western Isles and Ireland, and died in the land of their adoption.

To regard the coming of the Norse to these lands merely as the pirate visits of raiders and plunderers is totally to misconceive the history of a very interesting period. They came in part on Viking expeditions, but they came at a later period as settlers ; centuries of intermarriage and of constant intercourse in all the departments of life made them a part of the nation ; and on both sides the literatures have benefited by the alliance. The destruction of books with which the ancient writers charge them applies, not to books in the native tongue, but to the Latin church books in the monasteries destroyed by them ; had it been otherwise, King Brian could not have replaced them from abroad ; while the idea that they were the cause of the downfall of the office of file, or the ruin of the native poetry is, as we have tried to show, purely imaginary. The official poets were never so prosperous or so much held in honour as during the Norse period of occupation, and their downfall in later times is to be ascribed to natural causes ; while it is frcm the most troublous times of Norse invasion that much of the most exquisite poetry and much of the finest and most spirited prose that Ireland produced in ancient times is found to date. The ruin of the native literature at this time is purely mythical; it never actually occurred. Rather, the wider outlook attained by fixing the attention on foreign wars, instead of on the interminable provincial and tribal raids to which the people were accustomed, and the inter-mixture of interests, led to a great intellectual quickening in the nation. The long period of Irish and Norse inter-communication need be regarded by the literary historian with no unfriendly eyes, however it may have been regarded by the contemporary annalists of Munster. That there was burning of monasteries and destruction of schools is true, but that they proved in the long run so detrimental to art, learning, and religion as is usually supposed, is shown by the facts to be an exaggeration.

So far as the literature is concerned, the period between the seventh and the eleventh centuries may be regarded as a time of production in poetry, and of arrangement into literary form of the prose. To the next centuries we owe the chief of the compilations which have preserved for us the existing materials, whether romance, poetry, genealogical and topographical verse and prose, or religious and hagiological matter, in great vellum volumes.

From the thirteenth century the power of the official poets was on the decline, but their place was taken by the schools of the bards and the families of the scribes. The industry of the hereditary scribes was primarily directed to the arrangement and collation of the annals and historical records, while the chief original literary output of the country is represented by the large mass of bardic poetry which continued to be produced until the loss of the language in the seventeenth century,

S

and the troubles of the time, brought it to an end. The full consideration of these matters must be deferred to another time.

APPENDIX

THE OLD BOOKS

It will be well to mention separately a few of the more important of the great compilations of manuscript literature and to give an idea of their contents. It is to be understood that these works are not books in the ordinary sense of the term, but are miscellaneous collections of material of different ages and varying value, written into large parchment volumes from time to time by the scribes who had them under their care; romances, history, genealogies, poems, biography, and religious matter being thrown together without much natural order. Thus, the contents of a single collection may contain material belonging to quite different ages, and composed by a great number of different writers. There is necessarily much repetition, certain pieces that were considered of importance having been copied into several different manuscript books by different scribes.

Besides the collections mentioned here, a great number of others exist, such as the *Leabhar Hy Maine*, or Book of the O'Kellys, the *Leabhar Branach*, or Book of the O'Byrnes, the Munster Book, etc., while a large number known to exist in the seventeenth century are lost.

The Book of Armagh.—This volume of ecclesiastical matter has always been associated with the Primordial See of Armagh and was for many centuries preserved in the library of the Cathedral in that city. It is now in Trinity College, Dublin. Its great value consists in the fact that it contains the only copy of the complete New Testament that comes down from ancient times and also the documents ascribed to St. Patrick. The book has always been greatly venerated, chiefly because it was believed that parts of it were written in St. Patrick's own hand. This is not so, but it contains a valuable collection of documents concerning him, some of which appear to have been copied from an original that was actually in St. Patrick's handwriting. They may have been collected and copied with a view to their safer preservation. Most of it was written by the learned scribe, Ferdomnach of Armagh (d. 845), and finished in 807. Besides the matter mentioned above, it contains a Life of St. Martin of Tours and some other ecclesiastical documents. An interesting entry on a blank space (fol. 16, *b*) records the visit of King Brian to the city in 1004 and his confirmation to Armagh of its ancient ecclesiastical supremacy and dues. The entry ends as follows: " This have I written, namely, Maelsuthain, in the presence of Brian, supreme ruler of the Scots (*i.e.*, the Irish), and what I have written be decreed for all the Kings of Cashel."

The Saltair Chaisil, or Psalter of Cashel, is ascribed to Cormac mac Cuileanan, King-Abbot of Cashel 837–903, who was killed at the Battle of Bealach Mughna, and also to King Brian, who probably revised it and had copies of the book distributed to the various Munster Princes. It was a composite book, containing among other matter the Book of Rights, Cormac's Glossary, the Calendar of Angus, a list of the Bishops of Armagh, lists of the Kings of Cashel, Aileach and Connaught, and other historical matter dealing chiefly with Munster. No complete copy of this book is known to exist but a good portion of it is preserved in the Bodleian Library, Oxford. Most of its contents have been published.

The Book of the Dun Cow.—This, the most ancient of the great collections of manuscripts which contain the old romances of Ireland, compiled about 1100 A.D. in the monastery of Clonmacnois, owes its curious name to a tradition that the parchment on which it was written was made out of the skin of a favourite cow that followed St. Ciaran (b. 516), the founder of the monastery, from his home when he went as a young student to study at Clonard, in the present County Westmeath, and which he afterwards took with him to Clonmacnois when he went there as first Abbot of the new foundation. It seems hardly credible that the skin was preserved for five centuries before being used for the purpose of this book, but in any case the story is a pretty one and it is quite possible that a special regard should have been paid to any memorial of the founder. The value attached to it in later times is shown by one of the entries in the volume which states that it and another (now lost) book called the " Short Book " (*Leabhar Gearr*) were " forcibly recovered from the men of Connaught " by a son of Niall Garbh O'Donnell, or Niall the Rough, " after it had been taken out of their keeping from the time of Cathal Og O'Conor to the time Rury, son of Brian O'Conor, and ten lords reigned over Carbary (Sligo) between them." To fight a battle for a book or to accept a book in ransom for a chief were no uncommon events, and show the value attached to them by their owners. The earliest part of this great compilation seems to have been made by Maelmuire, a grandson of the well-known Conn na mBocht, or " Conn of the poor," a culdee of Clonmacnois. This first scribe met a violent death at the hand of a party of robbers " in the middle of the great stone Church of Clonmacnois " in 1106 A.D. The contents are of a mixed character, religious, historical, and romantic. There is no kind of arrangement adopted for the material, and the most diverse subjects succeed each other with no other break than a capital letter affords. It may be well to give a fairly full account of the contents of this book, which may stand as a type of several other collections.

It opens, like most of the old volumes, with a fragment of the Book of Invasions (*Leabhar Gabhála*) containing the traditions relating to the ancient settlements of Ireland. Then follows the history of Nennius, poems to or by St. Columcille, the Story of Tuan, and a long list of romances, such as the Intoxication of the Ultonians, Cattle Spoil of Dartada, the Wanderings of Maelduin, the Vision of Adamnan, the Sickbed of Cuchulain, the Destruction of Da Derga's House, the Battle of Cnuca (an Ossianic tale), the Feast of Bricriu, the Battle of Carn Conaill, the Story of Connla of the Golden Hair, the Voyage of Bran, the Courtships of Emer and Etain, the Story of Mongan, and the earliest account of the Cattle Spoil of Cuailnge. A few semi-historical pieces, such as the Death of King Dathi and the banishment of the Deisi into Munster are included, also a couple of religious pieces, and Cineath O'Hartigan's long poem on the Burial Places of the Kings. On the whole, however, this book is devoted almost exclusively to romance, and it is satisfactory to reflect that even the monks looked with sufficient reverence on the old tales to desire their preservation. Nearly all these tales belong to the second or Cuchulain cycle ; there are only one or two belonging to the Fionn cycle and none exclusively to the mythological period.*

* This book has been published in *fac-simile* by the R I.A., with preface and description of contents.

The Book of Leinster.—This great book, drawn up and transcribed by Finn mac Gorman, a Bishop of Kildare (d. 1160), in the reign of Dermot mac Morrough, King of Leinster, and at the desire of Dermot's chief professor or fosterer, one Aedh, or Hugh mac Crimthann. A great number of the romances found in the Book of the Dun are also contained in this book, though frequently they differ a good deal in language and style. The Book of Invasions, as usual, opens the series, connected with which we have several groups of Historical and Geographical poems by the official poets of the tenth and eleventh centuries, such as Gilla Keevin, Flann Manistrech, Flann mac Lonain, Cuan hua Lochain, etc. As is natural, a large section of these poems and also of the stories and genealogies deal specially with the affairs of Leinster, of which this was evidently the official Provincial record. Besides the poems, there are a number of lists of Kings and Saints, Kingly precepts, etc. Among the pure romances not found in *L.U.* we may mention the Battle of Rosnaree, the Boromhean Tribute, Mac Datho's Pig and Hound, the Dialogue of the Two Sages, the Tragedy of the Sons of Usnech. Both the prose and poetical versions of the Dindsenchus are found in *L.L.*, also an adaptation of the Tale of Troy and some hagiological matter. The long version of the Cattle Spoil of Cuailnge occupies considerable space in the volume, and it is accompanied by several of the " Introductory Tales."

The Yellow Book of Lecan.—This title only properly applies to the first fragment of the book, which was written at different times by the Mac Firbis family, but chiefly by Gilla Iosa, son of Donnchadh Mór mac Firbis, about the year 1391 A.D. for Rory mac Donnell O'Dowda. The O'Dowds were chiefs of the Hy-Fiachrach, in the present Co. Sligo, and of these and the neighbouring families the Mac Firbises were hereditary scribes and genealogists. Again in this huge book we have a great quantity of the same material, especially as regards the old romance, but numerous short or fragmentary tales are added which fill up gaps in the series. Among the new romances not before mentioned are the Voyage of Snedgus and Mac Riagla and two or three other navigation stories, the Destruction of Dind-Righ, the Adventures of Cormac in the Land of Promise, the Tragical Death of Conlaech, the Death of Murtough mac

Erca, complete copies of the Battles of Magh Léana and Magh Rath and of Cormac's Glossary and the Book of the Ollamhs.

The Great Book of Lecan.—This book, also the work of Gilla Iosa Mór mac Firbis of Lecan, in Co. Sligo, where the family had a school, has never been printed or photographed. It belongs to the Royal Irish Academy, and contains material similar to that in the Book of Ballymote, but with an interesting tract added on the families with which the Mac Firbises were associated ; that is, the O'Dowds, chiefs of Tir Fiachrach (Tireragh) and Tir-Amhalgaidh (Tirawley) and the branches of their family. In the opening paragraph of the description of this book in the R.I.A. Catalogue O'Curry writes—" This volume, in its present condition, consists of 302 folios or 604 pages, all written in the Irish character, and, with the exception of an occasional line or sentence, in the Irish language . . . . It will be shown below that this book was compiled in the year 1417 when Rory O'Dowd was chief of his tribe and country."

The Book of Ballymote is another huge miscellaneous collection of materials, not arranged in any order but entered as the fancy or opportunities of the scribes suggested. It was compiled about the beginning of the fifteenth century by various scribes, three of whose names, Magnus O'Duigenan, Robert Mac Sheehy, and Solamh O'Droma, are mentioned. The O'Droma family belonged to Fermanagh, and the book was in the family of the chiefs of Ballymote for more than a century. But in 1522 the O'Donnells, who were evidently book collectors (see notes on *L.U.*), purchased the book for 140 milch cows from Mac Donogh ; on which transaction the scribe remarks that " Though in our judgment the book is good, buying a book from Mac Donogh is a purchase from a churl." The bitterness of parting with so treasured a possession, however, peeps out in a further note which seems to be a record of Mac Donogh's own attempt to reconcile himself to the sale of his volume. " Small," he says, " is the loss in O'Donnell's having forced the book from me, for it is a fame of foolishness that is come upon the book." No more is heard of the Book of Ballymote until the beginning of the eighteenth century, when it was in T.C.D. Library ; since then it has gone through further vicissitudes, but is now safely housed in the Library of the Royal Irish Academy.

There is not very much romance in this volume.   It may be
divided into (*a*) genealogies and synchronisms, including the
Invasions of Ireland ; (*b*) Historical matter, including a number
of early poems ; (*c*) Biblical and hagiological, including the
history of the Jews from the Old Testament, lists of genealogies
of saints ; (*d*) Several classical pieces, including the Irish versions
of the Æneid, the Wanderings of Ulysses, the Destruction of
Troy and the Exploits of Alexander, and (*e*) A miscellaneous
section including copies of the Dindsenchus, a copy of the Book
of Rights, and an interesting series of tracts on old Irish metric,
the various orders and schools of the Bards, the names of the
chief poets of Ireland, and the course of instruction in the schools
of the poets.

The Speckled Book (*Leabhar Breac*), called also the *Leabhar
Mór Dúna Doighre*, is chiefly ecclesiastical and religious, and is
written partly in Latin and partly in Irish.   It belonged to the
family of the Mac Egans and seems to have been written partly
at their Castle at Killyroe in Lower Ormond, and partly among
the other branch of the family at or near Dún Daigre (Duniry)
in Galway.   The Mac Egans were brehons to the families of the
O'Conors of Connaught, the O'Conor Faly, the Cineal Fiachrach,
the Mac Carthy Mores and other septs of the neighbourhood, where
they kept law schools, instructing their students in the ancient
laws of Ireland and kindred subjects.   The book was used by
Michael O'Clery in 1629 for his Life of St. Cellach ; it was then
in the Monastery of Cineal Fechan, Co. Galway, not far from Dún
Daigre.   It is not now quite complete, some of the pages having
become separated from the body of the work and bound up independently ; but, with the exception of two leaves, the whole of
it is in existence.

The larger part of this book is taken up with Homilies and
Passions, and Lives of Saints ; religious reflections, such as the
Discourse of the Soul and Body, the Visions of Adamnan, and
Monastic Rules and Litanies.   But it contains also a copy of
Cormac's Glossary and some classical matter, such as the Adventures of Philip of Macedon and of Alexander the Great.   A good
part of it seems to have been compiled before 1544, but there
are notes given in it up to 1595.   Nearly the whole of this book
has, in some form or another, been published.

The Book of Lismore, sometimes called the " Book of Mac Carthy Reagh."—This book has had a curious history. It was discovered by some workmen in a walled up passage in the Castle of Lismore, Co. Waterford, in 1814, lying in a wooden box along with a crozier, much injured by damp and gnawed by rats and mice. Nothing had been known of this manuscript up to the moment of its recovery except that in 1629, on the 20th of June of that year, it had been in the hands of Michael O'Clery, one of the Four Masters, at Timoleague Abbey. Its recovery was, therefore, as surprising as it was delightful, and leads to the hope that some of the still lost books of which Keating and O'Clery speak as having been used by them in the compilation of their historical works, may yet be found.

The book still remains as the property of the Duke of Devonshire at Lismore Castle, where it was discovered. It was compiled from the lost Book of Monasterboice and other manuscripts in the latter half of the fifteenth century for Finghin mac Carthy Reagh and his wife, Catherine, daughter of the eighth Earl of Desmond, and seems to have been written by three different scribes.

The larger part of this interesting book is devoted to lives of the Irish Saints under the form of homilies, but there are also in it a number of Ossianic and romantic poems and tales, most of them otherwise well known, a copy of the Book of Rights, a romantic life of Charlemagne, an abridgment of Marco Polo's Travels, a fragment of a history of the Lombards, and much semi-religious matter.

The Book of Fermoy.—Both the origin and title of this manuscript are uncertain ; as it contains a large number of poems on the O'Roche family it might with equal propriety be called the Book of O'Roche. It seems to have been at one time the property of Mr. W. Monck Mason, and was purchased by Rev. James Henthorn Todd, D.D., at a sale in London in 1858 for £70, and by him presented to the Royal Irish Academy, Dublin. It has unfortunately never been published in *fac-simile*, but an account of it, drawn up by Dr. Todd for the Academy, will be found in their Irish MSS. Series (Vol. I., Part I., 1870). To this the reader is referred for fuller information. It has been written at different times and by different persons, and the most interesting portions of it, outside the historical bardic poems on the O'Conors of Connaught, the O'Keeffes of Fermoy, the Mac Carthys, Roches and other families in the South of Ireland, are the curious legendary and mythological tales that it contains.　As is usual with these large books, it begins with a fragment of the *Leabhar Gabhála*, or Book of Invasions, and contains, besides the family poems and mythological tales alluded to above, several semi-historical legends, such as the Destruction of the Court of Mac Dareo and the Banishment of St. Mochuda from Raithin (Rahan in King's Co.) to Lismore, and of the Deisi from Meath ; poems by Cineath or Kenneth O'Hartigan, and Fothadh " of the Canon," and some legends of saints and religious matter.

INDEX.

T